Contents

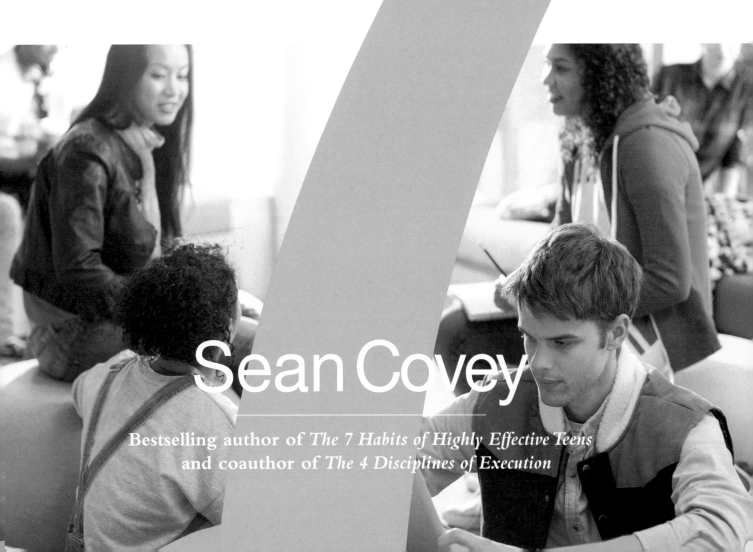

THE 7 HABITS®
OF HIGHLY EFFECTIVE
COLLEGE STUDENTS

Succeeding in College… and in Life

Sean Covey

**Bestselling author of *The 7 Habits of Highly Effective Teens*
and coauthor of *The 4 Disciplines of Execution***

ABOUT FRANKLINCOVEY

FranklinCovey is a global company specializing in performance improvement.

We help organizations achieve results that require a change in human behavior. Our expertise is in seven areas: Leadership, Execution, Productivity, Trust, Sales Performance, Customer Loyalty, Education.

Product and program catalogs can be requested by calling 1-800-331-7716 in the United States or by contacting your local representative outside the United States.

The 7 Habits of Highly Effective College Students

IMPORTANT NOTICE

Illustrated by Q-Power Communications and Mark Pett.   www.MarkPett.com

Manufactured in the United States of America

ISBN: 978-1-936111-61-9

The stories in this book are based on interviews, letters, or previously published materials. In some cases, names and other identifying details have been changed.

Welcome to College!
Now What?

"We ourselves feel that what we are doing is just a drop in the ocean. But the ocean would be less because of that missing drop."

-MOTHER TERESA

IN THIS CHAPTER, YOU WILL DISCOVER WAYS TO:

- Describe the College Success Formula.
- Give a brief overview of *The 7 Habits of Highly Effective College Students*.
- Get the most out of this book.

Welcome

Your first year of college might be the most important year of your life. You're making decisions that will affect everything from now on. This book will help you make the *best* decisions of your life.

What I Wish
I'd Known in College

"In college, I learned how to plan and prioritize, how to live on three hours of sleep, that pulling all-nighters to cram for tests doesn't work, and that it was one of the best experiences of my life."
–Stephanie, Brigham Young University

"Annoy your advisers, academic counseling, tutors, library people, professors. They're all paid to help you, so feel free to bother them. I went through my whole first year trying to figure things out all by myself. Then I found out about all these people I could talk to and get answers. I no longer had to suffer through math alone. My tutor could suffer with me!"
–Alex, McGill University

"Being out of school and working for 10 years actually helped me to be a better student."
–Denise, Pacific Union

"I wish I'd known that it is much easier to earn a degree when you are young. I did not complete my degree when I first attended college, and I have regretted it ever since!"
–Victoria, Nottingham University

REAL CHOICES:
Crossing the Finish Line

Imagine your mind is a TV screen. Now keep this image on the screen all the way through college.

It's a photo of John Stephen Akhwari crossing the finish line during the 1968 Olympics in Mexico City. Akhwari was a marathon runner from Tanzania. He had trained for years and was thrilled to be among the best in the world.

Shortly into the race, however, Akhwari took a severe fall. The tumble left his right knee badly cut and the joint damaged. Any hope of finishing near the top was crushed. Nevertheless, he got up, put on his grit, and step by step limped 26 miles through the city streets until he reached the gates of the massive stadium where the finish line was located.

At that point, Akhwari was a mere lap away from the line, yet still he had every reason to give up. A fourth of the runners had dropped out much earlier due to the punishing heat and the thin air at high altitude. Daylight had departed and so had most of the spectators, as the winner had been declared more than an hour earlier. Akhwari was the lone runner left. So why not quit?

Yet, as Akhwari entered the stadium, his eyes signaled he had no intention of bowing out. He edged his way along the track's inner lanes—first walking, then staggering, and finally attempting a trot. Gradually, the few remaining spectators took notice of him and started cheering him on. In the end, however, Akhwari's inner will—not the cheers—propelled his worn body around the track and across the finish line.

Today Akhwari's dramatic and inspiring performance lives on in Olympic history. Replays of his drive and perseverance stream on the Internet and still motivate people around the world. But here's the part I like best: When asked what had kept him going, Akhwari said, "My country did not send me 5,000 miles to start the race. They sent me 5,000 miles to finish it."

I love that statement.

Hi. My name is Sean, and I'm the author of this textbook. Let me start by congratulating you on making it to college. That's no small achievement. Think of all the schooling, time, money, and supportive people who have brought you to this

Look for John Stephen Akhwari's inspiring finish in the 1968 Olympics on YouTube.

moment. Just registering for classes can be a major feat, so good job. You've worked hard and achieved an important goal. Like Akhwari, you've made it to the big game.

If you happen to be the first in your family to attend college, give yourself an additional pat on the back. You have broken the barriers, beaten the odds, and are now forging a path for others to follow. Imagine how good it will feel when a younger brother or sister or a friend goes to college because of your example.

Or maybe you have been out in the workforce for some time and have now decided to go to college. If so, chances are you felt something missing in your life that you couldn't get without a college education. Whatever that "missing something" might be, I salute you for making the bold move to pursue it.

So, yes, no matter who you are or what hurdles you have overcome to get to this point, give yourself credit. I think you're making a smart choice!

"I just thought about my father and my mother. I just thought about my country. Once I am on the road, there is no way I am going to quit."

—John Stephen Akhwari

3

GETTING THE MOST OUT OF COLLEGE

While making it to college is great, your next goal is to graduate. After all, you didn't come all this way just to start. Like Akhwari, you came to finish. Right?

For you, finishing might mean two years and an associate's degree, four years and a bachelor's degree, or six years and a master's degree. Who knows? Maybe people will be calling you "Doctor" in a few years.

Regardless of how long the race, graduation will be a great day. But the path won't be easy; college can feel a lot like a marathon. I remember coming home after my first day at college feeling completely overwhelmed. The campus was huge, I didn't know anyone, and I wasn't sure if I could succeed there. Suddenly, high school didn't seem so bad. It took a while for me to feel comfortable in college, but gradually I did.

I think most students are shocked when they first start college. You might be living away from home for the first time, or you may be new at making so many decisions on your own, or maybe you're overwhelmed by a part-time job and school, or money is suddenly a huge issue. A single day of your new life might be full of questions like these:

> *Tuition is how much?*
> *What do you mean I need to get on my own phone plan?*
> *What were all those forms I just signed?*
> *What does this engine light in my car mean?*
> *Should I be cleaning the oven?*
> *Why is my computer making that noise?*
> *How do I tell my roommate that her socks smell like a dead animal?*
> *A hundred and ten dollars for one book? Seriously?*
> *Should I buy groceries or have a social life this week?*
> *Why won't anyone hire me?*
> *Should I stop staying out until 4 a.m.?*
> *What experience do I put on my résumé if I have no experience?*
> *How do people just know what they want to do?*
> *What is a "syllabus"?*
> *Why doesn't anyone prepare you for this?*
> *What does "analyze the character of Ahab in* Moby Dick*" even mean?*
> *Should I delete that tweet about my crazy English professor?*
> *Is it normal to cry when paying my rent?*
> *Should I do laundry or just buy more underwear?*
> *How do you cook a Lean Cuisine®?*
> *Should I try online dating?*
> *Can't I just have Red Bull® for dinner?*
> *Why am I crying?*
> *What the heck am I doing with my life?*

These questions are why I wrote this book. Although I can't help much with a lot of them (like should you clean the oven? Yeah, I think so), I'm mostly interested in the last question: "What the heck am I doing with my life?" After all, it is the big question, and going to college is a big part of the answer—but it's not the whole answer. This book aims to help you succeed not only in college, but also in life. That's the big marathon.

"You have set yourself a difficult task, but you will succeed if you persevere; and you will find a joy in overcoming obstacles. Remember, no effort that we make to attain something beautiful is ever lost."

—Helen Keller

David, a student at California State University, Long Beach, says he has two goals for college:

1. Getting as much out of college as he can.
2. Getting out of college as fast as he can.

David doesn't want to just put on a cap and gown and march across a stage at some distant point. He wants to do it effectively—to make the most out of the opportunity. He wants to learn from great thinkers, to meet students from all over the world, to expand his mind, and to be well prepared to get a job when done. But he also wants to do it efficiently. He doesn't want to wander aimlessly, miss opportunities, or take longer than needed and waste time and money. He wants to do it right and then move on.

My guess is that you feel the same way. You've worked hard to get to this point, so you want to get the most out of college, and you don't want to waste a lot of time getting it done.

So how are you going to make that happen? How are you going to succeed in college?

> "The mind is not a vessel to be filled, but a fire to be kindled."
>
> —Plutarch, ancient Greek historian

THE COLLEGE SUCCESS FORMULA

For starters, I've learned that successful college students have three things in common: (1) A compelling reason for going to college, (2) solid academic skills, and (3) effective life skills. These things make up what I call the College Success Formula.

College Success Formula

A COMPELLING WHY + SOLID ACADEMIC SKILLS + EFFECTIVE LIFE SKILLS = HIGHLY EFFECTIVE STUDENTS

College Success Formula: A Compelling *Why*

What kept John Akhwari going? It was his overwhelming desire to keep his commitment to his country and be a role model for the young people of Tanzania. He wanted to look back on his life and say, "I did it." Those compelling whys propelled him the full 26 miles across the finish line.

If you have a compelling why, you'll be more likely to finish college. Take the example of Jaime Lopez, a student in Southern California. Jaime grew up in a neighborhood where few students made it through high school. Rarely did anyone think of college. Every day he felt pressure to go the route of gangs and crime, but somehow he caught a vision. "I wanted something different for my life," he said.

John Akhwari's Olympic race earned him the title "King Without a Crown" in his home country.

Jaime saw college as his path to a better life. No one in his family had ever done it, and when he shared his dream with his high school counselor, he was told he wouldn't make it if he didn't earn a sports scholarship or join the military. When neither of those options panned out, Jaime refused to be stopped. At age 18, he left to fend for himself, got a job, and immediately began setting aside small amounts of cash for tuition. After four years and much personal discipline, he enrolled in college.

Today Jaime is as committed as ever to graduating. His compelling why—to attain a better life—keeps him working hard and sacrificing. I think these experiences will make his why even more compelling over time.

Do you, like Jaime, have a compelling why that will keep you going? Or is college just what you do after high school? Why are you dedicating some of the best years of your life to gaining more education?

Take a few minutes now to identify your compelling why.

ACTIVITY 1

Driving From Start to Finish

Because he had strong reasons for persisting, John Akhwari fought off injury, heat, and altitude to complete the Olympic marathon. Jaime Lopez worked and saved for four years to be able to attend college. But what about you?

What are your top three reasons (compelling whys) for attending college?

1.

2.

3.

Are your reasons for attending college strong enough to overcome obstacles that might get in the way of finishing your degree?

How do students answer these questions? Here are some examples:
- "My apprenticeship training was not enough for me and I had the desire to go to college to get better wages and a higher position."
  –Kerstin, Johannes Gutenberg University of Mainz, Germany
- "The parties." –Sonja, University of Alabama
- "I wanted to go to college because I didn't know what I wanted to do and I knew college was one way to find out. Then there are the obvious reasons: I wanted the advantage in the job market, money, and the prospect of more money in the future."
  –Justin, University of Utah
- "I went because I was knowledge-hungry; I always have been. As a kid, I read encyclopedias while other kids were playing. I know that's odd, but it's true. And college was an amazing feast of learning for its own sake. I loved it." –John, Boston University

College Success Formula: Solid Academic Skills

It's just as important to know how to succeed in college as to know why. You need two sets of skills: academic skills and life skills.

Academic skills include writing, reading, test taking, studying, note taking, critical thinking, researching, and presenting. Of course you also have to know how to navigate the campus, use the library, get help from your professors, and use online resources.

Some students already come with solid academic skills, while others need to develop them. Most colleges know this, so they set up academic-support centers—mostly at no cost to you—for tutoring, mentoring, and testing. There are also lots of resources on the Internet. Many colleges also have college-success courses you can take that will help you build study skills and life skills. You may even be using this textbook in one of these courses.

If you haven't developed good study skills, it's not too late to start.

Jeri had lousy study habits in high school. After two kids and a divorce, she decided to go back to school so she could qualify for a better job. That was when her study habits came back to haunt her. Reading in bed put her to sleep, and trying to study on the train to work was pointless. Then there was procrastination, which was her lifelong hobby. Plus, the two kids were darling little distractions.

A few changes were in order. Jeri moved out of her bed into what she called her "study home," a quiet corner where she could be alone for two hours a day after work. She used those hours for heavy reading and saved her train time for light reviews of what she had read. "When the kids are at daycare and I have the place to myself, I can study until my brain falls out."

As was the case with Jeri, good study skills can make all the difference, and it's your responsibility to develop them. No one can do it for you. While colleges can help you get academic support, you can't sit back and assume it's their job. Now more than ever you are responsible for your learning. In this book, I will share some basic study skills from some excellent professors that will help you get started. Because these skills are essential academic tips based on the principles in this book, I call them "Academic Protips." Beyond the protips, visit your school's academic support center, go online, talk with your parents, or lean on a friend for help.

College Success Formula: Effective Life Skills

You also need effective life skills—for managing time, setting goals, communicating well, managing finances, resolving conflicts, building friendships, caring for your health, dealing with difficult people, working in teams, and so on.

These skills are just as important as academic skills. You probably know students who are bright intellectually but struggle to control themselves, get along with other people, or manage their time and money. They might be smart, but they have a tough time making friends or holding on to a job.

In fact, a critical reason for gaining life skills is that employers look for new hires who have them. They like to know you did well in your classes, but

Napoleon:
"Nobody's going to go out with me."

Pedro:
"Have you asked anybody yet?"

Napoleon:
"No, but who would? I don't even have any good skills."

Pedro:
"What do you mean?"

Napoleon:
"You know, like nunchuck skills, bow-hunting skills, computer-hacking skills. Girls only want boyfriends who have great skills."

—From the film
Napoleon Dynamite

they also want to know if you're disciplined and good with people. While most employers are willing to train you for your job, they don't want to have to train you in life skills.

DID YOU KNOW?
Life Skills Make You Employable

Edexcel, a United Kingdom-based education firm, recently asked more than 2,000 employers from 22 countries what they looked for when recruiting. They responded with pleas for more life skills, such as:

- Problem Solving
- Positive Thinking
- Creativity/Innovation
- Trust
- Leadership and Management
- Multitasking
- Initiative/Responsibility
- Teamwork
- Empathy
- Communication Skills
- Professional Manners
- Cultural Sensitivity

(Playfoot and Hall)

Considering these life skills, how employable are you right now? What can you do to make yourself more employable?

JEANINE WORKS ON HER CRITICAL-THINKING SKILLS

> "Habits are at first cobwebs, then cables."
>
> —Spanish Proverb

THE 7 HABITS OF HIGHLY EFFECTIVE COLLEGE STUDENTS

So how do you improve your life skills?

You look at your habits. You might have habits that work against you, like victimization ("Why is everyone out to get me?"), procrastination ("I can't be out of gas already"), or impulsiveness ("Why did I eat all the pizza?"). You gain good life skills by changing your habits, especially if you have darker habits like addictions.

The purpose of this book is to help you form new habits—the habits of effective, successful students—habits that will help you lead a successful, effective life.

This textbook is based on, "The 7 Habits of Highly Effective People," a set of life skills originally identified by my father, Dr. Stephen R. Covey. As a university professor, he spent decades studying the habits of the most successful people and organizations. He reviewed hundreds of books and mounds of research, drawing on sources from all over the world and from both classic and modern literature.

He started sharing the 7 Habits with his students at the university. His classes grew so popular they were held in the basketball arena.

In 1989, the book *The 7 Habits of Highly Effective People* first came out. Overnight it became a worldwide sensation. It has since grown into one of the bestselling books of all time, with well over 40 million copies sold in more than 40 languages. Until his passing, Dr. Covey traveled the world teaching the 7 Habits to thousands, everyone from kings and CEOs to families and small children. Each year the book seems to grow more relevant and popular. Thousands of corporations around the world have also adopted the 7 Habits as a way to improve their cultures and build their leaders.

I translated the 7 Habits into teen language when I wrote *The 7 Habits of Highly Effective Teens*. Thousands of teens around the world are now taught the habits in school each year. Later, I wrote a picture book for children called *The 7 Habits of Happy Kids*, which is also used in many homes and schools.

Meanwhile, I've begun taking the 7 Habits to college campuses, talking to students everywhere about the success formula that has changed the lives of thousands of people. I thought if the 7 Habits are so helpful to the leaders of the world, why not teach the habits to college students like you who are the leaders of the future?

So, What Are the 7 Habits?

Each of the 7 Habits is a chapter in this book, but rather than keep you in suspense, here's a sneak preview:

HABIT	DESCRIPTION
1. Be Proactive®	I am responsible for my education and life.
2. Begin With the End in Mind®	I have a plan for what I want to accomplish.
3. Put First Things First®	I do the most important things first.
4. Think Win-Win®	I am considerate of others, but I also have the courage to stand up for myself.
5. Seek First to Understand, Then to Be Understood®	I hear people out before expressing my own opinion.
6. Synergize®	I value the strengths of other people and combine them with my own to solve problems.
7. Sharpen the Saw®	I regularly recharge my body, heart, mind, and spirit so I can stay sharp and improve myself.

The habits build on each other. When you were born, you were dependent on your parents or others for your survival. Gradually, you moved toward independence. The more you take responsibility for your life (Habit 1), work toward meaningful goals (Habit 2), and use your time well (Habit 3), the more independent you become. We call it "winning the Private Victory®" over self.

While it's good to be independent, there is a higher state to strive for. This is called interdependence. At home, at school, and at work, we must work well with others to be successful. Life is a team sport. Going for win-win (Habit 4), understanding others (Habit 5), and valuing people's differences (Habit 6) make you more interdependent. We call it "winning the Public Victory®."

So you move from dependence to independence to interdependence, as you can see in the 7 Habits Leadership Continuum below. I call it the Leadership Continuum because as you move up the continuum and become more and more interdependent, you truly become a leader—a leader of your life and a leader among your peers.

THE 7 HABITS LEADERSHIP CONTINUUM

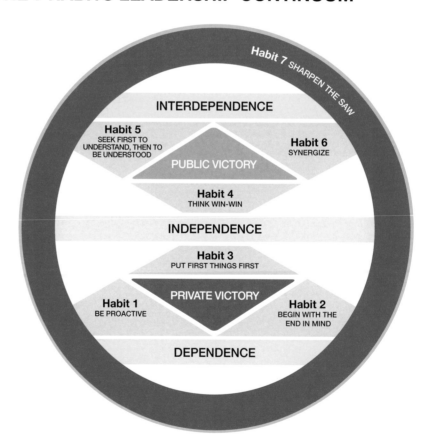

You can see that the Private Victory comes before the Public Victory. You've got to get your own act together, at least to some degree, before you can succeed with other people.

Notice also that Habit 7: Sharpen the Saw surrounds all the other habits. It's the habit of renewal. If you have Habit 7, you do something every day to recharge your body, mind, spirit, and emotional life. You can't practice the other habits unless you practice Habit 7.

To see how well you already practice the habits, take the 7 Habits Assessment below:

The 7 Habits Assessment

ACTIVITY 2

How well do you live by the 7 Habits? Take the following assessment to find out. It should take no more than 10 minutes.

		STRONGLY DISAGREE				STRONGLY AGREE
BE PROACTIVE						
1.	I take initiative to get things done.	①	②	③	④	⑤
2.	I control my moods and anger, even in difficult circumstances.	①	②	③	④	⑤
3.	I focus on things I can do something about rather than on things I can't control.	①	②	③	④	⑤
4.	I accept responsibility for my actions rather than blaming others or making excuses.	①	②	③	④	⑤
	TOTAL					
BEGIN WITH THE END IN MIND						
5.	I plan ahead.	①	②	③	④	⑤
6.	I have a sense of direction in life.	①	②	③	④	⑤
7.	I have a clear plan for finishing college in a timely manner.	①	②	③	④	⑤
8.	I begin papers and projects with a clear understanding of desired outcomes.	①	②	③	④	⑤
	TOTAL					
PUT FIRST THINGS FIRST						
9.	I organize my time so that I work on the most important priorities first.	①	②	③	④	⑤
10.	I am disciplined in carrying out plans; I do not procrastinate.	①	②	③	④	⑤
11.	I balance all aspects of life (i.e., work, leisure, family, etc.) to maintain overall effectiveness.	①	②	③	④	⑤
12.	I am organized; I keep good track of papers, notes, phone numbers, etc.	①	②	③	④	⑤
	TOTAL					

Continue to next page.

			STRONGLY DISAGREE				STRONGLY AGREE
THINK WIN-WIN							
13.	I do not undermine others for personal gain.		①	②	③	④	⑤
14.	I am fair with everyone; I do not play favorites.		①	②	③	④	⑤
15.	I work to find win-win solutions to conflicts.		①	②	③	④	⑤
16.	I have the courage to say no when appropriate.		①	②	③	④	⑤
		TOTAL					
SEEK FIRST TO UNDERSTAND, THEN TO BE UNDERSTOOD							
17.	I listen to people without interrupting.		①	②	③	④	⑤
18.	I seek to understand other people's viewpoints.		①	②	③	④	⑤
19.	I seek to understand problems before attempting to solve them.		①	②	③	④	⑤
20.	I express my viewpoints clearly and concisely.		①	②	③	④	⑤
		TOTAL					
SYNERGIZE							
21.	I seek out the strengths of others to get things done.		①	②	③	④	⑤
22.	I am creative and resourceful.		①	②	③	④	⑤
23.	I am open-minded in trying new ideas.		①	②	③	④	⑤
24.	I work well in groups.		①	②	③	④	⑤
		TOTAL					
SHARPEN THE SAW							
25.	I care for my physical well-being.		①	②	③	④	⑤
26.	I'm good at building and maintaining friendships.		①	②	③	④	⑤
27.	I am constantly trying to expand my knowledge.		①	②	③	④	⑤
28.	I spend time helping others and contributing in positive ways.		①	②	③	④	⑤
		TOTAL					

Continue to next page.

KEY

Add up your score for each habit.

IF YOUR SCORE IS...	THEN...
20	You've mastered this habit. Either that, or you're fooling yourself.
16—19	You're doing okay, but there's room for improvement.
12—15	You're dangerously close to being average.
8—11	Your success in college and life depends on making some important changes.
4—7	Don't be so down on yourself. From here, you can only go up.

Look at the total for each habit. Are some habits high or low? Which habits do you need to work on the most?

The 7 Habits sound like just good common sense, and in some ways they are. But common sense is not always common practice, and we all know we can do better. The good news is that living by the 7 Habits can help you:

- Be more self-confident.
- Plan out your life, education, and career.
- Use time more wisely.
- Make lasting friendships and improve family relationships.
- Prevent trouble and settle it successfully if it comes.
- Understand and communicate ideas better.
- Work better in teams.
- Balance your life so you're not overwhelmed.
- Do better in class.
- Complete your degree.

If you wonder how the 7 Habits can impact you, imagine what it would be like to live by their opposites, or what I call "The 7 Habits of Highly Defective College Students":

Habit 1: Be Reactive. Blame all your problems on your parents, professors, lousy roommates, or some other convenient scapegoat. Take no responsibility for yourself or your education. Be a victim.

Habit 2: Begin With Squat in Mind. Don't plan. Avoid setting goals—you won't follow through anyway. Don't think about tomorrow. Sign up for whatever classes sound easy. Live for the moment and party on.

Habit 3: Put First Things Last. Take only courses that start after noon so you don't have to miss any late-night parties. Put homework off until you're through surfing the Net or watching reruns on TV. Procrastinate.

Habit 4: Think Win-Lose. View school as a vicious competition. Don't help people because they might cheat off you and get credit. And remember, if somebody else succeeds at anything, it means you lose. So be sure to win at all costs.

Habit 5: Seek First to Talk, Then Pretend to Listen. Talk a lot because only your ideas count. Pretend to listen in class while you play with your phone.

Habit 6: Don't Cooperate. Assume that people are weird or inferior if they don't think the way you do. Teamwork is overrated.

Habit 7: Burn Yourself Out. Forget keeping your life in balance. It's too hard. You don't have the time to exercise or the money to eat right. You can't party and sleep. Burnout is cool and mono isn't as bad as they say it is.

So there you have "The 7 Habits of Highly Defective College Students." Can you imagine what your life would be like if you had these habits? I suggest sticking with the highly effective habits.

Obviously, you don't master all 7 Habits at once, so this book will help you practice the habits a step at a time until they stick with you.

> "No change in circumstances can repair a defect in character."
>
> —Ralph Waldo Emerson

Henry Morton Stanley

LESSON ON LEADERSHIP: One Step at a Time

Welsh journalist and explorer Sir Henry Morton Stanley is famed for his grueling expeditions along the Nile and Congo Rivers. When asked if the African jungle intimidated him, Stanley said:

I did not see the whole. I only saw this rock ahead of me; I only saw this poisonous snake which I had to kill in order to take the next step. I only saw the problem directly in front of me. If I had seen the whole thing, I would have been too overwhelmed to have attempted this. (Carter and Feeney)

The thought of tackling college and changing your habits all at once can be overwhelming. But if you take it one small step at a time, it'll be a lot easier.

GETTING THE MOST FROM THIS BOOK

More than any of your college textbooks, this one—and the course that goes with it—is about you. Literally millions of corporate executives, government leaders, school teachers, sports teams, and others have learned the 7 Habits, and now that opportunity is yours.

To get the most out of this textbook and course, study and review each chapter carefully. After this "Welcome" chapter, you'll read "Foundations of Leadership," which will help you understand how to lead an effective life. The next seven chapters are about the 7 Habits. The final chapter, "Putting It All Together," shows you how the 7 Habits combined can solve your most important problems as a college student.

In each chapter you'll find:

Activities. These are usually short-answer questions or brief self-assessments to help you apply the 7 Habits.

Lessons on Leadership. These are short stories about people—some well known and some students like you—who have used the 7 Habits to lead their own lives successfully.

Baby Steps. These are brief suggestions for applying the habits immediately. I call them Baby Steps. This comes from the classic movie *What About Bob?* starring Bill Murray and Richard Dreyfuss. If you've seen it, you might remember that Bob just about drives his psychiatrist crazy. Eventually the psychiatrist gives Bob a book called *Baby Steps*, which teaches him that the best way to tackle life is one "baby step" at a time. As he takes these baby steps, life becomes much simpler for Bob. "Look at me; I'm baby-steppin'," Bob likes to say. While I can't guarantee you a simpler life, I do encourage you to tackle the habits a little at a time by doing two or three of the Baby Steps at the end of each chapter.

80% of the final exam will be based on the one lecture you missed and the one book you didn't read.
–Third Law, College Laws of Applied Terror

"One, two, baby steps. Three, four, baby steps. Five, six, baby steps. I'm starting over again."

—Varsity Fanclub, "Baby Steps"

Academic Protip. In gaming, a protip is advice from an expert to someone new to the game. At the end of each chapter, you'll find a short article on a vital study skill that relates to the habit. While the protips don't go into academic skills in depth, they will help you deal with maybe 80 percent of the academic challenges you will face in your first years. The protips are written by prominent university professors who are experts on these topics:

- How to Study in College
- How to Use a College Library
- How to Write a College Paper
- How to Study for a Test
- How to Think Critically
- How to Make a Presentation
- How to Read College Textbooks
- How to Manage Your Money

LET ME PUT IT THIS WAY... HAVE YOU GUYS EVER HEARD OF THE 80/20 PRINCIPLE?

You can download a free version of the FranklinCovey Living the 7 Habits app for Android or iPhone. Use the code *Habits89* to unlock additional features.

Teach to Learn

Another great way to get the most out of this textbook (or any other) is to teach what you learn from it to someone else.

Everybody knows the teacher learns more than the student. San Jose State Professor Walter Gong studied that idea in depth and found that people who know they are going to teach a concept remember the concept much better. They're also better at applying the concept to life. So at the end of each chapter in the "Baby Steps" section, I challenge you to teach a key idea from the chapter to someone within 48 hours. You could teach it to a friend, a family member, a roommate, a co-worker, whomever. This process is called "Teach to Learn."

YOUR PROFESSOR OR TEXTBOOK	YOU	A FRIEND OR FAMILY MEMBER
TEACHER	TEACHER/LEARNER	LEARNER

To get a feel for the power of the Teach to Learn process, try this activity:

Teach to Learn

Teach a brief overview of the 7 Habits to a friend or family member. Do this within 48 hours. because you lose much of the learning after that. You don't need to be formal— it's best to stay simple and casual and use your own words.

Step 1: Study the concept. Review the 7 Habits Leadership Continuum.

Step 2: Teach the concept. From memory, teach the 7 Habits to a friend in less than 5 minutes. Explain why Habits 1, 2, and 3 are called the "Private Victory," while Habits 4, 5, and 6 are called the "Public Victory." As you teach, draw the 7 Habits Leadership Continuum by hand.

Step 3: Apply the concept. Share a personal example or insight into how one or more of the habits has applied to your life.

APPLYING THE 7 HABITS TO YOUR LIFE

Of course, the best way to get the most out of this textbook is to start applying it to your life. It's time to step up and be a leader. The type of leadership I'm talking about has nothing to do with holding a position, becoming a corporate CEO, winning an election, or having tons of followers. It's about leading your life.

Until now, school may or may not have required you to take the lead. Parents, teachers, or counselors may have done a lot of the thinking for you. They decided when your school day would start and end and what classes you would take. They monitored your homework, checked your grades, or stayed on your case to make sure you graduated.

College is totally different. There's not a lot of hand-holding. Counselors are happy to give advice if asked, but do not come looking for you. An instructor might take an interest in you, but won't call you each morning to make sure you wake up in time for class. Now you have to take the lead.

You might run into some hefty obstacles as you head out. College is meant to stretch your mind and capacity. The first year is often the hardest, so don't be alarmed if you have an occasional rough day or bomb a test here or there. If, for whatever reason, you find yourself facing more than you can handle academically, financially, or emotionally, take the lead and seek help. Asking for help is a sign of inner strength, not weakness. Top corporate leaders use advisors, and world-class athletes have coaches, so why not you?

Be picky about whom you go to for advice. Friends may be great listeners but lousy doctors or financial advisors. Most colleges have counselors who can help you or point you in the right direction for help. Whatever you do, take good care of yourself. Surround yourself with people who can help you. Then put your heart into your education.

Campus Voices

I asked a number of students what their biggest first-year challenges were, and this is what they said:

"It's hard to always get my work done on time." –Tiara

"Staying healthy. There is so much food on campus and in the dorms. It's challenging not to eat everything in sight." –Hannah

"Writing papers. I am not confident when it comes to grammar." –Kevin

"I have three children who play sports. I sometimes skip homework to go to their games." –David

"Managing classes, friends, sports, clubs, time for myself, time with God, and all the other stuff." –Clarissa

"Even though my car is teeny tiny enough to fit into those half-size, not-real parking spots, I managed to accumulate $300 in parking fines." –Enoch

"Making new friends and relating to people from different backgrounds." –Emma

"Getting up each morning." –Aaron

"Leaving my family and trying to adjust to sharing a small room with another girl." –Kristen

"There are so many distractions that are more fun than school." –Candace

"My last class ends at 2:40 and then I work from 3:30 until 11:00 p.m. No time for me or my homework." –Jamie

"Finding parking." –Jeff

"I have no money to afford any other things after tuition and buying books." –Keirra

My hope is that you'll have the time of your life in college. Trust me, in spite of the occasional marathon-like moments, college can be a lot of fun and incredibly worth your time and effort. Many people, including me, think back on their college years as some of the best. And they are not just thinking of the parties. They made lifelong friends, learned from great minds, overcame insecurities, had a lot of fun, and prepared themselves for meaningful careers.

They're even grateful for the challenges they faced that made them stronger and more road-tested for life.

So yes, welcome to college. In spite of your roommate's socks, your crazy English professor, and $110 for one book, you're going to do fine. You have potential you don't even know about, and college will help you find and unleash it. I predict you'll cross your finish line, and chances are it will turn out just how Dr. Seuss said it would back in kindergarten:

> *So be sure when you step.*
> *Step with care and great tact*
> *And remember that Life's*
> *A Great Balancing Act....*
> *And will you succeed?*
> *Yes! You will, indeed!*
> *(98 and ¾ percent guaranteed)*
> *KID, YOU'LL MOVE MOUNTAINS!*
> *-From Dr. Seuss, Oh, the Places You'll Go!*

COMING ATTRACTIONS

In the next chapter, you'll discover how your perceptions of yourself, others, and the world around you govern everything you do and the results you get. You'll also get some great tips on how to take advantage of all the resources your campus has to offer. So read on!

References

Carter, John Mack, and Joan Feeney, *Starting at the Top*, New York: William Morrow & Company, 1985, p. 110.

Covey, Stephen R., *The 7 Habits of Highly Effective People*, New York: Simon & Schuster, 2012.

Dr. Seuss, *Oh, The Places You'll Go!* New York: Random House, 1990, 42.

Playfoot, Jim, and Ross Hall, *Effective Education for Employment: A Global Perspective*, Edexcel, Apr. 2009, 24.

What About Bob? Dir. Frank Oz, Touchstone Pictures, 1991. Film.

Foundations of Leadership

"Sow a thought, reap an action;
Sow an action, reap a habit;
Sow a habit, reap a character;
Sow a character, reap a destiny."

–SAMUEL SMILES

IN THIS CHAPTER, YOU WILL DISCOVER THAT:

- What you do depends on how you see the world.
- What you get in life depends on what you do.
- A highly effective life is centered on principles.

Also, look for the Academic Protip...

- How to Study in College

Foundations
of Leadership

In this chapter, you will discover where your habits come from and how to change them so you can succeed in school and in life.

What I Wish
I'd Known in College

"How much the decisions I made while I was there would impact my ENTIRE life."
–Loretta, Illinois Wesleyan University

"Cramming never produces results as good as studying throughout the semester. I had a terrible first semester and spent the next seven semesters trying to make up for it."
–Mary, Illinois Wesleyan University

"College life is all about the quality of our relationships—with professors, roommates, mentors, etc. We build lasting relationships by keeping our commitments, showing proper respect for authority and position, and treating others as we would like to be treated."
–Richard, University of Waterloo, Canada

"Before I went to college, I wish I'd known more about me."
–Nicki, University of Texas

"I wish I'd known that if your meal plan runs out before the end of the semester, you will be forced to survive on microwave popcorn and metallic-tasting, off-brand sodas."
–Enoch, University of Toledo

"I wish I had known that college wasn't preparing me for life, it IS life. If I had it to do over again, I would work harder and play harder."
–Kim, University of Arizona

REAL CHOICES:
Thinking About How You Think

The great leaders of the past were supposedly blessed with great foresight. Yet, consider what these visionary leaders of the 20th century had to say about their fields of expertise:

- "Man will not fly for 50 years."
  -Wilbur Wright to his brother Orville two years before they went airborne at Kitty Hawk
- "The talking motion picture will not supplant the regular silent motion picture."
  -Thomas Edison, inventor of the movie camera
- "[Before man reaches the moon] your mail will be delivered within hours from New York to California, to England, to India, or to Australia by guided missiles."
  -Arthur E. Summerfield, U.S. Postmaster General, in 1959 (I think I prefer text messaging.)
- "People will soon get tired of staring at a plywood box every night."
  -Darryl F. Zanuck, head of 20th Century-Fox motion-picture studios, speaking of a new device called television

- "If excessive smoking actually plays a role in the production of lung cancer, it seems to be a minor one."
  -Dr. W. C. Heuper, National Cancer Institute in 1954 (Then why are smokers up to 23 times more likely to get lung cancer?)
- "There is practically no chance communications space satellites will be used to provide better telephone, telegraph, television, or radio service inside the United States."
  -T.A.M. Craven, Commissioner of the U.S. Federal Communications Commission in 1961
- "We don't like their sound. Groups of guitars are on their way out."
  -Decca Recording Company executive upon rejecting the Beatles in 1962
- "There is no reason for any individual to have a computer in their home."
  -Ken Olson, President, Digital Equipment Corporation in 1977

George Eastman and Thomas Edison. Courtesy, Library of Congress.

23

"Computers in the future may perhaps only weigh 1.5 tons."

—*Popular Mechanics*, 1949

At the time they were made, these statements sounded reasonable. Today they sound absurd.

Often such misguided thinking results in nothing more than a good laugh, or perhaps an ego-enema. Other times, the errant thinking leads to disastrous and very costly results. Think about what it cost the Decca Recording Company to turn down the Beatles. Ouch!

Of course, this chapter is not about the crazy things people used to think. Rather, it's about you. It's about how you think and act.

The results you Get in life flow from the things you Do, which in turn flow from the way you See things. We call this the See-Do-Get Cycle. The Decca executive saw groups with guitars losing popularity, so he turned down the Beatles. We all know the results he got—or rather, *didn't* get.

The same See-Do-Get Cycle is at work in your life. How you See things will impact what you Do, and what you Do will impact the results you Get. Then the results you Get will impact how you See things, and so on.

It works like this:

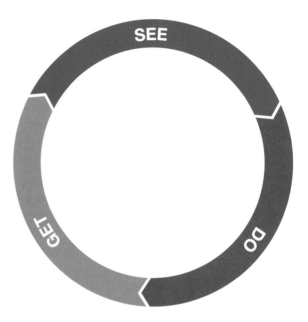

I SEE	I DO	I GET
My professor is a big jerk.	I check out whenever he/she lectures and give him/her the glare from time to time.	Not much learning.
Math is too hard for me.	I give up easily when I don't understand the assignment at first.	A lousy grade.
I can do math. I just need some help.	I work with a tutor twice a week on my math assignments.	A good grade.

It's a cycle. To you, the professor is a jerk, so you either check out or give him/her the glare and tell everyone what a jerk he/she is. He/She senses you don't like him/her, and he/she glares back at you, which makes him/her more of a jerk, right?

If you think math is too hard for you, you give up on tough problems and get a lousy grade, which again reinforces the idea that math is too hard for you, and so on.

Now imagine that you See yourself differently: "I can do math. All I need is some help." Then instead of giving up, you find a tutor and spend the effort to do well. You Get a good grade. All of a sudden, you *can* do math!

Clearly, what you See is what you Get in life. If you See yourself as a loser, you'll probably lose. If you See yourself as a confident person who can succeed with the right kind of help, you probably will succeed.

WHAT YOU SEE—THE POWER OF A PARADIGM

The way you see things is called your *paradigm*. Other words for paradigm are mindset, perception, belief system, frame of reference, or point of view.

Your brain is packed with paradigms. You have political, religious, moral, racial, and social paradigms. You have paradigms about sports, music, art, movies, parents, drugs, sex, dating, studying, drinking, leadership, and college. Lots of paradigms are in our heads about ourselves, other people, and the world in general:

- "Country music is awful."
- "My roommate is really cool."
- "I'm not a morning person."
- "My professors don't care about anyone but themselves."
- "I'm good at overcoming challenges."

DID YOU KNOW?

The word "paradigm" comes from the Greek παράδειγμα (paradeigma), "pattern or example."

Your paradigms are like lenses through which you view the world. If you see college through positive lenses, you will see it as a great opportunity to build lifelong friendships—to tap into great minds, and to prepare yourself for a meaningful career. By contrast, if you look at college through negative lenses, you'll see it as an obnoxious rite of passage to get a good job. You will see exams as meaningless games and research papers as tree-killing wastes of time. So your paradigms of college matter a lot.

A paradigm is a mental map. Suppose a friend gives you a map on the first day of school and tells you it's a map of the campus. Running late, you whip out the map and start making your way to class. Fifteen minutes later, frustration hits. Nothing makes sense. Only then do you realize that your fun-loving friend has given you the wrong map. Hilarious. So even if you try really hard and think positively, that map won't help you find your class.

If you have the wrong mental maps, you're not going to make it to your destination. You've got to have accurate paradigms of what college requires of

> "Representation of the world, like the world itself, is the work of men; they describe it from their own point of view, which they confuse with the absolute truth."
>
> —Simone de Beauvoir, French intellectual

25

you—how to write a paper or take a test, how to get along with others, how to work in study groups, and so forth.

If you start now in getting the right mental maps of your college experience—the campus, the policies, the resources, the events, the graduation requirements, the pace, the deadlines, etc.—you can avoid all kinds of detours, costly delays, and emotional wrecks.

The same is true of your life. What are your paradigms of finding success, of managing time, or of getting and keeping a good job? You can save yourself a lot of grief in the coming years if you examine your paradigms; and if they're off target, work to make them as accurate as possible.

ACTIVITY 4

Mapping Out Your Campus

Paradigms are like mental maps. Bad maps can steer you wrong. Good maps can make all the difference. One correct map or paradigm you should adopt is to realize how many resources are available to help you succeed in college. With that in mind, grab a friend and journey to at least 10 of the locations below. Identify what major services are provided at each. At your college, the names might be different from these, but do your best to find as many as you can.

__ Academic Support Services
__ Bookstore
__ Campus Museums (if any)
__ Campus Security/Police
__ Career Counseling Services
__ Employment Office
__ Financial Aid Office
__ Graduation Office
__ Internship or Foreign Study Services
__ Library
__ Medical/First Aid Office

__ A Professor's Office
__ Psychological Counseling Services
__ Performing Arts & Music Ticket Office
__ Physical Fitness/Athletic Facilities
__ Scholarships and Grants Office
__ Student Activity Center
__ Testing Center
__ Writing Center
__ Crisis Support Center
__ Student Government Center

Also, go on your campus website and check out the academic and activities calendars. Search out your college's policies on attending classes, cheating, driving, adding/dropping classes, drinking, parking, retaking classes, dress and grooming, smoking, using drugs, registering for classes, appealing grades, participating in student leadership, etc. Choose at least three of the policies and describe them below:

1.

2.

3.

The more accurate your paradigms of available resources on your campus, the better use you can make of them.

Grade Your Paradigms

Your most important paradigm is your paradigm of yourself. For Brianna, a student at New York University, the first year of college was a major shock. She was stunned by the tremendous workload and the talents of her classmates. Intimidation set in fast. "I just knew that I wouldn't ever be able to keep up with them," she said. "So when they asked me to join their study sessions, I turned them down. I started focusing instead on extracurricular activities."

Fortunately for Brianna, midterms brought a pleasant wakeup call: she discovered that she had managed to keep up with her class after all. "At that point, it began to dawn on me," she said, "that I could compete, and that I could do even better if I stepped up my effort." And she did. She worked harder, and at semester's end, she had scored better than average in each of her classes. But the biggest payoff for Brianna was her new self-paradigm. "I became a force to be reckoned with!" she now says with a smile of fresh confidence.

Do you have any of these self-paradigms?

> "You yourself, as much as anyone in the entire universe, deserve your love and affection."
>
> —Buddha

NEGATIVE SELF-PARADIGMS	POSITIVE SELF-PARADIGMS
I'm terrible at making new friends.	I like meeting new people.
I'm awful at taking tests.	If I study intelligently, I can do well.
Appearance is everything in a relationship, and I'm not beautiful, so...	I'm comfortable in my own skin.
I don't know if I'm the college type.	I'm going to be the first in my family to graduate from college.
College is way too expensive. I'll never be able to pay for it.	With a little help, I can work my way through college.

What paradigms do you have of your SELF?

As you can imagine, your self-paradigms directly impact your self-esteem. In fact, your self-esteem is made up of the self-paradigms you've built up over the years. Low self-esteem can lead to poor decisions; high self-esteem can take you successfully through life.

So examine your paradigms. Are they accurate? Are they complete? Or do they need an overhaul? Give them a grade. Is it an A paradigm, a B, a C, or a D? Base the grade on this question: Will this paradigm really work for you in the long run? If you see yourself as unfriendly, what will be the consequences for your college experience, your relationships, and your career? Is that paradigm going to work for you?

Shift Your Paradigm

> "We see the world not as it is, but as we are—or as we are conditioned to see it."
>
> —Stephen R. Covey

No one's paradigms are totally accurate. That's one reason you go to college—to be educated and expand your paradigms.

Which paradigms do you hold on to as real and accurate, and which do you discard as bogus? Not long ago, bloodletting (draining blood) was the accepted paradigm to rid the body of disease. For many years, people lived by that false paradigm and made bad decisions as a result. Today that paradigm has been corrected, but even in our high-tech world, the paradigms keep changing. For example, debates rage on about whether or not the Internet is melting our brains and making us unable to concentrate. Some say maybe, some say maybe not—and then some on both sides are totally certain.

So if you say, "I'm not the college type; it's just not me," is that an accurate statement? Is it really a fact? Or have you just talked yourself into believing it? I'll bet it's a paradigm, and a paradigm is not reality, just like a map is not the same thing as the territory it represents. You can *change* a paradigm.

In fact, don't be surprised if you encounter two highly regarded professors in the same department with very different paradigms about what is "true" in their field. Professors are human and are also striving to make their paradigms more accurate and complete.

When a person's paradigm changes, it's called a Paradigm Shift. If you've come straight out of high school, college can be a huge Paradigm Shift, especially if you move away from home. People talk differently and behave differently. Demands are higher, and more responsibility shifts from parents and teachers to you. Moving from dependence to independence is a Paradigm Shift.

Or maybe you've been out in the workforce for years. Going back to school is another big Paradigm Shift! School might not be what you remember. You might be stunned that you have to work harder and longer than you did on the job. You might find you're older than your teachers. You might be blindsided by technology: "What's with all this online stuff? We did fine without it when I was in school!"

"Going to college was the scariest thing I've done," said Marisol, a military spouse. "We had three kids and I had a job. But when I looked at who got laid off at work and who didn't, I saw school was the important difference. I needed that degree.

"The first thing I learned was that college isn't high school—thank heaven. But it was a big adjustment to be in class with people younger than me. I felt so old! I also had to adjust to the idea that nobody was going to tell me what to do. But then I got into it and nobody seemed to care how old I was. Plus, I was paying for it, so I cared a lot more!"

IT'S EASY ONCE YOU SHIFT YOUR PARADIGM!

Student Voices: Shifting From High School to College

When first-year students in Georgia were asked to identify the differences between high school and college, these were their answers:

PARTICIPATION IN HIGH SCHOOL	PARTICIPATION IN COLLEGE
It's mandatory and free.	It's voluntary and expensive.
Parents and teachers prod you along.	You set your schedule and manage your priorities.
The number of classes are mostly set for you.	You attend part-time or full-time; you set the pace.
Teachers monitor attendance.	Professors may or may not track attendance.

CLASSES IN HIGH SCHOOL	CLASSES IN COLLEGE
Choose from a limited list of classes.	Choose from a wide variety of classes.
You proceed from one class directly to another.	Class times vary throughout the day and evening.
Generally no more than 35 students are in a class.	Classes may number 300 students or more.
Up to 30 hours a week are spent in class.	6–18 hours each week are spent in class.

TEACHERS IN HIGH SCHOOL	PROFESSORS IN COLLEGE
Approach you if they see you need help.	Expect you to initiate contact for assistance.
Give help before or after school.	Set scheduled office hours.
Are trained in teaching methods.	Are trained as researchers and content experts.
Teach the material in the textbook.	May or may not follow the textbook.

STUDYING IN HIGH SCHOOL	STUDYING IN COLLEGE
If you hear a lesson once, you learn all you need.	Review notes and textbook regularly.
Study 0–4 hours a week outside of class.	Study 2–3 hours for each hour in class.
Homework is mostly short assignments.	Large amounts of reading and writing required.

TESTS IN HIGH SCHOOL	TESTS IN COLLEGE
Are frequent and cover small amounts of material.	Are infrequent and cover large amounts of material.
Mostly multiple choice is the norm.	More open-ended essays are common.
Mastery is shown by reproducing what you have been taught and in the form it was presented.	Mastery is shown by applying what has been taught to new situations or unfamiliar problems.

GRADES IN HIGH SCHOOL	GRADES IN COLLEGE
Homework scores may overcome low test scores.	Tests and major papers provide most of the grade.
Extra credit is often available.	Extra credit is seldom available.
First test may have little impact on final grade.	Tests may account for large part of final grade.
Effort counts. Show up, you get a good grade.	Results count. Attendance doesn't equal good grades.

SOCIAL LIFE IN HIGH SCHOOL	SOCIAL LIFE IN COLLEGE
You know a lot of people, many for years.	Feel like a stranger at first, then make friends.
1,000–4,000 students are on campus.	1,000–30,000 students are on campus.
School activities are mostly "fun" sports, dances, choir, etc., attended by students and parents.	Fun activities abound, but many are more cultural, attended by community, alumni, and students.

While Paradigm Shifts might make you nervous, they're mostly changes for the better. Many first-year students arrive a bit insecure; some are in a panic. They find the first few weeks tough—maybe extremely tough. But as their paradigms shift, they discover that college is in many ways better than they expected. Gradually, they learn to like the extra freedom. They get excited about what they're learning and what it can mean for the future. Then people say to them, "Wow, you've matured," or "Hey, I can tell you have learned a ton." Their confidence grows.

Campus Voices

I asked a handful of first-year students to share their favorite Paradigm Shift about college, and here is how they responded:

"I was surprised to learn how much professors are willing to help."
–Leann

"It is not as scary and hectic as I thought it would be."
–Amber

"I am more intelligent and determined than I thought."
–Bonita

"The work was easier than I thought it would be."
–Emma

"There is so much more freedom than I thought there would be."
–Ryan

"How nice the faculty members are."
–Beau

"How fast a semester goes by."
–Sven

"I never guessed how much fun I would have in my classes."
–Colin

"I've been in the workforce for a while and I found it a lot easier to socialize with a young crowd than I thought it would be."
–Lloyd

"I love the diversity at all levels."
–Jeremy

"Professors aren't as bad as I had heard. You've just got to pay attention."
–Tiarra

"In high school, I was a terrible student. Now I am getting all A's."
–Jason

"You don't have to go to class every hour of every day."
–Elizabeth

Naturally, not all of your Paradigm Shifts will come easily. In his classic book *The Structure of Scientific Revolutions*, Professor Thomas Kuhn of the University of California, Berkeley, invented the term "paradigm shift." He showed that scientific breakthroughs come only when people "break with" old ways of thinking—old paradigms. Sometimes those "break-withs" take time and effort.

As hard as it can be to shift your own paradigms, shifting others' paradigms tends to be even harder. Many of the most historic Paradigm Shifts were strongly resisted. For example, in the 1850s, about 1 in 10 new mothers died from a galloping infection they called "childbed fever." Then a Hungarian obstetrician named Ignaz Semmelweis noticed that when doctors washed their hands before examining new mothers, the death rate plummeted to nearly zero. But when he suggested that doctors who didn't wash their hands were passing germs on to their patients, he was laughed at, humiliated, and forced out of his job. Of course, now we know that Semmelweis was right about his "germ theory" of disease.

Life is made up of Paradigm Shifts. Whether you're trying to change your own paradigms or the paradigms of others, you need patience and effort. But in the end, if you're open to those shifts, you are more likely to succeed in college and life.

Ignaz Semmelweis

> Thomas Kuhn argued that scientific advancement is not evolutionary, but rather is a "series of peaceful interludes punctuated by intellectually violent revolutions," and in those revolutions "one conceptual world view is replaced by another."

"Man's mind, once stretched to a new idea, never goes back to its original dimensions."

—Oliver Wendell Holmes, American jurist

Shifting Paradigms

Describe a time when you had a positive Paradigm Shift:

What was your paradigm before the event?

What was your paradigm after the event?

What caused it to shift?

ACTIVITY 5

31

WHAT YOU DO—THE POWER OF A HABIT

Why have I made a big issue about paradigms? Because paradigms drive behavior. They influence everything you Do.

When Brianna saw herself as capable as her peers, she started behaving differently. She worked harder, became more confident, and focused more on school. How she saw herself greatly impacted what she did.

Assume for a moment that this is your paradigm of yourself: "I stink at school." With such a self-paradigm, how will you handle taking a test, talking to a professor, choosing classes, or working with a study group? You'll probably apologize for your faults, make lame excuses, procrastinate, or forget to try. After all, what's the use?

By contrast, try on this self-paradigm: "I can do well at school." Now how do you handle taking the test, meeting the professor, choosing a career, or joining a study group? Chances are, things will go much better. You'll speak with confidence, look people in the eye, and even laugh and learn from your mistakes. Because how you See things impacts what you Do.

And so I ask: What are your self-paradigms? Do you see yourself doing well in college? Do you see yourself in charge of your life or as a victim of life? Your answers are important—you choose how well you do in school and in life.

> "Live your life by doing things that are beneficial."
>
> —Jimmy Fallon

ACTIVITY 6

Contrasting Self-Paradigms

You've probably had times when you felt either good or bad about yourself.

1. Describe a time when you felt down on yourself. How did you act at that time? What was the result?

2. Describe a situation when you felt confident or upbeat about yourself. How did you act at that time? What was the result?

When you change the way you think, you change the way you act. The same applies to your relationships with others. The way you See people impacts how you behave toward them. Consider what happened with Gayle, a student from Alabama:

When I started college, I was quite critical of others, especially my roommates. Every time one of them left dishes unwashed, I noticed it and I fumed. Every time one of them made too much noise at night, I noticed it and I fumed. I could point out anyone's flaws. And the truth was that I really didn't have any close friends.

Then one day I got caught in an emergency and one of my roommates went out of her way to help me. I couldn't believe someone would do that for me, much less my most annoying roommate.

I felt obligated to repay her and so tried to do nice things for her. The more I did nice things, the kinder she was to me. I began to realize that she really was a talented and caring individual. I also began seeing her strengths and ignoring her petty annoyances. We became best friends, doing most everything together.

It was a while before it hit me that maybe the reason I was still annoyed with my other roommates was that I had remained focused on identifying their flaws. I determined to find out more about them and to try to identify their strengths. In some cases it was hard, but gradually I found the good in them, and it was about then that they warmed up to me. Before long, I couldn't believe how lucky I was to have such good roommates and friends.

When Gayle shifted her paradigm from negative to positive, she changed the way she treated her roommates, and they changed the way they treated her. On both sides, a Paradigm Shift changed behavior.

DID YOU KNOW?
Theory X and Theory Y

A classic study of leadership paradigms comes from MIT Professor Douglas McGregor. In the 1960s, he found that leaders have one of two paradigms of other people: Theory X or Theory Y.

X LEADERS VIEW PEOPLE AS:	Y LEADERS VIEW PEOPLE AS:
• Lazy. • Unchanging. • Incapable of self-management. • Followers not leaders. • Having few valuable ideas. • Working only for money and security.	• Wanting to work. • Motivated by meaningful goals. • Self-starters. • Able to handle responsibility. • Full of ideas and suggestions. • Working for an important purpose.

Assume you're a leader with a Theory X paradigm. How would you treat your employees? Would you trust them to work on their own? Would you listen to their ideas?

Now assume you're a leader with a Theory Y paradigm. Now how would you treat your employees? Would you trust them and listen to their ideas? Would you need to constantly check up on them?

How leaders perceive people influences how they lead. Likewise, how you perceive people impacts how you treat them.

I WOULD DEFINITELY SAY HE'S AN X-PARADIGM LEADER

You act according to your paradigms—the way you See things—in everything you Do. Your paradigm of "clean" impacts how you groom yourself and how you organize your stuff. Your paradigm of alcohol impacts how much—or if—you drink. Your paradigm of grades impacts how much you study. That's because your paradigms drive what you Do every day.

DID YOU KNOW?
The Top 10 Bad Habits

1. Lying
2. Being late
3. Forgetting and other acts of carelessness
4. Knuckle cracking
5. Belching and passing gas
6. Obsessing over orderliness
7. Being unable to make a commitment
8. Being a skinflint (cheapskate)
9. Procrastinating
10. Cigarette smoking

-From *The Complete Idiot's Guide to Breaking Bad Habits*

"I get home, I got the munchies

Binge on all my Twinkies

Throw up in the tub

Then I go to sleep."

—Tove Lo, "Habits"

Get in the Habit

As I said earlier, what you repeatedly Do is called a habit. Some habits grow on you over time, such as brushing your teeth, exercising daily, or being late to class. You might not be conscious of more subtle habits, such as putting yourself or other people down or letting your fears rule your actions.

If you have a string of ineffective habits, you're habitually ineffective. If you have a habit of staring at the television for six hours a day, you're using up about three months a year. Over four years, that's the equivalent of an extra fifth year in college. By contrast, if you have a habit of exercising and eating right, you'll be more alert for class and study time. Your habits can make or break your college career.

Where do your habits come from? From your paradigms. Deeply rooted paradigms lead to deeply rooted habits. Too often people try to change their behaviors without changing their paradigms. What are the most popular New Year's resolutions?

• Lose weight.
• Pay off debts.
• Quit smoking.

They're also broken the most.

Why? Because people try working on the behavior rather than the paradigm that drives the behavior. To lose weight, they try eating less. To quit smoking, they try cutting back on the cigarettes. But the change is only temporary—soon they're right back where they started.

If you want to hugely improve your effectiveness, work on changing your paradigms.

WHAT YOU GET—THE POWER OF EFFECTIVENESS

Just as how you See things impacts what you Do, what you Do ultimately impacts what you Get.

Let me illustrate using a well-known fable—Aesop's tale of *The Goose and the Golden Egg.* A poor farmer wakes up one day only to discover that his goose miraculously laid an egg of pure gold. Delighted, he takes great care of the prized bird, ensuring its safety and good health. In turn, day after day the goose delivers a single golden egg, which brings the farmer and his wife good fortune.

One day, in a moment of greed, the farmer kills the goose to get all of the golden eggs at once. To his dismay, however, he finds no gold inside and the bird is now dead. And the farmer and his wife did not live happily ever after.

So, what happened here? The farmer's flawed paradigm (See) was that all the gold was inside the bird. So he killed (Do) the goose to obtain the riches faster. In the end, however, the results (Get) proved disastrous.

In contrast, imagine the farmer had a better paradigm and believed that his bird could only produce one golden egg per day and no more (See). With that in mind, the farmer would have cared for and protected the goose at all costs and been very happy cashing in one golden egg per day (Do). And he and his wife would have taken long cruises in the Mediterranean happily thereafter (Get).

> "Bad habits are easier to abandon today than tomorrow."
>
> —Yiddish Proverb

What He Saw

What He Did

What He Got

Sometimes we're like the farmer. We kill the goose, so to speak. For example, we work so hard in school—taking no time for rest or fun—and end up burning out. Or we work so hard at a job that we have no time for ourselves or the people in our lives, and end up with broken bodies and relationships.

Effectiveness, by contrast, means getting what you want in such a way that you keep getting what you want over time.

When Gayle changed her paradigms about her roommates, her behavior changed, and so did her results. She went from having no friends to having "the best roommates ever." How? She changed her paradigms, not her address. Likewise, when Brianna changed her paradigm about her own abilities, her behavior changed and her grades improved. Because these women now See things differently, they Do things differently and Get different results.

After 20 years of research, Stanford Professor Carol S. Dweck confirmed in her book *Mindset* that most people have one of two mindsets (or paradigms) about their ability to learn: a "fixed" mindset or a "growth" mindset. People with a fixed mindset believe that their intelligence is limited and can't get better. People with a growth mindset believe their intelligence is unlimited and they can learn forever.

According to Dweck, it really matters if you have a fixed or growth mindset. Here's the difference:

	FIXED MINDSET	GROWTH MINDSET
What They *See*	My intelligence and personality are fixed; I am who I am. Effort on my part is fruitless.	My intelligence and qualities can be improved with effort. I'm in a constant state of becoming.
What They *Do*	• Avoid challenges. • Get defensive or give up easily when faced with opposition. • Ignore useful feedback. • Feel threatened by the success of others.	• Embrace challenges. • Persist in the face of setbacks. • Learn from criticism. • Find lessons and inspiration in the successes of others.
What They *Get*	Plateau early and achieve less than their potential.	Reach ever-higher levels of achievement.

Know that your paradigms (mindsets) really do influence the choices you make and the actions you take. Hopefully you'll adopt a growth mindset. Now take a few minutes to examine some of your paradigms about college and life.

See-Do-Get

Read the following See-Do-Get examples, then insert a few examples from your own life. In each case, identify the paradigm (See), the behavior (Do) that the paradigm leads to, and the results (Get) you might expect.

SEE	DO	GET
I hate math.	I skip math as often as I can.	I failed math and have to retake the class.
My instructor is a bore.	I bring other things to do in class or doodle a lot.	The instructor seemed frustrated with me and the way he/she graded me reflected it.
Exercising regularly helps me to study better.	I work out four times a week.	I got sick less and stayed alert longer while studying.

Put Principles at the Center

The best way I know to produce healthy, accurate paradigms and effective habits is to center them upon timeless, universal principles of effectiveness. Let me explain what I mean by "center."

While people have many paradigms, one or two tend to become the more dominant "center" of their attention, or the main lens through which they look at life. A person's center, therefore, becomes the prominent source from which he or she gets security, guidance, strength, and wisdom.

Consider a few examples of students who are centered on things other than principles, which leads to an unstable foundation.

Stuff-Centered. If we center our lives on stuff, then we measure our happiness by what we own. We need the latest of everything. When a new piece of technology is launched, we've got to have it. New fashion? We're wearing it first. Why? Because *things* drive our choices, we base our self-esteem on what we possess.

Screen-Centered. TV, computer, movie, and cell-phone screens have flooded much of the world. If we center our lives on screens, we spend endless

> "There's never enough of the stuff you can't get enough of."
>
> —Patrick H. T. Doyle, author

hours watching TV, playing games, and texting relentlessly. Sometimes we juggle multiple screens at once. We don't have time for much else.

ZITS   ***BY JERRY SCOTT AND JIM BORGMAN***

ZITS © 2010 Zits Partnership, Dist. By King Features

Boyfriend/Girlfriend-Centered. This is a common center. However, if we center our lives on a boyfriend or girlfriend, our schedules and decisions are determined by someone else. An offhanded comment can ruin the whole week. Our sense of self-worth depends on how our boyfriend or girlfriend treats us.

School-Centered. If we center our lives on school, we spend all our time studying with no breaks—no time for friends, family, fun, or even sleep. Meals intrude on study time and tend to be fast food. Failing a test can ruin our lives, because our grades determine our self-worth.

While attending business school years ago, I became school-centered at one point. I was obsessed with performing well in class at the expense of my health. I didn't take time to exercise or get fresh air each day because I wanted to be a step ahead the next day in class and it seemed like a waste of time. This was fine for a while, but after a year of this kind of focus, I didn't feel too well, I became more stressed than ever, and it negatively impacted how I was doing in school.

Job-Centered. If we center our lives on a career, we measure our self-worth by how the job is going. Our only friends are co-workers, and all we ever talk about is work. We work long hours. Even when we go on vacation we're constantly on our phones.

Drug-Centered. If we center our lives on drugs such as alcohol, narcotics, or painkillers, the only thing that matters is getting that next high.

DID YOU KNOW?
Screens R Us

The average teen consumes no less than 10 hours and 45 minutes across all platforms every day, including an average of 5 hours a day on the Internet.

IT'S YOUR DAY OFF, KEVIN. MAYBE YOU'RE TOO WORK CENTERED.

People might center their lives on sports, money, or fun, and end up neglecting family, friends, school, and work—everything that makes life meaningful. But you can't count on any of these "centers." At any time, you could lose all your money, your friends, your health—even your phone—and have nothing left at the center of your life.

The only thing you can center your life on that will never let you down is *principles*.

What is a principle?

Principles at the Center

Imagine a world where everything occurs by chance. Sometimes the sun rises in the morning; sometimes it doesn't. Water running over the edge of a cliff might fall down or rise up. An apple seed might produce an apple or maybe a rose. Who knows? Such is life in a "chance world."

Fortunately, even though life isn't predictable, we do not live in a chance world. There are some things we can depend on. They're called principles, or natural laws.

Principles are timeless. They're as true today as they were during the Middle Ages. Principles are universal; they apply whether you are in Minnesota, Malta, Madagascar, Morocco, or Mongolia. Principles are also self-evident—they're true whether we like it or not.

"Important principles may and must be inflexible."
—Abraham Lincoln

39

PRINCIPLES
• Are timeless and universal.
• Produce predictable outcomes.
• Are not religious.
• Are external to ourselves.
• Operate whether we believe in them or not.
• Are self-evident.

Gravity is an example of a principle. Gravity has always existed, so it is timeless. Gravity applies wherever you go in the world—north or south, east or west—and regardless of your age, religion, nationality, or ethnicity, it is universal. Gravity doesn't care if you believe in it or not. And it is self-evident, since it is hard to argue about the existence of gravity. Just jump off a chair and see what happens.

DID YOU KNOW?

Gravity is the force that attracts objects toward each other. The equation is $F = mg$.

- F is the force pulling an object toward the earth.
- m is the mass of the object.
- g is the acceleration due to gravity; this number is constant for all matter in the universe.

mg is the product of m times g.

So you can let the principle of gravity work for you or against you, but you can't eliminate it from your life.

Suppose you want to grow a garden. If in the spring you plant a healthy seed in good ground, feed it, weed it, and water it, you can expect some nice vegetables at harvest time. But suppose you don't plant the seed, flake off during the growing season, and then try to cram everything in just before the harvest season. Will it work? No, because nature has its laws. That's how principles work, whether you like it or not. It's called the law of the harvest.

In your studies, you'll probably come across many scientific principles like these. But what about your personal and relationship success? Are there principles at work there too?

Of course. Take honesty, fairness, respect, integrity, and kindness. Do these principles change across national borders, time zones, or centuries? Can you even imagine a healthy relationship based on their opposites—dishonesty, unfairness, disrespect, lack of integrity, or cruelty?

"Every person has free choice—free to obey or disobey the natural laws. Your choice determines the consequences. Nobody ever did, or ever will, escape the consequences of his choices."

—Alfred A. Montapert, author

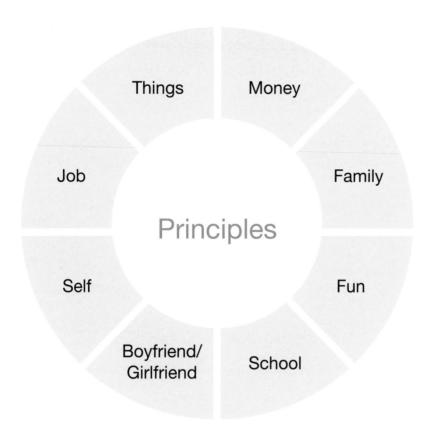

My experience is that people who center their lives on timeless, universal principles are more successful. They're more stable. They don't change their values from day to day or from crowd to crowd, like social chameleons trying to fit in wherever they can.

It is fascinating to note that the key to succeeding in the other centers, all of which have a place, is to put principles first. In other words, if you want to be a better boyfriend or girlfriend, put principles first. If you want to be a better mother or father, put principles first. The more you put principles like honesty, respect, hard work, empathy, and service at your center, the more friends you will have, the better student and employee you will be, the more effective you will become at leading your own life, and so on. It's called principle-centered leadership, and it always leads to success in the long run.

That isn't always the case in the short term. After all, we've all seen some people prosper by lying, cheating, or stepping on others. But it won't last in the long run. In the long run, principles always win.

"Be thou incapable of change in that which is right, and men will rely upon thee. Establish unto thyself principles of action, and see that thou ever act according to them. First know that thy principles are just, and then be thou."

—Akhenaton,
King of Egypt,
14th century BCE

LESSON ON LEADERSHIP: Lighthouse Principles

>> When people ask me to define a principle, I like to tell this apocryphal story:

One foggy night at sea, the captain of a great battleship saw what looked like the lights of another ship heading toward him. He had his signalman send a message to the other ship: "Change your course 10 degrees to the south."

The reply came back: "Change your course 10 degrees to the north."

Then the captain answered: "I am a captain. Change your course 10 degrees to the south."

Reply: "I am a seaman first class. Change your course 10 degrees to the north."

This last exchange really infuriated the captain, so he signaled back: "I am a battleship. Change your course 10 degrees to the south!"

Reply: "I am a lighthouse. Change your course 10 degrees to the north!"

Guess who changed course.

Rank meant nothing. Opinions meant nothing. The lighthouse was not going to move. Principles are like lighthouses—they do not change. Like the captain, we can only choose whether or not we will steer clear or smash ourselves against the rocks.

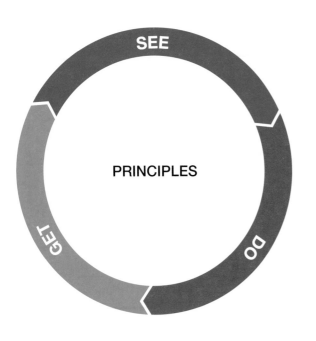

So, what does it mean to be principle-centered? What does that look like?

Principle-centered people make decisions based on principles. They don't make decisions based on what their boyfriend likes or what will make them the most money. It's called principle-centered leadership.

Take the principle of honesty. If you're principle-centered, you tell the truth regardless of how it affects you. You don't cheat on a test, even if it means a better grade. You don't make up a phony excuse if you have a late paper. You don't steal stuff from your roommate.

If you have timeless, universal principles at the center of your life, you'll become a highly effective person. For example, you'll See yourself as an honest person, so you won't Do dishonest things. As a result, you will never Get in trouble for being dishonest and you will always feel good about yourself.

In this book, I introduce each of the 7 Habits with this picture of the See-Do-Get Cycle. I want to show you how each habit is centered on principles that will always work for you. If you act on those principles, you won't crash into the rocks of life and crack up.

So, what are the timeless, universal principles that make people most effective? When Dr. Stephen Covey researched centuries of success literature from around the world, he was trying to identify them. It took him many years, but he finally boiled down certain key principles into "The 7 Habits of Highly Effective People."

DID YOU KNOW?
Stay Golden

The Golden Rule, or "Do unto others as you would have them do unto you," has a history that goes back before the term "Golden Rule" (or "Golden Law," as it was called in the 1600s). It was present in varied forms in the philosophies of ancient Babylon, Egypt, Persia, India, Greece, Israel, and China.

Over the years, many people have come up to me and said something like, "You know, the 7 Habits remind me of my own cultural traditions, or sacred literature, or the teachings of this philosopher or that philosopher." And all I can say is, "Yes, they do, don't they?" Principles belong to us all. They are part of the human experience. All the great cultures and all the great thinkers throughout the ages have taught the importance of principles.

So the 7 Habits don't come from any one culture, religion, or philosophy—rather, they are based on universal, timeless principles that work everywhere for everyone. They never have and never will go out of style. You can count on them to make you successful regardless of what happens to you.

> "The ideas embedded in the [7 Habits] framework are timeless. They are principles. This is why they work, and why they speak to people in all age groups around the globe."
>
> —Jim Collins, *Good to Great*

IN SUMMARY

The key to success in college and life is to develop the habits of effectiveness. Changing your habits isn't easy. But you can do it if you first change your paradigms.

You See the world through lenses I call paradigms. You hold paradigms of yourself, others, and the world around you. Sometimes the paradigms are accurate. Sometimes they're not. When a paradigm changes, I call it a Paradigm Shift.

Your paradigms, especially your self-paradigms, drive your habits. For example, if you See yourself as incurably shy, it will probably be a habit with you to avoid meeting new people. But if you See yourself as confident, your behavior will change. The magic here is that you can choose how you See yourself—it's up to you.

Your habits make you effective or ineffective. Effectiveness means getting what you want now in such a way that you can keep getting what you want— harvesting the golden eggs and taking care of the goose. The best way to break

"Propensities and principles must be reconciled by some means."

—Charlotte Brontë

a bad habit or gain a good habit is to shift your paradigms. And the best way to develop effective paradigms is to center them on timeless, universal principles. The more you place principles of effectiveness at the center of your life, the more stable, balanced, and effective you become. Each of the 7 Habits is based on these self-evident principles of effectiveness.

To begin applying these concepts, try taking some of the Baby Steps on the next page. I also recommend carefully studying and applying the information found in the Academic Protip: "How to Study in College."

COMING ATTRACTIONS

Coming up next, you'll learn about how to make sunny weather, even if the conditions outside are bad. You won't want to miss it!

Baby Steps

1. Teach to Learn. Teach the See-Do-Get Cycle to a friend or family member. Give an example of how your paradigms (See) impact your behavior (Do) and the results of your behavior (Get).

2. Think of a limiting paradigm you have of yourself, such as "I'm not a friendly person" or "I can't wake up in the mornings." Sometime today do something that totally contradicts that paradigm.

3. Consider all the potential life centers mentioned in this chapter: friends, money, fun, parents, school, self, possessions, boyfriend/girlfriend, work, principles, and so forth. Which of these would you consider to be your center? _____
    What is the impact of that center on your life?

4. Principles are timeless, universal, and self-evident. Try to name 10 principles or natural laws.

5. Are you violating a principle in your life right now? If so, what are you going to do about it?

6. Think of a person who annoys you or whom you simply don't like. What is your paradigm of that person? _____ Is your paradigm accurate? _____
    Do you need to shift it?_____

7. The next time you look in the mirror, say something positive about yourself.

8. Name three people you would consider principle-centered:
    a. _____

    b. _____

    c. _____

9. Where in your life are you having problems? Identify the paradigms that might be behind these problems. How could you shift those paradigms?

Academic Protip

I searched all over the world for the perfect person to talk about general study skills, because those skills are foundational to succeeding in college. And I think I found what I was looking for. Her name is Eileen Tracy, and she holds degrees from distinguished universities. But more important, her advice is real and practical, and she has some insightful ideas on how to approach your studies in college. I'd encourage you to read her words carefully, as she may be able to create a mini Paradigm Shift in your own mind about studying in college. Enjoy!

Eileen Tracy,
B.A. Honors,
Oxford University;
M.A., University of
East London

How to Study in College

By Eileen Tracy, B.A. Honors, Oxford University; M.A., University of East London

College is where reading lists, syllabuses, and coursework assignments come in big sizes. It's therefore incredibly helpful for students at this higher academic level to apply some study skills in their work: even just a little study skill can slash workloads and boost grades.

And yet, many students shun study skills, preferring to struggle on regardless, with an attitude something like: "If I've managed so far on no skill, why bother now? Can't you see I got enough to do as it is?" There's no doubt that taking on new skills can be stressful.

So rather than dish out study tips that you may not wish to hear about, I will present you instead with 10 "don'ts" guaranteed to make you feel like dropping out tomorrow. In other words, here's a tried-and-tested guide to failing at college.

1. **Learn passively.**
   Passive learning may make you go blank in your exams, but it's truly wonderful in every other way. It means avoiding all active learning. You learn something actively if you reproduce it in a form that's wholly yours. Active learning is saying it in your own words,

perhaps from memory; turning it into a quick illustration, mind map, or graph; summarizing it; reducing it to a list of points or key words; spending 10 minutes planning your answer to an exam question on the topic—these are all examples of active learning. But as you can imagine, they require work. Passive learning merely requires that you reread your notes, maybe transfer them to the computer, certainly highlight them all prettily. It stays "secretarial," sparing you the pain of learning anything, yet relieving you of the guilt of doing nothing: after all, you've spent hours at your desk, right?

2. **Never review anything you've learned.**
   Let's say you've just learned something. Great! So now, what are you going to do to remember it? Here's a very efficient strategy:
   - **Take a short break.** Then quickly review what you learned (in other words, check that you know the essentials by heart). Then leave it: a night's sleep will deepen your understanding and aid recall, because it is through sleep (and also through breaks) that your brain processes what you've learned and gives you a sense of where it fits with what you already know.

- **The next day, review a second time.** It shouldn't take more than a few minutes, thanks to that magic night's sleep. This second review seals the information in your memory for a week.
- **Review it a third time after that week.**
- **Then give it a fourth review one month later.**
- **A fifth and final review at the end of the term** commits the information to your long-term memory.

Note that this is a guideline and need not be followed exactly. The main point is that we tend to forget what we learn unless we review it about five times, at increasing intervals. But honestly! Who has time to organize five little reviews of a topic when the entire syllabus can be crammed into one simple last-minute, pre-exam panic?

3. **Give yourself no breaks.** Just aim to sit at your desk until the work's all done. Because academic work expands to fill all time available, your task will never end, so you'll get much sympathy from friends and family. After 40 minutes, concentration decreases, particularly when you're trying to read for information; so the most efficient students tend to work in half-hour bursts broken by short breaks, and briefly reviewing what they learned after each break. But then, these students get such good grades, they have no friends.

4. **Learn everything through logic.** Passed down to us from Ancient Greece, successfully used over millennia, all memory tricks, or "mnemonics," involve the use of imagination. Let's say you have to learn a list of key words, such as the 12 signs of the zodiac, but you have only one minute. Logic, obviously, would fail you here. But now just picture a caper (Capricorn) falling into an aquarium (Aquarius) at the zoo—and being promptly eaten by a fish (Pisces). Imagine that fish then filling with air (Aries). (As a sort of allergic reaction to capers, if you like.) A couple of bulls' horns sprout out of this poor fish's head (Taurus). Two fish-loving twins (Gemini) raise the alarm. But they can't be heard because at that precise moment, a tiny crab (Cancer) is pinching one of the zoo's largest lions (Leo)—much roaring, etc. Richard Branson (Virgo) is called in to throw money at the problem, but decides that on balance (Libra), he'd rather keep spending his money on space travel. Whoa! This kind of psychedelic storytelling is for kids, not serious college students. Leave mnemonics well alone.

5. **Fear deadlines.** Anything with the word "dead" in it should be avoided, right? The writer Mark Twain confessed that his secret for getting complex, overwhelming jobs done was to break them all down into small, manageable tasks and then get started on the first one. In other words, he gave himself many little, teeny-weeny, friendly deadlines. Maybe he even put these little deadlines into some sort of schedule, and presumably, scheduling his tasks in this way gave him time to do things other than write great American literature all the time. But Twain is now dead. See what deadlines did to him?

6. **Be perfect.**

Take your as-long-as-your-arm reading list. It may have been designed by a college professor to impress his or her colleagues rather than to serve your student needs—but let's not think too deeply here. Let's just read each and every single listed book from cover to cover. Effective students aren't so conscientious, and will settle for a "good enough" approach instead, which enables them to decide which reading is most important and prioritize it, skim instead of read, browse, find summaries on the Internet, get a sense of the main points, and still have time for tennis—cheats!

7. **Get hyperstressed studying for exams.**

Prepping for exams doesn't need to be this big enterprise. If you've been paying attention in class, just brush up on your weak spots. Start with the likely exam questions and then fill in the knowledge you need. Review what the professor is most likely to ask you about. Take 10 minutes and sketch a mental answer to a question. People get hyperstressed "studying for exams." They think of it as trying to memorize every brick in the wall, so they cram and reread everything, a lot of which is irrelevant to the exam. Nobody can work like that. It's crazy. But a student who knows the basic stuff will score points. The basic information is always what the professor is looking for—it's the easiest to score and the most relevant.

8. **Lose sleep.**

Persistent sleep deprivation has been found to lower people's IQ and, with it, their ability to do difficult tasks. This is why brain surgeons are absolutely required to sleep regularly. Well, never mind, you're not studying brain surgery, and anyway, you can work through the night and sleep after the term's over.

9. **Sleep during lectures.**

Your mind can process up to 800 words a minute; the average person can only speak at a quarter of this speed. One way to stay alert in lectures and classes is to sketch out the outline of the talk or discussion, perhaps putting together a few exam-style questions based on what you hear, and making selective notes accordingly. But it's easier just to doze—or scribble down everything you hear. If you can make out your own scribbles, that is.

10. **Listen to your ego.**

Your ego's main purpose in life is to connect your identity and self-worth to your grades. It makes you take everything too seriously: "This class is essential to my survival." It makes you see only the future: "I can start to enjoy life in three years' time once I've got my degree"—or the past: "I've failed before, I'm bound to fail again." It will try to make you feel special but alone: "I don't need help"; "There's no one to turn to." Another way in which your ego can spoil an otherwise perfectly pleasant day is to make you squirm (sometimes smirk) by comparing you to others:

"So-and-so here is better/worse than me because they're older/younger/the same age/more advantaged/less advantaged/enjoy the same advantages but do less/more work…" and so on. The ego is quite a talker and loves extremes. Seen through its eyes, a good grade makes you a winner. A bad grade or a moment's procrastination proves you're a loser. Nothing could be further from the truth. Life is full of helpful people and second chances, and in the long run, attitude matters more than grades. But don't take my word for it.

Eileen Tracy is a study-skills counselor and runs a private practice in London to help students in the United Kingdom and internationally to study effectively. Author of *The Student's Guide to Exam Success*, Eileen has appeared on BBC television, has written many articles, and gives talks for parents, teachers, and students at schools and universities. She holds a B.A. with Honors from Oxford University and an M.A. from the University of East London. See her website at www.eileentracy.co.uk.

References

Cerf, Christopher and Victor S. Navasky, *The Experts Speak: The Definitive Compendium of Authoritative Misinformation*, Villard, 1998, 35, 171, 182, 208, 209, 237, 261.

Dweck, Carol, *Mindset: The New Psychology of Success*, Ballantine Books, 2007, 245.

Gutelle, Sam, "Social Media Habits of Teenagers," *Social Media Week*, June 11, 2013.

Kuhn, Thomas, *The Structure of Scientific Revolutions*, University of Chicago Press, 2012.

"The Lighthouse," Reader's Digest, Dec. 1983, contributed by Dan Bell.

1

HABIT 1
Be Proactive
The Habit of Choice

"Success isn't a result of spontaneous combustion. You must set yourself on fire."

–ARNOLD H. GLASOW

IN THIS CHAPTER, YOU WILL DISCOVER WAYS TO:

- Take initiative.
- Carry your own weather.
- Use proactive language.
- Grow your Circle of Influence.
- Break negative cycles.
- Avoid addictions.

Also, look for the Academic Protip...

- How to Use a College Library

Habit 1:
Be Proactive

is the foundation of all the other habits. It is the habit where college students like you learn to take responsibility for your life and education more than ever before.

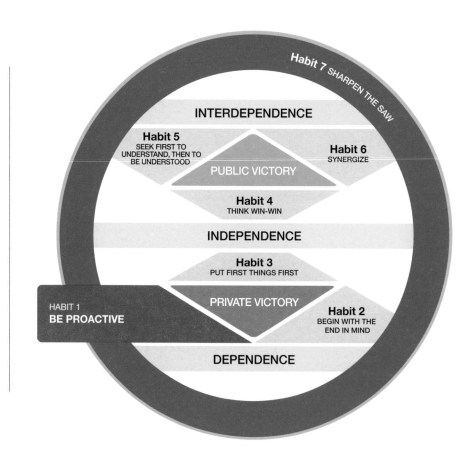

What I Wish
I'd Known in College

"It really is true: 90 percent of life is showing up! So make the most of attending class—even the early ones!"
–Courtney, Boston College

"I think freshman year is the hardest. There is no one there to force you to go to class and no parents breathing down your neck to get your homework done. Make it a point to never miss class and to get your homework done as soon as you can. It's no fun spending the last three years of college trying to make up for poor choices in your first year."
–Jordan, University of Utah

"Persistence is more important than talent or knowledge in college, and in life. Study more than you party. You don't have to be the smartest person in the room, just one of the hardest-working."
–Jennifer, Purdue University

"You really have to take control of your own education. Don't just 'get by,' but make an effort to think about what you're reading or studying and what you're doing. Take advantage of everything in front of you."
–Janita, University of Technology, Mauritius

"It isn't as hard as you think, especially if you show up to class and do your homework."
–Baruti, University of South Africa

"This isn't high school anymore. It's up to you to 'show up' in every sense of the word."
–Jackie, University of Hawaii

REAL CHOICES:
Creating Your Own Life

Frank McCain was hungry. It was nearly dinnertime for the young man who was in his second term at North Carolina Agricultural and Technical University, known as "A&T." So he and three friends decided to grab a bite at a nearby diner.

It's the sort of thing millions of students do every day without even thinking about it. But on this day, February 1, 1960, Frank and his friends were taking their lives in their hands. They were African-American students, and it was against the law for them to sit down and order a meal in this whites-only restaurant in Greensboro, North Carolina. They knew the reaction might be a violent one.

They did not make this decision lightly. Frank had been reading about Gandhi and Martin Luther King and the idea that injustice doesn't have to be met with violence. Injustice could be overcome by peaceful, nonviolent protest.

"Fifteen seconds after I sat on that stool, I had the most wonderful feeling," Frank said later. "I had

a feeling of liberation, restored manhood; I had a natural high. And I truly felt almost invincible."

The students asked for service, but the manager ordered them out and a police officer stood by with a blackjack in hand. Everyone stared at each other for a long time. Abruptly, the manager closed the restaurant early and the young men left with empty stomachs.

Word of their daring deed spread quickly, and the next day 20 more African-American students joined them in a second attempt to get service at the restaurant. Within a week, more than 300 black students were participating in lunch counter "sit-ins," with many white students joining them. The movement spread across the country.

The students "sitting in" were viciously abused. People poured sugar, mustard, and ketchup on them and shouted obscenities and death threats. People spat on them and hurled eggs and milkshakes at them. Many of the students were carried away to jail. But like Gandhi, not one ever fought back or said a word of protest to their tormentors. They simply and politely kept asking for service.

Four African-American college students sit in protest at a whites-only lunch counter during the second day of peaceful protest at a Woolworth's in Greensboro, North Carolina. From left: Joseph McNeil, Franklin McCain, Billy Smith, and Clarence Henderson.

> "Do what you think is right for your happiness. If you're not happy with what you're doing, change studies. If you think the direction you've taken for the last five years is no longer suiting you, start something else."
>
> —Erlijen, student, University of Amsterdam

This shameful spectacle caused many people to look into their hearts, and it wasn't long before the law changed across the entire United States. Today a plaque marks the lunch counter in Greensboro where Frank McCain and his friends sat down for the first time. The lunch counter itself is on view in the Smithsonian Institution, and a statue on the A&T campus pays tribute to the four college freshmen who changed a nation.

"We didn't want to set the world on fire. We just wanted to sit down and eat like everybody else," Frank said many years later. "We wanted to be included in the round table of humanity."

Frank McCain and his friends weren't satisfied with standing back and letting the future happen to them. They took steps to create their own future. And that's what Habit 1: Be Proactive is about—taking responsibility for your life and choosing the future you want to have.

You probably don't face the dreadful barriers Frank faced, but in your own way, you have a serious choice to make: Will you stand back and let life happen to you, or will you step up and make it happen the way you want it to happen?

If you're a proactive student, you take charge of your life. You take charge of your education. You choose your classes, your major, your career. You choose when to wake up and go to sleep. You choose your friends and how you will spend your time. You face up to obstacles and beat them, as Frank McCain did. You are captain of your own ship.

The opposite of proactive is reactive. If you're a reactive student, you avoid responsibility for your life and your education. You blame other people ("I would have aced that test, but my roommate wouldn't lend me his notes") or circumstances ("It was too cold to go to class") for your problems. You act like a victim ("That professor's out to get me"). You need somebody else to do everything for you ("Mom, would you take the bus over here and do my laundry for me? I just can't do it. I know it's 200 miles, Mom…").

In this chapter, we'll find out how proactive you are and what you can do to become more proactive. If you practice Habit 1, these See-Do-Get elements become your reality.

PEOPLE WHO PRACTICE HABIT 1:

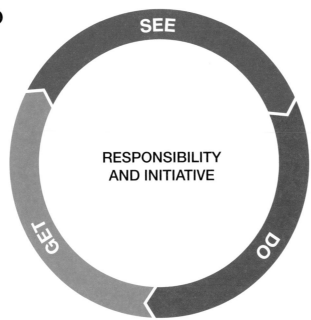

RESPONSIBILITY AND INITIATIVE

SEE

GET

DO

SEE
- You are free to choose how to act, regardless of what happens to you.
- Your future is a product of your own choices.

DO
- Take initiative.
- Carry your own weather.
- Use proactive language.
- Grow your Circle of Influence.
- Break negative cycles.
- Avoid addictions.

GET
- The future you want.

THE PARADIGMS OF PROACTIVITY

Proactive people think differently. If you're proactive, you have these paradigms:
- You are free to choose how to act, regardless of what happens to you.
- Your future is the product of your own choices.

The Freedom to Choose

You are free to choose your own actions. Nobody can make you do anything.

Imagine being in a situation where you're completely helpless, where other people are totally in control of you. And these people hate you and want to make you suffer.

That was the situation of the great Jewish psychiatrist Viktor Frankl when he was imprisoned in the Nazi death camps during World War II. In his famous book *Man's Search for Meaning*, written after the war, he describes many atrocities, including watching his parents, brother, and wife sent off to die in gas chambers. Only he and a sister survived.

As a medical student, Frankl had been schooled in genetic determinism and environmental determinism, two prevailing theories of why people behave as they do. Genetic determinism suggests that you are who you are because of your genetics. The convenient thing about this theory is that it allows people to blame their bad habits on their genes. "My grandfather was hot-tempered, my dad was that way, and so am I. There's nothing I can do about it."

By contrast, environmental determinists argue that genes are not the whole answer. Your environment makes you who you are—your home life, your neighborhood, your friends, your school, the economy.

Viktor Frankl

Clearly, your genes and environment both play a role in who you are. But Frankl saw things in the camps that he couldn't explain with either theory: "We who have lived in concentration camps can remember the men who walked through the huts comforting others, giving away their last piece of bread. They may have been few in number, but they offer sufficient proof that everything can be taken from man but one thing: the last of the human freedoms—to choose one's attitude in any given set of circumstances—to choose one's own way."

Frankl discovered that people are free to choose their own attitudes. This discovery excited him. It meant that his captors could jail him, kill his family, and torture his body, but only he could choose how to respond to it all. They could not take that choice from him. Only he—neither his genes nor his environment—could choose what he would do.

Frankl was fortunate to survive the war. Afterward, Frankl taught his students about their freedom to choose their own response to life. He pioneered the cognitive theory of human behavior: You are not simply a product of your genes and your upbringing. You are a product of your own choices. You're free to choose what you will do about what has happened to you, what is happening to you, and what will happen to you in the future.

Three Theories of Human Behavior

GENETIC DETERMINISM	ENVIRONMENTAL DETERMINISM	COGNITIVE THEORY
"I am the product of my genes."	"I am the product of my environment."	"I am the product of my choices."

The Creative Force of Your Life

If you are proactive, you see yourself as completely free to choose what you will do with your life. You also see yourself—nobody and nothing else—as the creator of your own future. That's the second paradigm of proactive thinking.

Richard de Charms, a professor of education and psychology at Washington University, taught that people are either "pawns" or "origins." In the game of chess, the "pawn" is the least powerful piece on the board. It gets pushed around and sacrificed. The player who controls all the moves is called the "origin." The origin acts; the pawn is acted upon.

Do you see yourself as more of a "pawn" or an "origin"?

If you see yourself as a pawn, you get pushed around by luck, fate, or circumstances you can't control. Life just happens to you. You're a victim of society or your upbringing. By contrast, if you see yourself as an origin, you're in charge of your life, you control the moves, and you are responsible for your success—or lack of it—in school. De Charms says by choosing one of these two paradigms, you decide what your life will be like.

Of course, no one controls everything in life. Lots of stuff happens—good and bad, genetic and environmental—that you have absolutely no control over. But if you have the proactivity paradigm, you create your own future.

WHAT PROACTIVE COLLEGE STUDENTS DO

Remember, your paradigms drive what you Do, so here's what you Do differently if you have the proactivity paradigm:

- Take initiative.
- Carry your own weather.
- Use proactive language.
- Grow your Circle of Influence.
- Break negative cycles.
- Avoid addictions.

Take Initiative

Proactive people act rather than become acted upon. They are self-starters. They take initiative to make things happen.

Taking initiative does not mean being pushy, aggressive, or annoying. Rather, it means being resourceful and creative in making things happen the way you want them to happen.

I like the example of Ute, a student at the University of Göttingen in Germany. She needed a place to live, but all the affordable places near the university were run down and falling apart. She could have just coped with it like most students, but instead, she hopped in her VW Käfer and looked in a better section of town. When she found a good neighborhood, she put a note in each postbox that told people who she was and what she wanted. An elderly patent lawyer responded and offered her a guest room in his nice home for a very affordable rate. It even had a garden view. Ute spent three great years there.

The point? Ute didn't just sit back, accept the status quo, and let life happen. She took the initiative to make things happen her way.

During my senior year of college, I was a few credit hours short of a language requirement I needed to graduate. I wasn't excited about the classes offered, so I drew up my own curriculum for a class, showed it to the dean of the college, and asked for credit. He not only approved my plan but enthusiastically endorsed it. As a result, I got what I wanted and received credit for it—all because I took the initiative.

If you don't like your circumstances, go out and make your own.

Once when Napoleon was preparing for battle, one of his soldiers asked him what he thought the battlefield conditions would be like. Napoleon was curt in responding: "Conditions? I create my own conditions."

Like Napoleon, proactive people create their own conditions. They take seriously the words of George Bernard Shaw, the English playwright, who said: "People are always blaming their circumstances for what they are. I don't believe in circumstances. The people who get on in this world are the people who get up and look for the circumstances they want, and if they can't find them, make them."

If you're proactive, you take the initiative to get the classes you need, take care of your health, or get a job. When life says no to you, you don't take no for an answer. You create the conditions for a positive and fun college experience.

> "Whatever you're meant to do, do it now. The conditions are always impossible."
>
> —Doris Lessing, author

Napoleon Bonaparte

"7 Rights" for Successful Studying

Create a good study environment by doing these seven things right.

1. **Right Attitude.** Good grades are your responsibility. You own them and no one else does, not even your mom. You can get good grades. You may need to get help, but it is within your control. Believe that you can do it because you can.

2. **Right Energy.** Your brain is connected to the rest of your body. To work well, it needs food and sleep. So if you're starving, grab a bite to eat before you jump into studying. Staying up all night to study puts your body in the same state as drinking and driving. Instead, exercise, drink water, and take breaks.

3. **Right Location.** Find a quiet place where you can spread out all your stuff, such as the library. Stay away from places where you are tempted to slack off. Make sure you have everything you need readily accessible—paper, pencils, laptop, snacks, and water—so you don't have to get up constantly.

4. **Right Time.** Set regular times for studying. Pick times when you are most alert and least likely to get distracted. Make it a routine.

5. **Right Pace.** Determine how long you will study. Stretch yourself, but break down your study times into doable chunks. Build in breaks to catch some fresh air and recharge.

6. **Right Sequence.** Prioritize your work. First, focus on the now: do whatever is due today or tomorrow. Second, focus on the later: look ahead and chip away at upcoming projects, papers, readings, and tests. Don't put them off—do a little bit at a time.

7. **Right Response.** You have the right to say no: NO to incoming text messages, NO to a crazy party, NO to your friend asking for a favor, and NO to the same video you've seen 10 times already. Don't be afraid to say no. It's okay.

Now reflect: How effective are your study conditions? Think about your habits and patterns: where, when, and how long do you study? How well do you organize your study materials and plan your time? What could you do better?

"On starting out a gloomy day: First you must realize that it is the day that is gloomy, not you. If you want to be gloomy, too, that's all right, but it's not mandatory."

—Nora Gallagher, author

Carry Your Own Weather

Have you ever known people who mirror the weather? If it's sunny outside, they're cheerful. If it's overcast, they're gloomy. If it's really stormy, watch out!

If you're a reactive person, you allow the outside world to determine how you feel. You let other people spoil your moods. You let the weather decide if you're going to have a good day. You feel awesome if your team wins and snarl at people if your team loses.

By allowing the outside world to decide how you feel, you empower it to control you. You've heard of road rage. Driver A cuts off Driver B, so Driver B goes into a rage—horns sound, fingers fly, and Driver B's day is ruined. To top it all off, while Driver B stews all day, Driver A is off and sailing, enjoying life.

You waste time and energy when you allow others' weaknesses to control your emotions. Comedian Buddy Hackett put it this way: "I've had a few arguments with people, but I never carry a grudge. You know why? While you're carrying a grudge, they're out dancing."

Proactive people choose their own weather. They choose to be pleasant, positive, and principle-centered, regardless of the circumstances or the moods of those around them. They're like the four freshmen from A&T who sat politely and quietly at the lunch counter while angry people spat on them. They're like the concentration-camp prisoners Frankl wrote about, giving away their last piece of food for the day, creating hope even in the darkest circumstances.

Marci, a student from Kentucky, shared this experience:

Over the Christmas holidays, I flew home to spend time with family. On a previous visit, I had met a young girl named Emily. She was 11 and I was 20. She was stricken with juvenile rheumatoid arthritis that had progressed to the point that it was crippling her ability to use her arms and legs. We had periodically stayed in touch, so I thought I would try to see her.

I called Emily's home the day after Christmas and learned she was in the hospital having surgery. The muscles and tendons in her hips had tightened so much that it was like she was always squatting down. The doctors were going to cut the muscles and tendons in her stomach and pelvis to release her hips and let her legs straighten.

As I went to the hospital, I wanted so badly to have something to say that would lift her spirits. Instead, as I walked into that room, there was my little friend—wrapped like a mummy from the waist down, with a huge smile on her face. She was lifting the spirits of all who entered her room. She was taking all her physical challenges and choosing to deal with them in such a way that brought smiles and strength to those around her. She totally lifted my spirits.

Emily had many reasons to be miserable: a horrible, chronic disease; surgery over Christmas, and a hospital stay while friends were playing with new toys. But she was free to choose how she felt, and she chose to be happy.

In contrast, I am reminded of a student who left her apartment for school one day and a neighbor called out, "Have a good day," to which the young woman replied, "Thanks, but I have other plans."

Do you know people like that? They choose to be miserable and try to bring others down with them. But whether it's raining outside or not, you can choose your own inner weather.

> "Happiness doesn't depend on outward conditions. It depends on inner conditions."
>
> —Dale Carnegie

DID YOU KNOW?
Becoming Authentically Happy

Dr. Martin Seligman is a distinguished psychologist at Princeton. In his book *Authentic Happiness*, he says your happiness depends on (1) genetics, (2) circumstances, and (3) things you control. However, his research says genetics and circumstances have less to do with happiness than the third category—the things you can control.

So to be happy, Seligman suggests, focus on things you can control, which he divides into three categories: past, present, and future. See these categories below:

The Past	You cannot change or control the past. However, you can change your paradigms about the past. • **Express Gratitude.** Think about the good things in your life. Keep a gratitude journal for 30 days. Record good things that happen each day, such as people who have helped you, gifts you got, or fun moments. Try to also express that gratitude to others. • **Extend Forgiveness.** Constantly stewing about what others have done only reignites anger—which is the opposite of happiness. Let go, move on. You don't have to trust people who have hurt you, but you should forgive them—for your own sake.
The Present	• **Add Variety.** Why do the same things all the time—eating the same crummy pizza, watching the same videos, playing the same games? Break up your routine now and then. • **Savor Enjoyable Moments.** You may be swamped, but make time to enjoy nature, listen intently to a friend, or go to a play. "Smell the roses." Don't rush through college so fast that you never get a chance to enjoy it. • **Do Meaningful Work.** Get involved in your studies or projects that take you outside yourself. Lazy loafing does not equal happiness.
The Future	In viewing the future: • **Argue for Your Strengths.** Focus on what you can do—not on what you can't. Don't dwell on your weaknesses. • **Become an Optimist.** Focus on the positives ahead. Don't be a pessimist who worries all the time. Look for silver linings in the clouds.

But it's not easy. Life is full of dumb problems like these, not to mention serious problems that really make things hard:

- You slog through snow to get to class and the professor doesn't show up.
- That annoying girl in the library won't shut up.
- Some idiot keeps setting off the fire alarm in the residence hall.
- Your boyfriend has your car and forgets to pick you up after work.
- Your study group blows off the assignment, and now the whole thing lands in your lap.
- This guy on a bike nearly runs into you and makes you drop your stuff in the gutter.
- Your sister chokes on a burrito, gets kidney stones, and you have to sit up with her in the emergency room all night; you have your midterm exam on chemical bonds in the morning; and your phone is dead.

Most people just react without thinking, and they "lose it." It's normal to get mad at other people and the weather and your own life. But you don't have to. Being normal is not required; you need to be effective. If you want to start carrying your own weather, imagine that you have a big pause button in the middle of your forehead.

When someone hurts my feelings, cuts me off while driving, or otherwise ticks me off, I imagine myself hitting that big pause button. Then I ask myself, "What is the right thing to do here? What's the best thing to do here? Do I really need to strike back in some way?" Sometimes hitting that pause button is all it takes to calm me down.

> "The professor is not merely an information dispensing machine, but a skilled navigator of a complex landscape."
>
> —William Badke, librarian

Pause Button
Stop, Think, and Choose

Have you ever "hit the pause button" when you were faced with a tough choice? Describe the situation and how you acted.

What was the situation?

When did you pause?

What did you do then?

What was the result?

ACTIVITY 9

> "It is our choices, Harry, that show what we truly are, far more than our abilities."
>
> —Professor Dumbledore, *Harry Potter and the Chamber of Secrets*

Your freedom to choose how you act—your personal pause button—can save you from endless problems. When might you need to push the pause button? When someone makes fun of your outfit? When your date doesn't show up? When your roommate messes up the kitchen and doesn't clean up? You need to be proactive during these moments. Imagine yourself hitting the pause button in those moments and responding in a way you won't regret later. It's within your control.

Remember Frank McCain sitting at the lunch counter day after day. People spat on him, threw eggs at him, and called him dirty names. But he looked on calmly and waited for a menu. Instead of striking back, he paused and thought about his real purpose and what he truly believed in.

And in the end, he got what he valued most—the respect of others, the respect of a nation, and a revolutionized way of treating his people.

When Put in This Position, I...

ACTIVITY 10

Describe how you would typically act in these scenarios. Write "P" if your typical response is proactive, or "R" if your response is reactive. If you respond with an "R," decide now how you will respond more proactively in the future.

THE SCENARIO	YOUR TYPICAL RESPONSE	P	R
While you're driving, someone cuts you off in traffic.			
Your instructor gives you a low score on a paper you worked really hard on.			
You're watching or playing a sport and the referee makes a bad call.			
You get asked to go to a movie, but you know you have homework.			
You sense you are about to lose your job.			
A roommate eats your food and leaves the package on the counter.			
You hear someone gossiping about you.			

Use Proactive Language

How can you tell instantly if people are proactive or reactive? Just listen to their language. Reactive people talk about how helpless they are, while proactive people are in charge of their lives.

REACTIVE LANGUAGE	PROACTIVE LANGUAGE
He makes me so mad.	I don't let him get on my nerves.
I have to do my homework.	I'm going to get this paper done now.
There's nothing I can do about it.	There's got to be a way I can do it.
If only I were taller…	I'm okay with the way I am.
I can't change.	Where there's a will there's a way.
It was his fault; he gave me the first drink.	I didn't take a drink. It was my choice.
I failed math because my professor was a lousy teacher.	Next time, I'll turn in my assignments on time.
I was born [insert ethnic origin]; nobody will ever give me a good job.	If I am prepared, someone will hire me no matter what race I am.
I have to drop out of school.	I'll find a way to stay in school.

Can you sense the drastic difference between these statements? For reactive people, all the responsibility is outside themselves: "He makes me so mad," "It was her fault," or "I can't help myself." Reactive language:

- Takes power away from you.
- Blames or accuses other people.
- Makes excuses.
- Makes you feel helpless.

By contrast, proactive people accept responsibility. They say, "I will…," "There's gotta be a way…," "If I do my part…," or "Let's look at the alternatives." Proactive language:

- Keeps the power where it belongs—in you.
- Avoids blaming other people.

"So much stress, so much to do. Problems to solve but they don't have a clue… What can we find that will see us through? SELF WORTH!"

—Better Than a Thousand, "Self Worth"

- Finds a "way."
- Gives you hope.

As you listen to conversations around campus, you'll hear a lot of reactive language.

If you catch yourself using reactive language, try turning it around and making it proactive. Make proactive language your native tongue, and speak the language of optimism. You can practice by completing the activity below.

Turning Reactive Language
Into Proactive Language

People are surprised when they realize how often they say things like "You ruined my day," or "She made me mad!" When you hear yourself using reactive language, replace it with proactive language. Give it a try:

REACTIVE LINE	PROACTIVE REPLACEMENT
Sample: She ruined my day.	I let her get on my nerves and ruin my day.
I have to go to class today.	
My roommates were too loud; I couldn't study.	
Laziness runs in my family. We're all slackers.	
Sorry. My boss brings out the worst in me.	
No one told me I had to pay utilities.	
The school's food is making me gain weight.	

Reactive language can literally ruin your life. A friend told me about his sister-in-law, a fine and capable woman who did well in high school. But in her first month in college she began to tell herself, "I can't do this. It's too hard." Eventually, she came to believe it and dropped out after one month. And she never went back. After 20 years of low-paying, backbreaking jobs, she lost her health and went on welfare.

Grow Your Circle of Influence

Like everyone else, you live in a circle inside a circle. The inner circle is your Circle of Influence—the things you can control in your life. The outer one is your Circle of Concern—the things that worry you that you can't control.

Your Circle of Concern might include the high cost of tuition, your mother's health, the price of gas, bad weather, climate change, or the color of your skin. You're concerned about those things, but what can you do? Not much.

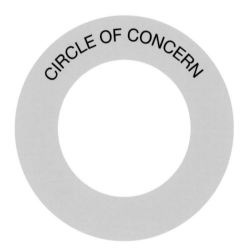

But you can do something about the things in the much smaller Circle of Influence.

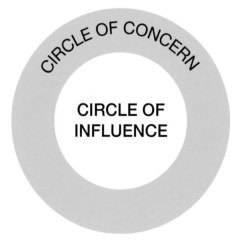

"Whether you prevail or fail, endure or die, depends more on what you do to yourself than on what the world does to you."

—Jim Collins, *How the Mighty Fall*

ACTUALLY, COME TO THINK OF IT, THERE'S NOT MUCH THAT'S IN MY CIRCLE OF INFLUENCE.

Do you worry too much about things in your Circle of Concern?

Imagine for a minute that you are Frank McCain. You have a lot in your Circle of Concern. For hundreds of years, African Americans like you have been shut out of the mainstream of society. You can't get decent jobs, so you're stuck in poverty. You have to live in a separate, run-down part of town, go to separate schools, and even drink at separate drinking fountains.

Nobody you know has ever broken through those barriers. Your parents didn't and your grandparents didn't. Unfortunately, your own future looks the same. You're 19 years old, just another first-year student in a black college. What can you do?

You could stay focused all your life on your Circle of Concern and grow old and bitter about it. Or you could focus on your Circle of Influence. Your Circle of Influence is extremely small, but within that circle you can do something. You can take the small step of sitting down to order dinner in a whites-only restaurant.

It was a tiny step, but it was within Frank's power to take it. As a result, his Circle of Influence began to grow, and it grew every hour—like ripples from a stone dropped in a pool—into the great American civil rights movement.

That's how you grow your Circle of Influence.

Let's say you're worried about a big math test coming up. The professor is tough and obviously plays favorites. You've never gotten good math scores; when you were little, your mother said, "Our family's no good at math." What do you do?

If you're reactive, you agonize over all the stuff in your Circle of Concern: You waste time bad-mouthing the professor, calling Mom for sympathy, wishing you had a different teacher, and crying in the bathroom.

But if you're proactive, you focus on your Circle of Influence. You can't control the professor; you can only control what you do. So you meet with her and ask for help, you get free tutoring at the student resource center, and you take practice tests and brush up on the problem areas. You might never be a math genius, but you get better. And you feel better about yourself.

Feel the difference between reactive and proactive people?

LESSON ON LEADERSHIP: Golda Meir

Golda Meir

Golda Meir is one of the great women of world history. In reflecting on her younger years, she said:

"I was never a beauty. There was a time when I was sorry about that, when I was old enough to understand the importance of it and, looking in any mirror, realized it was something I was never going to have. Then I found what I wanted to do in life, and being called pretty no longer had any importance. It was only much later that I realized that not being beautiful was a blessing in disguise. It forced me to develop my inner resources. I came to understand that women who cannot lean on their beauty and need to make something on their own have the advantage."

By disregarding what she couldn't control and focusing on what she could control—her education, strengths, and skills—Golda Meir grew her Circle of Influence to worldwide proportions. Eventually, she became the first woman to serve as Prime Minister of Israel.

What would change for you if you focused more on your Circle of Influence and less on your Circle of Concern? Do you have weaknesses? Of course you do. But can you stop dwelling on them so you can move forward?

So get to work on growing your Circle of Influence. Here's how:
- Rather than trying to "fix" other people, go to work on your own problems.
- Rather than complaining about the teacher, do the best coursework you can.
- Rather than bad-mouthing your annoying roommate, change your own annoying habits.
- Rather than blaming your parents, the fast-food industry, the school cafeteria, or your zodiac sign for being overweight, start doing what you must to lose a few pounds.

Do you know that when you focus on your Circle of Concern, your Circle of Influence shrinks? You have less influence on yourself and less influence with others. You get more and more helpless and hopeless. But when you focus on your Circle of Influence, which you can do something about, your influence on yourself and others expands! You get more power over what happens to you.

Remember the examples of Frank McCain and Golda Meir. Your influence might not spread across nations, but you'll shape your future instead of letting it be shaped by others. You grow from the inside out instead of shrinking from the outside in.

"Self-reliance is the key to a vigorous life. A man must look inward to find his own answers."

—Theodore Roosevelt (Robin Williams), From the movie *Night at the Museum*, 2006

DID YOU KNOW?
The Fundamental Attribution Error

When things go right, people tend to take credit for them. When things go wrong, people tend to blame someone or something else. This is called the fundamental attribution error. It's a convenient—but ineffective—habit. It's useless and dishonest to take credit for things outside our Circle of Influence or blame others for mistakes we make inside our Circle of Influence.

> "In any family, measles are less contagious than bad habits."
>
> —Mignon McLaughlin, *The Neurotic's Notebook*

Break Negative Cycles

Sometimes we inherit bad habits from our families. These habits might go back generations; if your father is an alcoholic, there's a good chance his father was an alcoholic. The same is true of drug addictions, poverty, violence, abuse, or a lack of education. Some families have traditions of yelling, getting up late, or watching TV all day. A bad habit can pass through multiple generations and become a vicious, unending cycle.

Are there negative tendencies from your family or upbringing that you want to stop from being passed on?

The good news, however, is that you have a choice. You can choose to be proactive and to break the cycle. The bad stuff can stop with you—within your family, friends, school, and even your community. When Frank McCain and his friends sat down to order a meal, a vicious cycle that trapped an entire society stopped right there in that Greensboro diner.

You can turn tragedy into hope. Listen to writer and teacher Walter Anderson describe an ugly slice of his upbringing:

The kitchen door opened—and I was caught, cold. It was too late to hide the evidence; the proof was in the open, plain as could be, right there in my lap. My father, drunk, his face flushed, reeled before me, glowering, menacing. My legs started to tremble. I was nine years old. I knew I would be beaten. There could be no escape; my father had found me reading….

An alcoholic like his parents before him, my father had hit me before, many times and harder, and in the years that followed he would hit me again, many times and harder, until finally I quit high school at sixteen and left home. His persistent rage about my reading when I was a boy, though, frustrated me more than all other abuse; it made me feel squeezed in the jaws of a terrible vise, because I would not, I could not, stop reading. I was drawn to books by curiosity and driven by need— an irresistible need to pretend I was elsewhere…. Thus I defied my father—and sometimes I paid a price for that defiance. It was worth it.
–*Walter Anderson,* Meant to Be, *Harper-Collins, 2006, p. 8*

"The great courageous act that we must all do, is to have the courage to step out of our history and past so that we can live our dreams."

—Oprah Winfrey

Can you imagine that? Your father beating you because you want to read? Fortunately, Walter's passion for learning was so great that he was able to break the cycles of alcoholism, abuse, and illiteracy that plagued his family. He literally read himself out of poverty. Walter is now the editor of a national magazine and the author of four books.

LESSON ON LEADERSHIP:
Lincoln, a Cycle Breaker

Abraham Lincoln

Abraham Lincoln's greatest achievement was to break a violent cycle of hatred and warfare.

When running for president of the United States, one of his challengers and greatest critics was Edwin M. Stanton. Stanton went so far as to call Lincoln a giraffe with "no token of any intelligent understanding." When Lincoln was elected, however, to the shock of everyone, one of his first official acts was to appoint Stanton as Secretary of War, declaring that "he was the best man for the job."

A woman once asked Lincoln, "How can you speak kindly of your enemies when you should rather destroy them?" After a brief pause, Lincoln replied, "Madam, do I not destroy them when I make them my friends?"

Lincoln made decisions based upon what he felt was best, not based on how others acted toward him. What negative cycles in today's world could a great leader break? What negative cycles in your own world could you break?

What other people do does not determine what you do. You can choose your own way. If something bad happens, reactive people take it out on others, like the guy who gets a lousy grade on a test and goes home and bad-mouths the professor.

But proactive people turn setbacks into triumphs. Instead of giving up, they take initiative and find the resources to turn things around. For example, Sam's first semester of college was a disaster.

I got a scholarship to go to Tech, took 18 hours, and was playing football. The first semester, I got D's, which was really, really bad for me. It was too much for me, way too overwhelming. I realized I couldn't handle it alone. Moving forward, I found out all the resources I had. Tech had tutoring available, and after that first semester, I never missed a tutoring class, never, not one time. I also went to the mental-health counseling center. I started building a relationship with each of my professors. My goal was that every professor would remember me and know my name, so when I got behind and needed help, I would ask for it, and amazingly, they would help me!

I never got below a 3.3 from then on and graduated with honors because I took advantage of the tools that were right there. They don't want you to fall out, they want to help you succeed.

> "You can't move forward because you've got your eyes in the rearview mirror."
>
> –Aaron Eckhart, in *Love Happens*

ACTIVITY 12

Turning Setbacks Into Triumphs

In the following scenarios, what proactive advice would you give your friend to turn the setback into an opportunity?

SCENARIO	PROACTIVE ADVICE
Your friend gets a sports scholarship, but after record-setting performances in the first two games has a career-ending knee injury.	
Your friend has a hard time concentrating in class. Away from home for the first time, the abuse she took from her father while growing up continues to haunt her.	
Your friend has always wanted to be a nurse and help people, but just found out she did not get accepted into the program.	
Your friend has no experience with happily married people. She watched her mother go through three divorces. She now has no confidence she can ever be happily married.	

Avoid Addictions

Nothing takes your freedom away faster than an addiction. Alcohol is the top addiction among college students. Tobacco, illegal drugs, and gambling are also common. There are more and more addictions to prescription drugs, video games, and pornography, as well as addictive behaviors with eating disorders and compulsive buying.

Anybody can become an addict—addiction can strike any age, race, income level, or educational level. Some say, "It's my choice. It doesn't affect anybody else." That's a lie—addiction impacts a lot of people: family, friends, and society. The prisons are full of addicts to booze, drugs, and pornography. Addiction impacts everyone.

IT'S LIKE HE DOESN'T EVEN THINK ABOUT THE CONSEQUENCES BEFORE HE ACTS.

DID YOU KNOW?
How Alcohol on Campus Affects Other Students

STUDENTS WHO…	PERCENT
Have had study or sleep interrupted	60.5
Have taken care of a drunken student	53.6
Have been insulted or humiliated	29.3
Have been pushed, hit, or assaulted	9.4
Have had a serious argument or quarrel	18.6
Have had their property damaged	13.6
Have experienced an unwanted sexual advance	20.1
Have been a victim of sexual assault	1.3

(NIH, "College Drinking.")

We are free to choose an addiction, but we are not free to choose the consequences of that choice.

One in four college students has trouble in school because of alcohol, and first-year students drink more than anyone. One in five college students drinks and drives. More than 97,000 college students are sexually assaulted in the United States each year because of alcohol. And about 1,825 students die from drinking alcohol (NIH Report, 2013).

One excellent student I know of chose to give "crack" a try. She thought just doing it once couldn't hurt. One try and the next thing she knew she was shoplifting and stealing from family to sustain her addiction. Next came prison and rehabilitation. College was a broken dream. So, yes, she was free to try crack once—but she lost her freedom in that very moment.

Addiction steals your freedom and always leads to bad consequences.

If you're proactive, you'll do anything to keep from losing your freedom of choice. It's precious to you. That's why you get an education—to expand your choices in life. That's why you avoid even the chance of getting addicted and watch your opportunities dry up and blow away.

ACTIVITY 13

The Case of the Vanishing Roommate

Addictions come in many forms. How would you respond to this student's concern?

I've got a roommate who is addicted to video games. Seriously. It's scary. I met him at the start of the semester and he seemed nice enough. He's from a small town, and this is his first time away. The first week of school he would talk with me and the other guys in our apartment, but then he virtually disappeared into his room. He gets home from work around 10:00 at night, says hi, goes in his room, shuts the door, and at 6:00 a.m., I can still hear him talking to himself while playing a game. I have no idea how he is surviving his classes, but I can't imagine he is doing very well. I don't know if I should say something or not.

Do you have any proactive advice for him? Should he say something to his roommate? Should he get help? If yes, what specifically should he say or do?

WHAT YOU GET: IT PAYS TO BE PROACTIVE

When I was growing up, my dad made me take responsibility for my life. If I said something like, "My girlfriend makes me so mad," he would come back with, "Now come on, Sean. No one can make you mad unless you let them. It's your choice."

Sometimes those conversations drove me crazy and I'd find myself thinking, "I like blaming other people for my problems. I like being reactive. It's fun and easy. So just leave me alone, Dad!" And then I'd go find my mom.

Well, I hope you don't think that way, because being proactive pays off. For example, a while ago I read about the stress levels of pilots in the military. When war comes, who do you think is more stressed out—fighter pilots or cargo-plane pilots? If you guessed the cargo-plane pilots, you are right. Their planes are slow and hard to maneuver, so they can't do much to avoid enemy attacks. The faster, more nimble fighters have a lot more choices.

The fighter pilots have what psychologists call an inner locus of control; that is, they See themselves as in charge of their lives. Proactive people have that inner locus of control. On the flip side, people with an external locus of control do not See themselves as in charge of their lives. Instead, they See themselves as subject to forces outside themselves—luck, fate, or other people's whims.

Because of their inner locus of control, proactive people enjoy:
- More job productivity and satisfaction.
- Less stress.
- Greater work ethic.
- Higher student achievement.
- More ability to adapt.
- Higher pay.
- Greater general happiness.

(Maltby, Day, and Macaskill)

Of course, reactive people tend to be less productive, stressed out, low-achieving, low-paid slackers. It's your choice.

Would you rather pilot a fighter jet or a cargo plane in battle?

What I Want to Get

Think back on the principles of Habit 1 and the activities you have completed in this chapter. Identify one or two actions that would help you most as a first-year student. What results do you hope to Get as a result of doing these things?

What I Am Doing Well

What I Hope to Do Better

What I Hope to Get by Doing Better

IN SUMMARY

As a college student, you might be on your own for the first time. For some students, this can be uncomfortable, especially if they have "helicopter parents" who always hovered around and made all the decisions. (The rise of the cell phone is often blamed for the explosion of helicopter parents—it has been called "the world's longest umbilical cord.") Then suddenly, they're off to college and making their own decisions. A student named Rebekah confessed, "College gave me a sense of freedom that literally overwhelmed me."

Proactive people step up and use their freedom. If you want good grades, take the initiative to study hard. If you want a good job, be ready when recruiters come looking. If you want to be a good parent, learn what it takes. You can't afford to wait for someone else to make life happen for you. Take charge and make it happen for yourself.

Granted, you are not responsible for everything that happens to you. You may, for example, have been the victim of a tragic accident or abuse. And, yes, both genes and environment do impact your life in ways you cannot control. But you're still responsible for what you do with what you have. Focus on your Circle of Influence and work to control the things you can control.

Here's a summary of the key points of Habit 1:

Habit 1: Be Proactive
Principles: Responsibility and Initiative

	INEFFECTIVE STUDENTS	EFFECTIVE STUDENTS
What They *See*	• I am a product of my genetics and environment. • What I get out of life is mostly a result of luck and fate.	• I am free to choose my actions and attitudes. • I am the creative force of my life.
What They *Do*	• Sit back and let what happens happen. • Let other people control them. • Use victim language. • Focus energy on things they can't control. • Allow old baggage from the past to impede progress. • Get pressured into addictive behavior.	• Take initiative: make things happen. • Carry their own weather; control their own feelings. • Use proactive language. • Focus energy on things they can control. • Break negative cycles from the past. • Say no to anything that could be addictive.
What They *Get*	• Dreams that stay dreams. • Out-of-control lives. • Increasing stress. • Crappy grades, broken relationships, a lame job.	• Dreams that become reality. • Control over their lives. • Less stress. • Better grades, better relationships, a better job.

In conclusion, Habit 1: Be Proactive is the key to an effective life because it is the key to living Habits 2 through 7. You have to be proactive to develop the other habits.

Try some of the Baby Steps on the next page. I also recommend carefully studying and applying the tips found in the Academic Protip: "How to Use the College Library."

COMING ATTRACTIONS
Just around the corner, you will be asked to think deeper than ever before about your motives, the purpose for your life, and why you want to go to college.

Baby Steps

1. Teach to Learn. Using the summary chart on page 75, teach the key concepts of Habit 1 to a friend, classmate, or family member within the next 48 hours.

2. The next time someone gives you the bird, give them the peace sign back.

3. If you did poorly on an assignment or a test, take the initiative to talk with your professor to find out how to improve.

4. Sometime today catch yourself using reactive language, such as "I have to," "He makes me so mad," or "I can't help it." Replace it with proactive language, like "I choose to," "I'm not going to let his bad mood ruin my day," or "I can do better."

5. The next time you have a problem with somebody, be the first one to apologize.

6. Get to know one of your professors whom you admire. Visit the office, have a talk after class, or do some research on him or her via the Web.

7. If someone is mean or rude to you, kill him or her with kindness.

8. Pick something that is really bothering you, such as a poor relationship with a friend or a class you are struggling with. Now, think about those things that lie within your Circle of Influence. Choose to focus on what you can control and forget about what you can't.

9. Identify a negative pattern you may have inherited from your family. What is it? _____ How might you be able to break that cycle and turn it into a new, positive pattern? _____

10. Identify the most proactive person you know. Write down his or her name and what that person does that is so different. _____

Academic Protip

If you live by Habit 1, you'll want to know about the college library. I used to think, "Why do you need a library when you have Google? Who needs all those dusty books when you can find what you want with a couple of clicks?"

Well, after talking to Professor Trevor Dawes, one of the world's top experts on college libraries, I was stunned by how valuable the library is. It's much more than just a place to study or check out books. It's the place to go for everything. Here you can get help with your assignments, your tests, your class projects, and even your personal problems. It's the perfect place to practice Habit 1. Here you'll find the resources you need to succeed in college. So take the initiative to get to know your library.

How to Use a College Library

By Trevor A. Dawes,
President of the
Association of College
and Research Libraries

The library can be intimidating. It's often a big building with long hallways, endless stacks of books, and hundreds of students reading, working on computers, or just sleeping.

But the library can actually be your best friend if you want to succeed in college.

Today's college librarian is not the person at the desk with a pencil behind her ear who glares at you if you start talking and tells you to shush. Today's librarians are actually there to help you find whatever you're looking for. Sometimes, they're the best people on the whole campus to talk to—and believe me, you're going to need them.

Think of a librarian as a personal coach. He is not going to do your schoolwork for you, but he's going to show you how to do it and where you can get help. The whole purpose of the university is to find the answers to questions, and the library has the answers. Maybe the librarian doesn't know everything, but he knows where to find it.

Suppose your professor says, "Write a five-page research paper on women characters in Shakespeare." (Or it could be a paper on political science, economics, or chemistry—it doesn't matter.) It's your first year of college, first class, first research paper. You don't have a very clear idea of what to do. You're not even sure what "research" is.

Come to the library. Find a librarian and ask her to sit down with you for a few minutes and help you understand what to do.

First, she'll probably ask you, "What question do you want to answer with your paper? What do you want to know?"

"Well, I suppose I want to find out what Shakespeare thought about women."

"Okay, let's see what we can find that will help you answer that question."

Now, the librarian has access to far more stuff on any question you can ask than you will ever be able to use. In fact, her resources are so vast that the problem isn't finding things, it's choosing things.

First, she will probably show you one of many subject guides that list recommended places to go for information. There might even be a subject guide called "Shakespeare and Women." The subject guide will point you to core resources that list a

Trevor A. Dawes,
President of the
Association of College
and Research Libraries

lot of material that's been published on the subject. For example, if you're taking an English class, the Modern Language Association Bibliography is a core resource. For chemistry, it would be Tetrahedron, which is published by Elsevier. Every academic subject has its own bibliography, which is a list of books and articles.

If there is no subject guide, she might show you how to use a "discovery service," a dream-come-true for people who do research. An online resource, the discovery service can give you a list of books and articles on any subject. The more you narrow down your search, the more helpful it is. Suppose you want to know "what is the symbolic meaning of the flowers Ophelia sings about in Shakespeare's play *Hamlet*?" Ask the discovery service, and if anybody's ever written anything on the subject, it will tell you where to look.

You might be asking yourself, "The discovery service sounds a lot like Google, which I already know how to use. Why do I need the library's discovery service?"

Think of Google as a gigantic pile of information. The problem with Google is that some of that pile is helpful and reliable information, but much of it isn't. Suppose you're taking a botany class and the professor wants you to write a research paper on trees. So you Google "trees." Obviously, you're going to get a billion hits. You'll find ads for tree services, programs for Arbor Day, a map of Tree Street, and Grandpa Jack's plan for a tree house. You might even find a website called "allabouttrees.com." That sounds just right. But you go there and find that it's the report of some fifth grader who had to do a science project on trees.

Of course, none of that will help you with your research paper. But the library's discovery service gives you only trustworthy and relevant information that you can use in your research paper. It lists only scholarly materials, articles or books that have been "peer reviewed"—which means that many scholars have already studied the material and pronounced it worthwhile. You can use it without worrying if it's bogus or not.

"Okay, I've found several articles on Shakespeare's attitude toward women. Now what do I do?"

Articles in the library generally follow the same format. First, pay close attention to the "abstract." It appears at the beginning and is usually a one-paragraph summary of the article. The abstract will tell you what question the author was trying to answer and a short answer to that question.

"Here's an article by Professor Smith that says Shakespeare's real heroes were women, not men."

Very interesting. Now you can skim or scan the article to find out why the author thinks that way. You might even be convinced he's right. But you can't just repeat in your paper what the author said in his. So you need to look further.

The librarian says, "Let's search the discovery service to see if anyone has written an answer to Professor Smith."

There it is. An article by Professor Jones that says Smith is totally wrong. Jones thinks Shakespeare's women are not heroes and some of them are downright evil, like Lady Macbeth. Jones sounds pretty convincing too.

"Now what do I do?" you ask. Well, you enter "heroic women in Shakespeare" into the search box on the discovery service and look for more opinions. You'll find lots of them, and eventually you'll come up with your own opinion, maybe somewhere between Smith and Jones. That's when you can start writing your paper.

College research is not that difficult: You look at what others have said on a subject, think about it for yourself, and then present your own opinion. The librarian can help you every step of the way.

"Can the librarian help me write the paper?"

Some libraries have writing services, but even if they don't, the librarian can point you to the college's free tutoring service. The point is, the librarian can be your research partner and sometimes even your writing partner.

"How about preparing for exams? Can the librarian help me there?"

Of course. Suppose you're preparing for a test and you run into something you don't understand. You could ask the teacher, but he or she might not be available. Especially during exam weeks, most college libraries are open early and late, and you can even instant message or email the library for help at 10 o'clock at night and sometimes later. Somebody is usually there to help you.

This might sound unexpected, but the librarian can often help you even with personal problems. If you're sick or you have money problems or an issue with a teacher, ask the librarian. He or she will point you in the right direction to someone who can really work with you.

I can't emphasize enough that librarians are available and would love to help you. If at any point you feel stumped, reach out, stop by, call us, send us a text or an email. Many students hear about the library at orientation, but they don't use it. They suffer alone, thinking there's no place to go for help.

But you can always go to the library. Your college library is the center of the campus for a reason—it's the one place you can go that crosses all the boundaries between people.

You can even take a nap there. Go ahead.

Trevor A. Dawes is a university librarian at Washington University in St. Louis, where he is responsible for research and acquisition services. Before that, he was circulation director at Princeton University Library and held positions at Columbia University libraries in New York City. Trevor has earned three master's degrees in library science: one from Rutgers and two more from Teachers College, Columbia University. The editor of two major publications, *Twenty-First Century Access Services: On the Frontline of Academic Librarianship* and *Marketing and Managing Electronic Reserves*, Trevor served as president of the Association of College and Research Libraries (ACRL) in 2013–2014.

References

De Charms, Richard, "Personal Causation and the Origin Concept," in C.P. Smith, ed., *Motivation and Personality: Handbook of Thematic Content Analysis*, Cambridge University Press, 1992, 325–333.

Frankl, Viktor, *Man's Search for Meaning*, Rider, 2011.

Maltby, John, Liz Day, Ann Macaskill, *Personality, Individual Differences, and Intelligence*, 2nd ed., Prentice-Hall, 2009.

Phillips, Donald T., Lincoln Leadership: *Executive Strategies for Tough Times*, Warner Books, 1993, 31.

College Drinking, National Institute on Alcohol Abuse and Alcoholism, National Institutes of Health (NIH), 2013. http://www.niaaa.nih.gov/alcohol-health/special-populations-co-occurring-disorders/college-drinking.

2

HABIT 2

Begin With the End in Mind

The Habit of Personal Vision

"The problem with not having a goal is that you can spend your life running up and down the field and never scoring."

–BILL COPELAND

IN THIS CHAPTER, YOU WILL DISCOVER WAYS TO:

- Discover what matters most to you.
- Write a Personal Mission Statement.
- Set meaningful, realistic goals.
- Map out a graduation plan.
- Begin with a résumé in mind.

Also, look for the Academic Protip...

- How to Write a College Paper

Habit 2:
Begin With the End in Mind

is the habit of personal vision. It's about identifying your dreams and goals, and planning your college experience.

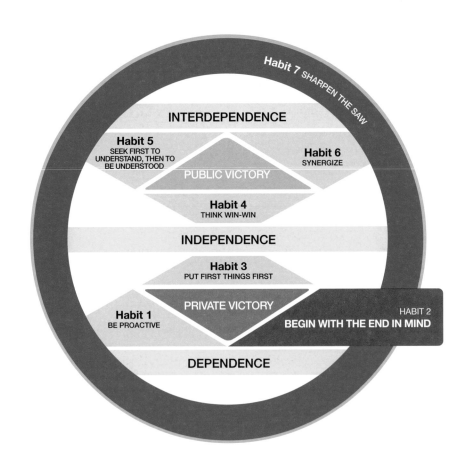

What I Wish
I'd Known in College

"The key to success is simply believing in YOURSELF."
-Julie, University of Kentucky

"I wish I had gone to college right after high school. But walking down the aisle and receiving my diploma at age 50 was a great accomplishment. You're never too old to learn." –Deb, University of Ohio

"What I learned in university was to always pursue a higher purpose in life rather than chasing a short-term goal."
-You-Jeong, Seoul National University, Korea

"That getting a degree and getting an education are not the same thing. You can pass all your tests and learn very little, or you can immerse yourself in the love of a particular subject and begin the education of a lifetime."
-Catherine, Flinders University in Australia

"Always begin college with the end in mind. Ask yourself, 'What lifestyle do I want to have three to five years after graduating from college?' Once you figure that out, figure out what degree you will need to support that lifestyle."
-Scott, Iowa Community College

"I wish that I hadn't rushed through college. I wish I'd taken more time and learned more about philosophy, art, history... all the 'impractical' stuff."
-Beth, Vanderbilt University

REAL CHOICES:
Influencing a Billion People

Have you heard of Dr. Norman Borlaug? Most people haven't.

It's strange that more of us don't know about him. After all, *The Wall Street Journal* once reported that he "has arguably saved more lives than anyone in history. Maybe one billion."

So who was this unknown hero?

Growing up on a small Iowa farm, he was known simply as "Norman." He went to a one-room, one-teacher school, then in high school he joined the football team. His coach really had an impact on him, encouraging him to give "105 percent" to everything he did.

When the Great Depression struck, he was still young. It was a shock to see his neighbors lose their farms to foreclosure. Though his family's farm was spared, he didn't have the money or the grades to get into college. (He flunked his college entrance exam.) But his grandfather told him, "Fill your head now if you want to fill your belly later on." With the help of a government grant, he finally got into the University of Minnesota.

College awakened a new spirit in Norman. He worked hard, and along with studying he found time to meet his wife, coach the wrestling team, work in a café, and lead a program that put unemployed young men to work. He noticed that many of the young men were starving as they started the program, but their morale and health got visibly better with good nutrition. "I saw how food changed them," he said later.

College was tough, and his plan to get a job as a forest ranger fell through. Then one evening he went to a lecture called "Those Shifty Little Enemies That Destroy Our Food Crops." The professor talked about crossbreeding wheat to prevent the diseases that ruined crops and brought hunger to millions. The thought of helping hungry people intrigued him, so he changed his major to plant pathology.

Finishing his Ph.D., Dr. Borlaug was hired by DuPont for lifesaving work

Norman Borlaug as a college wrestler. Photo courtesy of University of Minnesota Archives, University of Minnesota – Twin Cities

The Norman Borlaug Congressional Gold Metal

during World War II. Two years into his job, another type of battle called for his talents. Entire wheat farms were being destroyed across Mexico by stem rust, a parasitic fungus. Doomsayers predicted widespread starvation.

Stem rust was uniquely interesting to Borlaug, so—despite DuPont's offer to double his salary—he moved his family to Mexico. All kinds of trouble—such as hostile farmers and a lack of equipment—greeted him there; but after a few years and 6,000 sophisticated crossbreeding experiments, he found the ideal rust-resistant strain to match Mexico's needs. He also found time to be a dad and to coach Mexico's first Little League Baseball team.

Before long, 95 percent of wheat harvested in Mexico came from Borlaug's seeds. The predicted famine never happened, and instead of importing wheat, Mexico became a net exporter.

83

What do you think enticed Borlaug to leave the offer of more money to take the job in Mexico? Where do you think your college studies will lead you?

Then Borlaug faced a far bigger problem: famine was spreading over South Asia, with hundreds of millions of deaths expected. Desperate governments called for Borlaug, and again he answered the call. Within a single season, those countries were producing crops on a scale nobody had seen before.

Soon Borlaug's techniques were used around the world. The resulting Green Revolution doubled the world's production of wheat and saved countless lives.

Eventually, Borlaug settled into teaching at Texas A&M University. In 1970, Dr. Borlaug was awarded the Nobel Peace Prize. In 2009, at the age of 95, he passed away quietly, still an unknown name to most people.

Habit 2: Begin With the End in Mind is about having a vision and a meaning to your life. If you practice Habit 2, you do everything with a purpose. If you're highly effective, you identify the meaningful goals and dreams you want to pursue in life. You plan how to get the most out of college. But you also "Begin With the End in Mind" on the everyday level: you go to class with a purpose, you write papers, study for tests, sign up for more classes, date, and even raise a family with purpose.

By contrast, ineffective students have no clear purpose for college or life. At best, they follow a plan made by their parents or academic advisors. They change majors often and can't decide what they want to do for a career. Graduation time—if they make it that far—is the end of a "Christopher Columbus voyage": They never knew where they were headed, or they don't know where they are, once they arrive.

Norman Borlaug and farmers in Ghana. Photo courtesy of University of Minnesota Archives, University of Minnesota – Twin Cities

This chapter will help you to think about your priorities in life and your goals and plans for college. It follows the flow of the See-Do-Get Cycle below:

PEOPLE WHO PRACTICE HABIT 2:

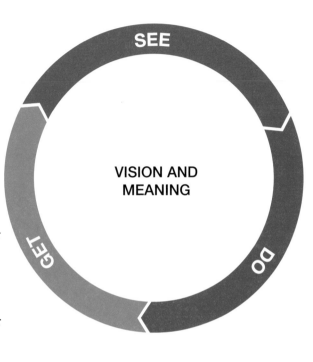

GET

- A greater sense of meaning and purpose.
- A feeling of greater self-worth.
- Accomplished goals.
- Criteria for deciding what is or is not important.

SEE

- The mental creation precedes the physical creation.
- You can make a meaningful difference.

DO

- Discover what matters most to you.
- Write a Personal Mission Statement.
- Set meaningful, realistic goals.
- Explore your career options.
- Map out a graduation plan.
- Begin with a résumé in mind.

THE PARADIGMS OF BEGINNING WITH THE END IN MIND

Life is never fully laid out for anyone. You can't see the end from the beginning.

Obviously, as a young farm boy Norman Borlaug had no idea he would get the chance to go to college, much less impact a billion people. When he heard the lecture on crop diseases, the seeds of a vision were planted—but even those early seeds didn't grow into a full vision of what he could accomplish. The big picture had to be filled in over time.

You might also need to take time to clarify your vision of what you want in college and in life. Don't expect to have it all laid out for you in this chapter. But you should be able to see that vision, even if it's fuzzy and out of focus, because now is a great time to be thinking about these questions:

- What have you always wanted to do with your life?
- What have you always been interested in?
- What noble causes inspire you?
- What talents do you want to develop or polish while in college?
- What do you want to become known for—or *unknown* for?

Habit 2: Begin With the End in Mind is based on two paradigms. The first is: "Everything is created twice, first mentally, then physically." The other is: "I can make a meaningful contribution in the world around me."

"Imagination is the beginning of creation. You imagine what you desire, you will what you imagine, and at last you create what you will."

—George Bernard Shaw, playwright

The paradigm about two creations applies to everything you do. Born in Italy in 1475, Michelangelo was already a well-known painter, sculptor, poet, architect, and engineer by his early twenties. In fact, he created two of his most famous sculptures, the *Pietà* and *David*, in his twenties.

How did he do it? "In every block of marble I see a statue as plain as though it stood before me, shaped and perfect in attitude and action. I have only to hew away the rough walls that imprison the lovely apparition to reveal it to the other eyes as mine see it."

When starting a project, Michelangelo first looked at the slab of marble and mentally pictured the statue inside, as if he had X-ray vision. Next, he physically chiseled the rough stone away to reveal the masterpiece. The mental creation was followed by the second creation—the work of art.

> "Genius is eternal patience."
>
> —Michelangelo

Michelangelo completed two of his most famous works, the *Pietà* (left) and *David* (right), while he was in his twenties. He saw the sculptures in his mind before he ever created them physically.

The same two creations apply to any profession. Homebuilders produce a blueprint before construction begins. Sports teams come up with a game plan before they play the big game. Business leaders develop strategic plans at the start of a new year. Teachers create lesson plans before teaching lessons. Engineers design cars on computers before production. Military leaders map out strategies before a battle. In each case, the first creation—the mental creation—precedes the second creation—the physical creation. It would be crazy to work the other way around.

So what about your life? Isn't your life far more important than any block of marble or any building, research paper, game, business venture, car design, or battle?

Just as you wouldn't start building a house without a blueprint, it makes no sense for you to go around every day without a plan for your life, your career, or your college years. Yet, too many college students do just that. They have no thought-out plans for their lives, and only a vague idea of what they want to get out of college. Some say they're too busy living to plan their lives. On the other hand, highly effective students know the value of pushing their proactive pause button long enough to plan their college career and to look ahead and make a plan for life. It's a "habit" with them.

More and more, the "traditional" way of attending college—starting right after high school and taking four or five years to graduate—is not so typical. In fact, nontraditional students are now in the majority. Nontraditional students include:

- Many first-time students who have been in the workforce for a number of years, or are planning to attend only part-time.
- Single parents and married students with families.
- Students who have been serving in the military.
- Students who are trying to finish up high school requirements or pass remedial skills requirements.
- Students who dropped out of college and have decided to return.
- …and more.

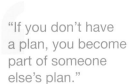

For such students, getting a degree can take much longer than the traditional timelines for meeting college-graduation requirements.

Whether you take a traditional route or attend college in a nontraditional way, having a plan from the beginning can save a lot of time and money.

The second paradigm of Habit 2 is: "I can make a meaningful difference in the world around me. My life has purpose." It's about knowing why you have a plan for college and life.

It means waking up each morning with a reason *why* you are going to class, *why* you are going to work, or *why* you have chosen a particular topic for your research paper—and feeling inspired by that reason. I believe every single person wants to make a positive difference in life. Everyone wants to make a contribution and to know his or her life matters.

Bethany was 22 and going nowhere—worse than nowhere, actually—to some very bad places in her life. But for Bethany, just one person, her son Noah, provided her with a "compelling why" for going back to school:

Upon graduating high school, I was going to take a year off. Four years later, I was still not in school and couldn't find a minute of "me time," let alone time for my education. When I was 22, tragedy struck, and sent me down a road from which I never thought I would return. Then, God gave me Noah. When he was born, it changed everything and gave me a reason to move forward. I am now a 27-year-old, first-time college student, single mom, and future educator…. It is crazy to think my reasons for not going to school back then are the exact reasons I now feel it is a necessity. I want my son to see how important and valuable education is, and I want to continue to improve our lives.

> "If you don't have a plan, you become part of someone else's plan."
>
> —Terence McKenna, philosopher

Whether your life directly impacts a billion people or a single person is not what really matters—the size of the contribution doesn't count. What does count is your belief in yourself: that your life is of worth and what you do is important. That's why this chapter will examine what is most important to you and what types of things you most want to accomplish.

So the first paradigm is about having a plan; the second paradigm is about having a purpose. Many students have plans but no purpose. Some are filled with purpose but have no plan for making it happen. Highly effective students have both.

Anne Sullivan

LESSON ON LEADERSHIP:
Impacting a Single Individual

Anne Sullivan's mother died at a young age, and Anne's alcoholic father abandoned the family. When relatives refused to take in the children, Anne and a younger brother were put in an almshouse, a place for the diseased and unwanted members of society.

Before long, Anne's brother died of tuberculosis, and Anne's health and eyesight began to fail. The one thing that did not fail her, however, was her spirit.

Anne wanted desperately to go to school. She was 14 before a government inspector helped her get that chance. She quickly became known as an ornery problem student. One teacher, however, took an interest in Anne and even arranged for operations to restore her eyesight. Anne felt a desire to do the same for somebody someday.

When Anne graduated from the Perkins School for the Blind, she stated in her valedictorian address:

And now we are going out into the busy world, to take our share in life's burdens, and do our little to make the world better, wiser, and happier…. Every man who improves himself is aiding the progress of society, and everyone who stands still holds it back.

Following graduation, Anne took a job as governess for a young girl in Alabama named Helen Keller. Helen had been born healthy, but after a few years, a disease left her blind and deaf. She turned into what some described as a wild creature. Many people before Anne had tried to work with Helen with no success.

Times were rough at first, but Anne gently worked miracles with Helen. In fact, in a remarkable show of devotion, Anne stayed with Helen for nearly 50 years. Helen was her only pupil. In that time, Helen wrote 12 books, was the subject of several movies and articles, and became a global spokesperson and champion for the blind and disabled. Royalty and leaders of nations asked her for advice. Anne was always quietly at her side.

Anne Sullivan chose to focus her career and legacy on the life of one person. Are there certain people whose lives you have recently touched?

WHAT STUDENTS WHO BEGIN WITH THE END IN MIND *DO*

Again, you probably won't finish this chapter with your future all figured out. But you'll move in that direction if you Do some of the things highly effective college students Do, including:

- Discovering what matters most to you.
- Writing a Personal Mission Statement.
- Setting meaningful, realistic goals.
- Exploring your career options.
- Mapping out a plan for college.
- Beginning with a résumé in mind.

Discover What Matters Most to You

Joan of Arc

Not long before and not too far away from where Michelangelo was born, Joan of Arc became a French heroine. Her courage brought strength to the men she led into battle. But she is most remembered for her staunch commitment to her beliefs and values.

In her final battle, Joan was captured, imprisoned, abused, put on trial, and threatened with execution. To preserve her life, all she had to do was to deny her beliefs and abandon her country. Yet, Joan was so committed to what she believed in and what she stood for that she refused, and at the age of 19 was burned at the stake.

Before meeting her fate, Joan declared, "I know this now. Every man gives his life for what he believes. Every woman gives her life for what she believes. Sometimes people believe in little or nothing, yet they give their lives to that little or nothing. One life is all we have, and we live it as we believe in living it. And then it is gone. But to sacrifice what you are and live without belief, that's more terrible than dying."

Joan saw living without a purpose as more terrible than dying. No one is asking you to put your life on the line for anything, but Joan's story raises questions: Are you giving your life to "little or nothing"? Do you have clear, meaningful purposes, goals, and dreams? Do you know what matters most to you?

These are deep questions, I know. Especially if you didn't get any sleep last night. But when you are clear about your priorities and compelling whys for going to college, you are more motivated as a student, you work harder, and you enjoy the journey more.

So how do you decide what matters most to you?

For Norman Borlaug, several events in his life stuck with him and caused him to think about what mattered most to him. Not until he attended the lecture on plant pathology did he sense what he wanted to spend his career doing. The willingness to go to Mexico and other parts of the world spun off from those feelings.

That's how it is for many people. Along the way, certain meaningful and enjoyable experiences stick in their memory like superglue. Over time, those memories grow into a unique bundle of experiences, and from it they eventually "detect" the things that matter most to them and how they want to spend their lives.

Richard was a smart-mouth in high school.

I hated the system. I would shout my student number instead of my name at roll call. I was lazy and didn't want to do the homework, so I mouthed off to the teachers about how stupid it was. I got what I deserved—no high school diploma.

But a certain teacher wouldn't let go of me. His name was Mr. Young. It was just about the end of high school when he pulled me into his office and told me how much potential he thought I had and how much I could "give" the world if I decided to.

I didn't think much of what he said, but he was actually trembling when he told me this. He really believed in me, which I couldn't believe at the time. Nobody had ever believed in me, including myself. It was the trembling that got to me.

That summer was the low point of my life. I kept thinking about Mr. Young and something happened inside of me. Here I was, a high school dropout, but I wanted to be a "Mr. Young" to somebody else. I decided I wanted to be a high school teacher like him. Ironic, I know. But I got my credits and went to college. Nobody could believe it—least of all me—but I did it. I'm now teaching history and caring about kids, just like Mr. Young.

> "A vocation [calling] does not mean a goal that I pursue. It means a calling that I hear. Before I can tell my life what I want to do with it, I must listen to my life telling me who I am."
>
> –Parker Palmer, author

Certain thoughts or experiences probably have stuck in your mind at times. You've felt compelled to do something out of the ordinary. A certain person has inspired you. Maybe a book or a movie has stirred up a strong feeling for a cause, something you'd be willing to sacrifice for. Maybe people have noticed you have talents. Think: How are you unique? What has energized you in the past?

As you think back on those things, I recommend that you find a quiet setting and complete the next five activities. They are short, but I challenge you to give them serious, undivided thought. Write your thoughts in the space provided so you can reflect on them later.

Most Influential Person

Think back on the people who have been positive role models or sources of inspiration for you. Select one who has had the greatest impact on who you are today.

• What did that person do to impact your life?

• What skills or qualities of that person's character do you admire?

• What other skills or qualities of character you admire in others would you also like to adopt?

80th Birthday

The following activity will help you define what you want people to remember about you.

1. Identify six roles you play in life (or plan to play) and write them in the spaces below.
2. Identify the name of a person who can talk about how you play that role in life.
3. Write a tribute statement you would like that person to give at your 80th birthday party.

PERSON	TRIBUTE
SAMPLE Role: *Spouse*	*As a spouse, he was always true to me. I never doubted his loyalty. He was a good listener who understood my heart.*
Role 1: Name:	
Role 2: Name:	
Role 3: Name:	
Role 4: Name:	
Role 5: Name:	
Role 6: Name:	

Your Thoughts on Success and Life

Harvard Professor William James (1842–1910) is called the father of American psychology. He wrote a lot about what it takes to succeed in life, including the thoughts below.

PART 1. Read through a few of William James's observations on how to find success in life. Highlight a favorite or two.

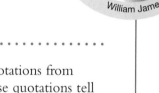

> *The greatest discovery of my generation is that man can alter his life simply by altering his attitude of mind.*
>
> *Act, look, feel successful, conduct yourself accordingly, and you will be amazed at the positive results.*
>
> *Lives based on having are less free than lives based either on doing or on being.*
>
> *It is our attitude at the beginning of a difficult task which, more than anything else, will affect its successful outcome.*
>
> *The great use of life is to spend it for something that will outlast it.*

William James

PART 2. Search in quotation books, online sources, etc., for 10 good quotations from various authors about what it takes to be successful in life. What do these quotations tell you about what is most important to you in life? Try writing a few original quotations to describe your thoughts on success.

Walking the Beam

Imagine a narrow steel beam stretched between two skyscrapers. What would you be willing to walk across the beam for? A million dollars? To rescue a little brother or sister? Fame? A date with a certain person? Think carefully.

- Make a list of what is most important to you—important enough that you would be willing to walk the beam to acquire or protect it. Rank each item on your list from top to bottom in importance.
- Now repeat the activity with three friends, family members, or other people you respect. Ask what matters most to them. What would they walk the beam for?

Getting to Know You

Write your first reaction to each question.

- I am at my best when…

- I am at my worst when…

- I want to be a person who…

- If I knew I couldn't fail, I would…

- My deepest positive emotions come when…

- My greatest talents and gifts are…

- When all is "said and done," the most important things to me are…

If you gave serious thought to each activity, you probably got some ideas about the purpose of your life—about the things that are most meaningful to you and the kind of person you want to become. Maybe now you've had a glimpse of how you want to spend your life and your college years.

Write a Personal Mission Statement

Over the years, I've met people from all walks of life who have captured what matters most to them and written it down in the form of a Personal Mission Statement. A Personal Mission Statement sums up what you want your life to be about. Think of it as a blueprint or personal constitution that directs your choices in life.

The process of creating a Personal Mission Statement challenges you to narrow your focus in life and commit to what matters most to you. A mission statement is not a list of goals; rather, it captures what you stand for and the type of person you want to become. Think of it as describing you at your best.

A student named Laney said her mission statement may seem overly simple, but it helped her live true to her values and to say no to things she didn't want to be involved with or waste her time doing. It reads:

> *My Mission Statement*
> *Be honest. Try your hardest.*
> *Do what's right. Give everything your all.*
> *Be kind to everyone. Have fun.*
> *And always remember who you are and what you stand for.*

Another example of a mission statement comes from Will, a student at Grand Rapids Community College in Michigan:

> *I have been given many gifts in life for which I am grateful. Gratitude alone is not enough, and it is my mission to use my talent and energy to honor God, my friends and family, and myself. I choose to serve others in ways that help them to become better and live fully. As a student, I will value what others teach me, so that one day I can work in ways that teach and serve others well.*

Here's an example from the United Kingdom. It comes from Charlie, a student at Canterbury University:

> *To live in the character and nature of who I truly am, kind, loving, and compassionate. Using the resources this life provides to help myself and those I choose to find happiness and be free from suffering.*

To mix things up a bit, let's look at an example from a well-known non-student named Mahatma Gandhi. He called his mission statement his *Resolution*:

"Life isn't about finding yourself. Life is about creating yourself."

—George Bernard Shaw

95

Let the first act every morning be to make the following resolve for the day:
- *I shall not fear anyone on earth.*
- *I shall fear only God.*
- *I shall not bear ill toward anyone.*
- *I shall not submit to injustice from anyone.*
- *I shall conquer untruth by truth.*
- *And in resisting untruth, I shall put up with all suffering.*

A student named Rose chose to make her mission statement a simple list of values that represent who she wants to be, using the letters of her first name:

Respect
Optimism
Solidarity
Entrepreneurial

My Personal Mission Statement is really short, and it changes a little from year to year. (No, I'm not going to share it with you! It's personal.) But it directs me in all of my choices and inspires me to be my best self. Your mission statement can do the same for you. If you haven't done so previously, I challenge you to develop a Personal Mission Statement and put it in writing. It does not need to be fancy or formal; often "less is more." It's meant to be for you, so don't write it to impress others; write it to inspire yourself.

Writing a Personal Mission Statement generally takes some time. The statement may evolve over a period of months, if not years, before you are totally satisfied with it. But don't wait that long to get started. In fact, you can get well under way in just a few minutes.

> "When I was a kid, only Batman had a cell phone. He had a car phone. I was like: Man, can you imagine having a car phone? But technology has not altered our lives, other than perhaps how we go about them. We are still in the position of waking up and having a choice: Do I make the world better today somehow, or do I not bother?"
>
> —Tom Hanks

Go to your *Living the 7 Habits* app to access a Mission Statement Builder tool.

Drafting a Personal Mission Statement

PART 1. Go back and review your responses to activities 15–19 in this chapter. Capture the major ideas in your mind.

PART 2. Write in the space below for 5 minutes without stopping. Don't worry about spelling, grammar, or handwriting. Just write whatever thoughts come to mind about what you want to include.

Once you have written a draft of your Personal Mission Statement, the next step is to make it a bit more formal—to mold and edit it into something tight and meaningful. Here are a few tips to help you improve your draft:

- Review inspiring quotations, literature, or poetry. Study the lives of people you admire. Listen to music that inspires you. From those sources, add any new thoughts to your existing draft.
- A first draft can be quite long, and that's okay. But eventually, you will want to edit until what is left is simple, covers only the essentials, and "rings true" to you. (Less really is more in many cases.)
- Aim high, but be realistic. Do you really plan to save every single whale in the world?
- Set it aside for a while and then come back and take a fresh look.

The mistake some students make is never finishing their Personal Mission Statement. It's exciting to write it, but it takes work. Just make it "good enough" for now and then revisit and improve it occasionally. Over time it will take the shape you want. Some people create their mission statements in the form of poetry, music, art, dance, and even clothes and jewelry. Regardless of its form, a Personal Mission Statement can be a powerful, constant reminder of the best of who you are and who you want to become.

Cameron graduated with honors from a major university, but he didn't start college that way. He was pretty typical—he felt stressed out, stunned by the size of the school, and crushed by the workload. But in a summer workshop before he started school, Cameron had written a "life mission" statement, and he says that statement got him through with flying colors:

My mission statement provided continuing direction throughout my college career. When you're in college, you're faced with really big life decisions that are going to impact the rest of your life. It's so easy to get sidetracked or distracted or overwhelmed with all these outside forces. To have a mission statement that you can get back to and kind of ground you—it was invaluable. It was invaluable in making decisions and not making myself get too overwhelmed and stressed out with assignments. It provided perspective, a long-term lens through which I could view my life 10 years from now and what I wanted it to be rather than being primarily focused on the problem or crisis right in front of me.

Roots to keep us grounded

Branches to set us free

Set Meaningful, Realistic Goals

A Personal Mission Statement is the "big picture" of yourself at your best. The next step is to turn your mission statement into reality. Setting meaningful, realistic goals can help you do that.

While they should be realistic, your goals shouldn't be low. Set them high enough that they excite and motivate you. One of my colleagues says, "When I was in my first year, I was satisfied with mediocre grades, since I didn't have any real ambitions. But then I heard about the honor society Phi Beta Kappa and its history of excellence. I became really motivated to become a member. So I started pushing for top grades, and finally I got through with nearly a 4.0 average. It was exciting and satisfying the day I got invited to the Phi Beta Kappa luncheon on graduation day and was able to sit down with other students I really respected. That Phi Beta Kappa key has opened a lot of doors for me since then."

Some time ago, when I was speaking to a big group of teens at a high school, I asked if anyone was willing to share their goals. A student named Ryan volunteered. I expected him to spout off a few goals he hadn't really thought about or to try to be silly to get attention, like some high school boys do. I was wrong. He reached into his wallet, took out a laminated card, and read his goals out loud:

> ## GOALS
>
> - Get and maintain a 3.7 GPA.
> - Get BFS (bigger, faster, and stronger). By senior year, weigh 200 pounds, run a 4.6 forty, bench-press 200 pounds eight times.
> - Be one of 22 starters on the varsity football team by senior year. Contribute to winning the state championship.
> - Be a good brother and example to my three little brothers.

Everyone in the audience was inspired by (and envious of) the commitment in Ryan's voice. They gave him big applause as he sat down. He was clearly going places in life.

I think most people understand the importance of goals, but coming up with a set of goals is not always easy. In fact, many college students don't have goals. Others set too many. Some set goals that are vague, "mushy," or impractical.

At FranklinCovey, we have shown thousands of people how to set and achieve goals. Believe me, we have seen all kinds of ways to do it, most of them too complicated. But we have found three simple tips that work:
- State the why.
- Be specific.
- Don't set too many goals.

> "The tragedy of life doesn't lie in not reaching your goal. The tragedy lies in having no goals to reach."
>
> —Benjamin Mays, minister and educator

99

Astronaut on the Moon

"I don't believe for a minute that everything that happens to you is your doing or your fault. But I do believe the ultimate quality of your life and your happiness is determined by your courageous and ethical choices and your overall attitude. You may get shipped some bad bricks and weak steel, but you are still the general contractor."
—Laura Schlessinger, talk-radio host

Before 1961, the United States had a vague goal with little meaning: "To lead the world in space exploration." The U.S. had dominated the "space race" for years and was involved in all kinds of space projects, but then Russia was the first country to send a man into orbit. People felt the U.S. was no longer the space leader and debated how to regain the lead. In 1961, in a famous speech before Congress, President John F. Kennedy galvanized the country with a specific goal: "This nation should commit itself to achieving the goal, before this decade is out, of landing a man on the Moon and returning him safely to the Earth."

He went on to point out the value of the moon project to national defense, job creation, and scientific knowledge. To achieve those whys, he picked a specific goal, one that had never been achieved before. He wanted a human being on the moon before the end of the decade.

In short, Kennedy took the original goal of being the best in the world in space exploration and made it more specific with the following simple formula:

From X to Y by When
- *From X (from a loss of space dominance and no man on the moon),*
- *To Y (a man on the moon and returned home safely),*
- *By when (before the end of the decade).*

Below are a few examples of how a college student might use the "From X to Y by When" formula to turn a vague goal into a more specific goal:

VAGUE GOAL	SPECIFIC GOAL
Do well in school.	This semester, I will achieve a 3.5 GPA.
Lose weight.	Go from 165 pounds to 145 pounds by June.
Do better at work.	Earn sales commissions of $1,000 in my summer job.
Be more social.	Participate in intramural basketball and join the Student Speakers Association this spring.
Graduate from college.	Within four years, graduate with a bachelor's degree in English.
Be a better husband.	Go on a date with my wife each week.

Can you see the difference in impact between the vague goals and the more specific goals? Can you see why it helps to identify "From X to Y by When"?

A friend of mine from South Africa, Treion Muller, shared how setting a specific goal helped him succeed in college:

On my first day at Southern Utah University, I walked into the admissions office and introduced myself. The staff already knew of me. As part of my application, I had sent an essay entitled "My Contribution," in which I confidently stated who I was and what I aimed to accomplish. This impressed them so much that they circulated the essay within the department, and were looking forward to meeting the new student from South Africa.

I came to America with the intention of going to college for four years. I had no family here, I had only one friend who wasn't expecting me, and I had barely graduated from high school. I was lucky the university had even accepted me.

I arrived with only enough money to get me through one year. So after the initial meeting in the admissions office, I returned later to see if they could help me start thinking of ideas for how to remain in school beyond the first year.

The admissions officer informed me that because I was a foreign student, I was not eligible for financial aid of any kind yet. She told me, "The only way you can get scholarship money from the university is to have a 3.9 GPA or better, and to be involved in as many activities and leadership opportunities as you can. At that point, you can apply for the university's Presidential Scholarship. But even then, we can't guarantee anything."

I looked her in the eye and said, "I'll be back in a year to apply for that scholarship." Then, one year later, I returned to her office as the Student Academic Vice President with a 4.0 GPA. I received and maintained that scholarship and other financial aid for the next three years.

Undoubtedly, there was more to Treion's success than just setting a goal. But without his clear why and his specific goals of getting a 4.0 and becoming a campus leader, I'm convinced that Treion would have achieved much less than he did.

I encourage you to keep Treion's example in mind as you set a few long-term goals of your own using the approach found in the next activity. Write your goals using the formula "From X to Y by When."

Long-Term Goals

Think of the roles you play in life such as student, friend, family member, employee, or others. For each role, set one specific long-term goal. For now, write a goal you can complete within a year.

ROLE	SPECIFIC GOAL
Student	
Friend	
Family	
Work	
Personal	
Other	

"Look. I just want to know exactly what the next 10 years of my life is going to look like, okay? And to have it organized on a color-coordinated calendar. Is that really too much to ask?"

—Emma Watson, actor

While some students have no goals, some have far too many. As the old Chinese proverb goes, "A man who chases two rabbits catches none."

Most college students pursue lots of tasks, projects, and dreams simultaneously. And that's okay. But I find it more practical to narrow down your goals and target two or three of them as your highest priorities. Ask yourself, "Which of my goals must be achieved, or nothing else I achieve will really matter much?" This kind of goal is called a Wildly Important Goal, or a WIG. A WIG is different from a Pretty Important Goal, or PIG. PIGs are not unimportant, but never let your PIGs get in the way of your WIGs.

Here are a couple of examples of WIGs from college students. The first comes from Beth, a young mom who has gone back to school part-time:

WIG 1: Get my B.A. in psychology and a counselor's certificate within four years.
WIG 2: Stay balanced by exercising three times a week, spending two hours an evening with my kids, and two hours a day studying.

From Tim, a full-time, first-year college student:

WIG 1: Get my core program finished in two years.
WIG 2: Get an internship at a top accounting firm.
WIG 3: Coach kids' volleyball once a week.

Of course, these students have other goals (PIGs), but they have identified these top priorities as their Wildly Important Goals. Now that you have seen a few examples of WIGs, give it a try. Identify your WIGs below:

Drafting a Personal Mission Statement

Look back at your mission statement. What goals do you have to achieve in order to accomplish your mission? List as many as you can on a piece of paper. You may also want to look back on the goals you set in Activity 21. Then identify the one, two, or three goals that you feel are your top priorities. Sometimes it helps to ask, "Which two or three goals must be achieved, or none of the other goals will really matter?" Once you have identified your Wildly Important Goals, record them here.

WIG 1:

WIG 2:

WIG 3:

ACTIVITY 22

You design your Personal Mission Statement for the long term, and it might change only a little over time. But WIGs, PIGs, and other goals are more flexible. Just as Norman Borlaug changed his goals and career directions after attending a lecture, you might change your goals from time to time as well. You might also want to set backup goals in case your WIGs don't work out.

DID YOU KNOW?
Headed in Unsure Directions

Goals can change from time to time, or they might just not work out. The following successful stars knew it was a long shot to make it in Hollywood, so they made backup plans for themselves:

Denzel Washington studied journalism, graduating with a degree from Fordham University.

Emma Watson has a bachelor's degree in English literature from Brown University.

Will Ferrell completed a degree in sports broadcasting at the University of Southern California.

Kevin Costner studied at California State University, Fullerton, where he graduated with a degree in business.

Eva Longoria got a master's degree in Chicano studies from California State University, Northridge.

Tommy Lee Jones, the Oscar winner, is an alumnus of Harvard University, where he completed a degree in English.

Tilda Swinton graduated in political and social science from Cambridge University.

Hugh Jackman has a bachelor's degree in communications from the University of Technology, Sydney.

Natalie Portman earned a bachelor's in psychology from Harvard University.

Jimmy Fallon studied computer science and received a bachelor's degree in communications from The College of Saint Rose.

"I believe there's a calling for all of us. The real work of our lives is to become aware. And awakened. To answer the call."

—Oprah Winfrey,

Explore Your Career Options

In your first year of college, your life is beginning again. You have a chance to Begin With the End in Mind by deciding on a career path. Of course, the ideal is to find a career that will help you fulfill your mission in life and your long-term WIGs.

There are three ways to look at work: as a job, a career, or a calling. A *job* is something you do as an assigned task and in an assigned amount of time. It can be temporary or full-time. At the end of it, you get paid and go home to relax. A *career* is a job with opportunities for advancement and personal growth, usually in a certain field, like law or engineering or media. A *calling* is a career attached to a meaningful purpose. It's your life's work. You feel passionate about it. You see how it benefits others. You love doing it. You might even accept less pay to pursue a calling over a career, as Norman Borlaug did when he left for Mexico.

DID YOU KNOW?
The Pay Factor

Although money isn't everything, you need to consider it when choosing a career. Look at this chart to see how money and education levels go hand in hand.

SKILL LEVEL	PAY	EDUCATION REQUIRED	TYPES OF JOBS
Professional Careers	Great money—upper-class lifestyle	High school (required) Bachelor's (required) Master's (usually required) Doctorate (often required)	CPA, advanced software engineer, lawyer, architect, business executive, college professor, doctor, dentist, successful entrepreneur, banker
Skilled Careers	Good money—middle-class lifestyle	High school (required) Bachelor's (usually required) Master's (sometimes required)	Computer programmer, police officer, lead mechanic, draftsperson, pilot, electrician, family farmer, financial analyst, real estate agent, schoolteacher, registered nurse
Semi-Skilled Careers	Fair money—lower-middle-class lifestyle	High school (usually required) Bachelor's (sometimes required)	Carpenter, auto mechanic, factory worker, store supervisor, truck driver, administrative assistant, insurance agent, car salesperson, enlisted soldier
Unskilled Jobs	Poor money—lower-class lifestyle	High school (occasionally required)	Retail sales clerk, fast-food worker, restaurant server, laborer, construction worker, custodian, lawn-care worker, security guard, most part-time jobs

What education and pay level do you need to achieve your aspirations and life-satisfaction level?

As you consider career options, do whatever you can to find a career you can turn into a calling. Any career or job can become a calling if you find meaning in it. That's why it's so important to decide what matters most to you and what goals you want to pursue in life before you choose a career.

Choosing a career is easier if you know about all the opportunities out there and what types of careers will best suit you. Most students are still learning about themselves and aren't sure what they'd like to do or do well. For that reason, most college campuses have career centers where you can take aptitude tests, learn about career opportunities, talk with career counselors, and explore your interests. Visit one of these centers even if you think you already know what you want to do for a career. When possible, do some pre-work before the visit. Think about your answers to these four questions:

- Talent: What are you really good at?
- Passion: What do you love doing?
- Need: What does the world need that you can get paid to do?
- Conscience: What do you feel you should do?

Where the four questions overlap represents your career "sweet spot," as shown below. On a tennis racket, the sweet spot is where you get the most power out of the racket. In this model, the sweet spot is where your career potential is greatest.

Talent involves doing what you do best.
- What are you really good at?
- What can you do better than most?
- What would those who know you best say are your greatest strengths?

Passion refers to what you like doing most. It's where your heart is.
- Since childhood, what have you always loved doing?
- What do you enjoy most about school?
- If money were no obstacle, what would you spend your time doing?
- If you could someday be famous for something, what would it be?

Need is the reality check.
- Where is there a need that you could get paid for?
- What is the biggest need in your family right now, and how can you help?
- Among your friends, who is in great need, and how can you help?
- What skills do you want to develop that people would be willing to pay for someday?

Conscience is the feeling that something "ought" to be done. The career might not be high-paying, but you choose it because you feel uniquely prepared for it and you can make a difference in other people's lives.
- How can you best help and serve others?
- Is there something you've always felt you should do with your life, even though you've ignored those thoughts in the past?
- What is life asking of you?

> "Where your talents and the needs of the world cross, there lies your vocation."
>
> —Aristotle

Oprah Winfrey described the "sweet spot" when she advised:

Have the courage to follow your passion—and if you don't know what it is, realize that one reason for your existence on earth is to find it. It won't come to you through some special announcement or through a burning bush. Your life's work is to find your life's work—and then to exercise the discipline, tenacity, and hard work it takes to pursue it.

How do you know whether you're on the right path, with the right person, or in the right job? The same way you know when you're not: You feel it. Each of us has a personal call to greatness—and because yours is as unique to you as your fingerprint, no one can tell you what it is.

Pay attention to what makes you feel energized, connected, stimulated—what gives you your juice. Do what you love, give it back in the form of service, and you will do more than succeed. You will triumph.
-Oprah.com

Now you might say, "I'm not Oprah." And you're right—you're not Oprah. Oprah was born in a small Mississippi town to a housekeeper mom and a soldier dad. She was an African-American girl raised in an age of segregation and discrimination and probably had far more to overcome than you will ever face in your life. No, you're not Oprah Winfrey. In fact, that's the point. You have unique qualities no one else has. So you need to find the best match for your uniqueness and the career options that are out there—to take your one-of-a-kind passions and talents and match them with the needs of society. Thomas Edison, who had lots of talents and passions, patented 1,093 inventions in his lifetime, including the light bulb, the record player, and the motion-picture camera. He said, "I never perfected an invention that I did not think about in terms of the service it might give others. I find out what the world needs, then I go ahead and try to invent it."

LESSON ON LEADERSHIP:
The Editorial Cartoonist

I attended college with an end in mind. I've always wanted to be a cartoonist and in my senior year of high school, I fell in love with editorial cartooning. I wanted to go to college, learn about art and politics, and work as an editorial cartoonist at a newspaper. In between classes on my first day of college, I went to the student newspaper and said, "I want to be your editorial cartoonist." They already had an editorial cartoonist, so I went to the city newspaper and said, "I want to be your editorial cartoonist." They didn't have a cartoonist, so I worked there until a spot on the college's newspaper opened up. I spent most of my years in college as their editorial cartoonist. I honed my drawing skills, studied politics, and three months after graduation, I landed a job drawing editorial cartoons at a newspaper. At that time, there were roughly only 200 editorial cartoonists working full-time at newspapers in the U.S. With hard work and planning, I achieved the end I had in mind. –Stacey

"Since every pleasure's got an edge of pain, pay your ticket and don't complain."

—Bob Dylan, "Silvio"

If you want to live in the sweet spot, it won't happen by accident. You'll need to Be Proactive about it. Too many people opt for a job that pays well without thinking about what they really want to do or how they can contribute to the world. Others choose careers that provide well for a family but eat them alive—and never give them time for the family! But then there's Norman Borlaug, whose career was right in the sweet spot with time left over to coach Little League.

So there's a lot to consider when you're making a career choice. And I'll give you a sneak look at the future: No job is the perfect job. You'll always have to do some things you don't want to do. Sometimes you will have to pay a price early in your career and make some sacrifices before getting to the position you really want. Often you'll encounter people you don't enjoy working with, bosses you struggle with, or clients who get on your nerves. That's part of life. But dealing with those problems is a lot easier when you've chosen a truly purposeful career that means a lot to you.

Exploring a Career

STEP 1: Go to the career center on your campus. (Some communities have career centers if your campus does not have one.)

STEP 2: Take an aptitude test recommended by the center staff.

STEP 3: Explore three careers that match the aptitude(s) identified by the test. Learn four "whats":
- What education requirements are necessary?
- What types of organizations hire for that career?
- What general job tasks are typically involved in that career?
- What are the general pay scales for that career?

STEP 4: Talk with someone in those fields about the pros and cons of each career.

Map Out a Graduation Plan

Let's say you have a personal mission, a set of goals, and a career as "ends in mind." Now you need to map out a graduation plan.

Traditionally, an associate's degree takes two years, a bachelor's degree four years, and graduate degrees two to four years beyond the bachelor's degree. Finishing on time or early requires planning.

But many students start college without an end in mind or a plan, so they take random courses that sound interesting. When they finally choose a major, they realize they should have taken different classes, or find they've left all the hard classes to the end. Sometimes they end up a class or two short of graduation, which means extra tuition, room, and board—and they wish they had thought things out better from the start.

Having a plan early on can save a lot of time and money later. For example, Rick and Jean started their major at the same time. Jean was single and wanted to enjoy the ride. Rick was married and wanted to graduate as soon as possible. Rick planned his classes so he could graduate a semester ahead of schedule, while Jean graduated a year behind schedule. Rick got a job paying $70,000 out of college and ended up hiring Jean when she graduated. As they talked one day, Jean realized that Rick had earned $105,000 during the year and a half she was still in school paying tuition—no small difference.

> "Hope is not a plan."
>
> —Anderson Cooper

You may want to be like Jean and take your time—that's a choice, and sometimes even a good choice. But be aware of the costs involved, some of which are not monetary. For example, when Jean started working with Rick, she noticed he had developed certain skills she didn't have. "What classes did you learn those skills in?" she asked. Rick had learned them all on the job and in some company training. So Rick had benefited not only financially but also professionally by gaining some great on-the-job training and experience.

You don't want to take classes that won't help you or come up short on classes you need, so creating a graduation plan is a smart choice even if you end up changing majors. A graduation plan is based on the career you're interested in and a major that will lead to that career; then you can map out classes you need for graduation.

To get a feel for this process, choose a career you might be interested in and do the following activity: "Mapping Out a College-Graduation Plan." Don't worry if you aren't sure it's the career you want to pursue—just pick one you might like and follow the steps.

ACTIVITY 24

Mapping Out a College-Graduation Plan

Select a career you find interesting—one you would seriously consider. It may be graphic design, nursing, engineering, athletic coaching—whatever you want. Then map out a plan to prepare yourself for that career. For the purpose of this activity, assume you are attending full-time and taking at least 12–15 credit hours per semester.

Which career you are seriously considering?

What college degree(s) do you need to be successful in that career?

__ Associate's   __ Bachelor's   __ Master's   __ Ph.D.   __ Other: _____

What college major(s) would help you pursue that career?

What college minor(s) would help you pursue that career?

Are there other special requirements, such as an internship?

In the spaces below, map out a possible schedule of classes you can follow. If your chosen career requires only an associate's degree, complete Years 1 and 2; if it requires at least a bachelor's degree, complete all four years.

	TERM 1	TERM 2
YEAR 1	1. 2. 3. 4. 5. 6.	1. 2. 3. 4. 5. 6.
YEAR 2	1. 2. 3. 4. 5. 6.	1. 2. 3. 4. 5. 6.
YEAR 3	1. 2. 3. 4. 5. 6.	1. 2. 3. 4. 5. 6.
YEAR 4	1. 2. 3. 4. 5. 6.	1. 2. 3. 4. 5. 6.

Even though you might ultimately choose a different major, planning can save you tremendous amounts of time, money, and sanity. Taking a class purely out of interest now and then is fun. But in general, good planning can help you graduate in less time than you ever imagined. Good things happen when you plan ahead.

Begin With a Résumé in Mind

Begin college with your résumé in mind. Creating the résumé you want to have someday will help you see into your future.

Suppose you want to become a nurse. The classes you take will look much like the classes every other nursing student takes, aside from a few elective or specialty courses. So, what will set you apart from all the other job applicants, other than your grades? Now is the time to start answering that question.

How? Think about what kind of nursing you want to specialize in, and focus your papers or projects on topics related to that area whenever possible. Having broad exposure to the whole field of nursing is good, but also keep a keen eye out for opportunities to intern, volunteer, or do projects in that specific area of interest.

Having good references on your résumé is important too. It's hard for professors or employers to write you a letter of recommendation if they don't know you or you never participate in class. Think now: Who would you like to recommend you? Start building relationships with those professors. Take more than one class from them. Don't be pushy, but do well in their classes, be punctual, make helpful comments, look sharp, and submit assignments on time. Jump on any chance to be a research assistant or attend special lectures.

You're probably familiar with "scratch and sniff" products. Most job interviewers can skim a résumé and smell a fake or a "smooth talker" in a heartbeat. Start building a genuine résumé now. Your experiences in your field of interest—jobs, internships, research assistantships, study abroad, student leadership, volunteer work— bring you the most credibility. You might have to proactively create such opportunities. Visit with people in your field. Volunteer. Join student associations.

If you plan to apply to graduate school, some graduate programs have specific entrance requirements that may not be a part of your college's general requirements. Find out what graduate schools want and gear your résumé toward their criteria.

Certain graduate schools may specialize in a particular area that isn't the best choice for your particular interests. Some graduate schools prefer your undergraduate studies to be in a field not directly linked to what you will study with them. Some graduate schools such as medical, law, or business put more emphasis on entrance-exam scores than they do on GPA or other criteria. Find out all of these things sooner rather than later—not after you have finished college, sent in your application, and been rejected.

To sum up, position yourself in the best possible light when you enter the workforce, apply to graduate school, or transfer to a different college. Often many people apply for a limited number of college slots or job positions. The more your résumé sets you apart and demonstrates your proactivity, the better your chances of being selected—so begin as soon as possible with your résumé in mind.

> "If you call failures experiments, you can put them in your résumé and claim them as achievements."
>
> —Professor Mason Cooley, College of Staten Island

HOW NOT TO ANSWER THIS JOB-INTERVIEW QUESTION:

"So why do you want to work for us?"

- "My parents told me to get a job."
- "For the benefits."
- "I need to buy a bike."
- "To subsidize my mud wrestling on weekends."
- "Because I got fired from my last job."
- "I'll need to text my mom on that."
- "How much do they pay you to ask these questions?"

THE REWARDS OF BEGINNING WITH THE END IN MIND

So where does beginning with the end in mind Get you?

Think about this: Where will having no end in mind get you? How much longer will it take and how much more will it cost you if you don't have a plan for college? What risks do you take if you have no goals? What will it cost you emotionally if you don't have a career that inspires you?

The costs could be high.

But if you do Begin With the End in Mind, you save time and money—and more important, you'll get more life satisfaction and the contentment that comes from living the life you want. Students who Begin With the End in Mind get better test scores, better grades, and better jobs upon graduation, as well as a more positive self-image and vision and a greater passion for the causes they care about.

Having a clear vision of what you want to do in college and in life is important, but it's even more important to have a clear vision of what you want to *be*.

I have no idea what your life has been like—mostly positive, I hope. But some of you have been through some horrible experiences or have grown up in awful environments. Some have faced severe learning challenges or struggled with school since childhood. Some of you have been away from school a long time and are just coming back. Some have battled loneliness or depression. Some have done things they wish they hadn't. Some have dealt with all of these things.

Sometimes people with tough lives end up with a negative self-paradigm. Don't let that happen to you. If you have made mistakes, don't let them hold your future hostage. If you have been abused, don't let your abuser's poor choices control your future choices. Picture the person you want to become and let that image guide you to the future. Writing a Personal Mission Statement, setting meaningful goals, having a plan for college, and creating a credible résumé—all of these actions can help you build a more positive view of yourself.

Above all, remember this: *You cannot have a feeling of worth if you are not doing things of worth.* Worthwhile things can come in small sizes: Complimenting someone. Reading to a child. Opening a door for someone. Letting another car go first at the stop sign. Taking notes for a friend who missed class due to illness. Size doesn't matter when it comes to feeling that you're worth something.

This textbook is not going to tell you the "right" purposes for your life. Determining that is up to you. That said, the happiest and most effective people I know are those who use their talents to make a positive difference in others' lives.

Ultimately, what you get out of life depends on your particular "ends in mind" and how aggressively you go after them. Look back over the activities you've done in this chapter. Identify one or two things you can follow up on that will improve your situation and capacity to grow as a college student. In the next activity, record those one or two things and what you hope to Get by doing them. How will they impact your life?

> "It's a dangerous business, Frodo, going out of your door. You step into the road, and if you don't keep your feet, there is no knowing where you might be swept off to."
>
> —J. R. R. Tolkien, *The Lord of the Rings*

What I Want to Get

Think back on the principles of Habit 2 and the activities you have completed in this chapter. Identify one or two actions that will help you most. What results do you hope to Get from doing these things?

	ACTIONS I WANT TO TAKE...	WHAT I HOPE TO GET...
ACTION 1		
ACTION 2		

SUMMARY

Again, no one fully knows the end from the beginning. Sometimes we must course-correct. Norman Borlaug did not know exactly where he was going when he entered college, and he ended up changing course. Eventually, he discovered that he wanted to help feed the world. He also wanted to satisfy his love for sports and family, and so he consistently made room outside of his career for both.

By contrast, Anne Sullivan chose to dedicate her life to a single individual, Helen Keller. Her pursuit eventually led to improvements in the lives of everyone with physical restrictions, particularly the blind and deaf. As for Joan of Arc, she literally gave her life for what she believed in.

So now you're at a point where you choose your life's goals and the plans you'll pursue. This chapter has focused mostly on the "big picture" of your life, but the same Habit 2 principles can apply just as much to planning a meal, preparing for a test, writing a paper, starting a relationship, or saving money. It all begins with a clear end in mind and viable goals and plans for achieving that end. The mental creation always precedes the physical creation.

Whether you're destined to impact a billion people or just one, Habit 2 helps you think about the contributions you want to make in life. You are the programmer for your life, so only you can write the program. Your success as a student depends, in large, on how you See, Do, and Get Habit 2: Begin With the End in Mind.

Here's a summary:

Habit 2: Begin With the End in Mind
Principles: Vision, Purpose

	INEFFECTIVE STUDENTS	EFFECTIVE STUDENTS
What They *See*	• Are too busy to stop and make a plan for life. • Think their parents, professors, and employers will let them know what is most important.	• Know that everything is created twice—first mentally, and then physically. • Want to live a life of purpose.
What They *Do*	• Plow forward without an aim or a plan. • Allow others to set their direction for them. • Spend a lot of time getting through college; do it inefficiently.	• Get clear on what is most important. • Write a Personal Mission Statement. • Set personal goals. • Find their voice—what they love to do and are good at. • Create a graduation plan for completing college on time, if not early. • Start thinking about what they want in their résumé from Day 1. • Begin research papers with a clear end in mind.
What They *Get*	• Aimlessness that leads to emotional pain and frustration. • Increased expenses from spending too many years in college. • A career they never intended to go into. • Less effectiveness and less efficiency.	• A compelling "why" for going to college. • A sense of meaning and purpose. • Less cost getting through college. • Better grades. • The satisfaction that comes with setting and completing goals.

In conclusion, Habit 2: Begin With the End in Mind is the habit of people who create their own lives. They see a clear vision of the future, whether it's 10 years from now, 5 years, or tomorrow.

Try some of the Baby Steps. I also recommend carefully studying and applying the tips found in the Academic Protip: "How to Write a College Paper."

COMING ATTRACTIONS

In the chapter that follows, you will learn the keys to becoming an organized person. I'll bet you can't wait!

Baby Steps

1. Teach to Learn. Using the summary chart on page 115, teach the key concepts of Habit 2 to a friend, classmate, or family member within the next 48 hours.

2. Give or take 10 years:

Ten Years Ago

Introduce yourself to someone as you were exactly 10 years ago today and tell him or her a few things about yourself. Do it with a family member, a roommate, or a friend, but you may want to tell the person it's part of a class assignment, so he or she doesn't think you've lost your mind.

If your name is Jack and you're 21, you would say something like, "Hi, my name is Jack. I'm 11 years old and I live in Vancouver, Canada, with my parents and a younger brother, who is 4. I just finished fifth grade. I have a cat named Rover, and I love to camp and play soccer. I'm a happy person."

Introduce yourself as you were 10 years ago, then give the other person a chance to do the same. If you find it too awkward, just fill in the blanks below.

The date 10 years ago today is _____.

My name is _____.

I am _____ years old.

I live in _____.

I live with _____.

My favorite things to do are _____.

I feel _____.

Ten Years in the Future

Now, shift gears. Introduce yourself to the same person as you would like to be 10 years into the future. Tell the person what you're doing and a little about yourself. Remember, this is how *you would like* to be 10 years from now. So Jack would say something like: "Hi. I'm Jack. I'm 31 years old and I live in Toronto, Canada. I just got married to a wonderful woman named Jacqueline. A few years ago I graduated in music from the University of Toronto and I teach piano at a private music school. I love my family and I hang out with them a lot. I'm feeling really good about where I'm headed with my life."

Now it's your turn:

The date 10 years in the future is _____.

My name is _____.

I am _____ years old.

I live in _____.

I live with _____.

My favorite things to do are _____.

I feel _____.

Debrief
When you went back 10 years, what memories surfaced? How did you feel?
Now what about the future? What did you see 10 years from now? What do you want to do and become over the next decade?

The good news is, where you end up 10 years from now is largely up to you and the choices you make. Remember, the best way to predict your future is to create it. Mental creation always comes before physical creation.

Academic Protip

College is all about asking the important questions of life. Why is the world the way it is? What is the good life? What can I do to make a difference? These are all Habit 2 questions. In college, writing papers is how we try to answer these questions. I've chosen one of the smartest college professors and best writers I know, my good friend and colleague, Breck England, to share insights on how to handle the task of writing college papers.

Dr. Breck England,
FranklinCovey

≫ How to Write a College Paper

By Dr. Breck England,
FranklinCovey

When you go to college, it's like walking into a party where lots of conversations are going on. Because a college is a big place, those conversations are about lots of things: psychology, history, chemistry, business—you name it. College is a place for people to think and converse about their thoughts on hundreds of subjects.

Now you get to join the conversation.

It's not very different from just talking with your friends. You've argued about sports teams and music and movies. You've debated your ideas about cars and clothes and money—and maybe even heavier topics like politics and religion. You've taken sides. Sometimes you've switched sides. But basically, you already know how to "converse."

In college, a paper is a way to join the conversation.

Your professors are going to ask you to write answers to lots of questions like these:

- "Does Shakespeare feel justice or mercy is more important in *The Merchant of Venice*?"
- "What are the survival advantages of prokaryotes over eukaryotes?"
- "What role does gross profit play in operating a business?"
- "Compare and contrast the views of Winston Churchill and A. J. P. Taylor about the origins of World War II."

Questions like these are important to the conversation because nobody is really sure of the answers. Supposedly, your professors have well-formed opinions but you will have your opinions, too, especially when you find out just how important and fascinating these conversations are.

And they *are* important. Take the question about the origins of World War II, which you might be asked to write about in a history class. You're jumping into a big argument there. The argument is about whether the Nazi leaders planned the war (as Winston Churchill believed) or bumbled into it (as the historian A. J. P. Taylor believed). Why is the argument important? Because in the future, people might run into the same kinds of conflicts, and it's crucial to know how to handle them.

Or suppose you're in biology class and the professor asks, "Is it better to be a prokaryote (like a bacterial cell) or a eukaryote (like a human cell)?" The question itself is full of questions: What does "better" mean? Is it stronger? Does it adapt to change better? Is it more "talented"? The point is, the conversation in college is finding the answers to important questions—and that's part of the fun. It's Habit 2: The "end in mind" for a college education is the search for truth and knowledge, which is arguably the most important thing human beings can do.

Many if not most of your classes will require you to write papers about questions like these. Some will be short one-pagers you can write quickly; others might take all semester and count heavily toward your grade. But nearly all of them will ask you to jump into the conversation.

Unlike a test, which usually asks you to repeat what you've learned, a college paper is your chance to say what you think. That's why the first thing you need is a point to make.

What's your point?

The whole point of writing a paper is to make a point. Sometimes it's called a thesis statement or a conclusion, but every paper needs a point. Your thesis is "your end in mind." Again, you're probably used to coming up with a thesis in everyday life: "Movie A is a lot better than movie B," "Team X can wipe Team Z off the field," and so forth. In a college paper, your thesis will sound something like this:

- "Prokaryotes are stronger and more adaptable than eukaryotes."
- "Shakespeare strikes a balance between justice and mercy in *The Merchant of Venice*."
- "World War II was not planned by the Nazis. They stumbled into it by mistake."

These are good examples of thesis statements. When you write your thesis, you're taking a side in a debate. You believe your side is right (although you know other people will argue with you, and they might also have good points to make; that's why college is a conversation).

Be careful not to confuse a "thesis" with a "topic." They're not the same. You might say, "I'm writing a paper on how World War II started." That's your topic, but that's not your thesis.

Usually, your thesis comes first in your paper. (There are times when it comes last; if you're reporting a lab experiment in a science class, your conclusion will end your paper.) Your thesis comes first because busy readers want you to get right to the point without delay.

Why do you think so?

Once you write your thesis, you'll need to give reasons for it. The whole idea of assigning you to write a college paper is to train you to come up with a strong point and then to support it with strong evidence. Why is Movie A better than Movie B? What makes you think Team X can wipe Team Z off the field?

Your reasons for your opinion will make or break your paper. It's good to have more than one reason—three is a good number. Make a simple outline with a thesis and three "because" bullets, like this:

Movie A is better than Movie B because…

- The characters are more realistic.
- The actors are more skilled.
- The music matches the story.

This thesis would make a pretty good paper. You can go on to explain why you think the characters are more realistic by giving examples. You might also talk about why you think realistic movies are better than unrealistic movies. Then you can go on to talk about why the actors are more skilled, give examples, and so forth.

Your grade will depend on how well you support your thesis, so spend

80 percent of your time writing good reasons for your point of view. Use examples, stories, statistics, and/or opinions from experts. Make sure you give the sources for any evidence you use. Put sources in footnotes or at the end of the paper in a source list or bibliography.

At the end of your paper, restate your thesis. Explain how you've proven that you are right (or at least that you have a good argument).

Now there are two basic rules for writing a successful college paper.

Rule 1: Don't try this alone.

You need help with your first college papers, so collaborate with people who can help you. I know you grew up with the idea that writing is "individual work." You might think getting help is cheating, but let's get clear on the difference between cheating and collaborating.

Cheating is getting the wrong kind of help. It means copying someone else's work without giving credit to them. So don't copy and paste stuff from the Internet without telling where it came from. Don't pay someone to do your paper for you. Cheating can get you thrown out of college—plus, it makes you a cheat.

Collaborating is getting the right kind of help. Go to the library and ask the staff to help you find the right sources to work from. Go to the writing center at your college where tutors will gladly help you get ideas, draft your paper, and edit it along with you. Go to your teacher as often as necessary—attend his or her office hours or make an appointment. Ask your teacher if your thesis is a good one. Ask how to improve it. Make sure you understand exactly what the teacher wants from your paper. Go back to the teacher with drafts and ask for suggestions.

Rule 2: Start early.

Many students have bad homework habits. They get an assignment on Monday that's due on Friday and wait until midnight on Thursday to start on it. This is a formula for disaster when writing a college paper.

If it's Monday and you have until Friday to write your paper, try the following manageable steps instead of taking one big step the night before.

1. As soon as you get the assignment, study it carefully. Get it in writing. Make sure you understand every word in the assignment. If you don't understand anything in the assignment, ask the teacher *immediately* to help you get it. Don't wait.

2. The same day, brainstorm a thesis statement. Then brainstorm another one. Keep at it until you feel good about it. Then show it to your teacher or a writing tutor. Get suggestions.

3. Once you have a good thesis, collect your supporting data. Get the librarian to help you find the right kind of sources. Go online and find what others have said about your topic. Go to Google Books™ and Google Scholar— you'll find good, reliable information there. Copy and paste good quotations and data from other sources. Be very careful to record exactly where you got each item of information—author, title, publisher, date, page number, and website name and address.

4. Draft your paper on Tuesday. Write quickly, as if you were brainstorming. It doesn't have to be perfect or even grammatically correct. At this point, you're just trying to get your ideas down. Take your draft to your teacher or to the writing center. Ask them to review it with you and make suggestions.

5. Rewrite your draft on Wednesday. Take good suggestions from others. Now let it sit for an hour or a day.

6. Edit and proofread your draft on Thursday. After letting it sit, you'll look at it with different eyes. You'll find problems you didn't see before. You'll clear up things that aren't so clear. Use spell check and grammar check—if there's a squiggle under a word or phrase, there's usually a problem. Click on the squiggle and fix it.

Some professors will tell you to use "Chicago Style" or "MLA Style" or "APA Style." This means you should follow the writing guidelines in one of these books:

*   *Chicago Style: A Manual for Writers of Research Papers, Theses, and Dissertations*, 7th edition, University of Chicago Press, 2007. Used by most college teachers.
*   *MLA Style: MLA Handbook*, 7th edition, Modern Language Association, 2009. Used by humanities teachers—English, art, literature, film, etc.
*   *APA Style: Publication Manual of the American Psychological Association,* 6th edition, 2009. Used by science teachers—biology, physics, math, psychology, etc.

You can order these books online, and there are apps available for each of them.

Obviously, you shouldn't try to take all these steps at once. That's why you can't leave the assignment until Thursday night. Start on Monday and finish by Thursday. You'll have peace of mind and your product will be much, much better for it.

So, in summary, if you want to write a good college paper, remember to:

*   Make your point with a good thesis statement.
*   Support your thesis with three good reasons for it.
*   Don't try this alone.
*   Start early.

Dr. Breck England has taught college writing for nearly 30 years. He was adjunct professor of business writing at the Marriott School of Brigham Young University and a writing instructor at the University of Utah. He has also taught writing skills to thousands of business professionals as a consultant for Shipley Associates, a worldwide communication training firm, and FranklinCovey. He is coauthor of *Presentation Advantage* and *The FranklinCovey Style Guide for Business and Technical Communication,* 5th edition, FT Press.

References

"Borlaug's Revolution," *The Wall Street Journal*, July 17, 2007.

Wrzesniewski, A., McCauley, C.R., Rozin, P., and Schwartz, B., "Jobs, careers, and callings: People's relations to their work," *Journal of Research in Personality*, 31 (1997), 21–33.

Put First Things First

The Habit of Integrity

"There can be no happiness if the things we believe in are different from the things we do."

–FREYA STARK

IN THIS CHAPTER, YOU WILL DISCOVER WAYS TO:

- Live in Quadrant 2.
- Plan weekly.
- Adapt daily.
- Organize your stuff.
- Dive into the courage zone.

Also, look for the Academic Protip...

- How to Study for a Test

Habit 3:
Put First Things First

is the habit of turning a vision into action.

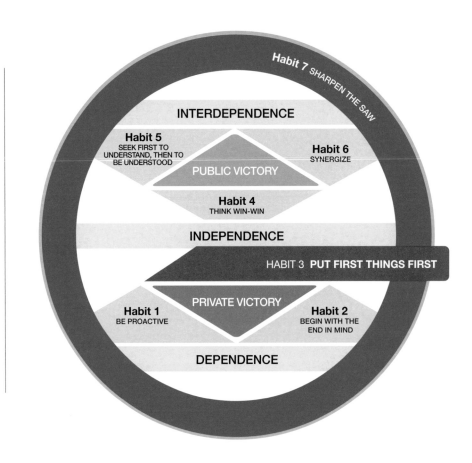

What I Wish
I'd Known in College

"Don't get overwhelmed. Take one class at a time, one assignment at a time, one problem at a time. Prioritize what needs to be done first, start there, and work your way down the list of work to be done."
–Steve, Utah State University

"Do the most important things first. Learn to be modest, not to have something all at once, and especially to be patient. Take care of your physical and mental health carefully."
–Irina, Charles University, Prague

"Take great notes in class. And if you really want to save study time, retype key points after class for an always up-to-date review guide. It only takes a few minutes and will make studying for the final that much easier."
–Jack, Bates College and Harvard Business School

"I wish I'd known that I could have had more time for fun in the evening if I would have cranked out my work in the daytime. I wish someone would have told me to just get it done. "
–Haydn, Lincoln Christian University

REAL CHOICES:
Saying No for a Deeper Yes

Are you the type of student who paints your face and acts crazy to cheer on your favorite college sports team? Even if you don't like college sports, I think you will like the story I'm about to share. Hint: It's not about sports; it's about the next 40 years of your life.

Though there are many great college basketball coaches in the world, none have led their teams to more victories than UCLA's John Robert Wooden. No one has equaled his 81 percent win record, mostly against top-ranked opponents. No one has beaten his record of 10 U.S. national championships. Yet, perhaps the biggest victory of them all came the day he was faced with a sizeable and tempting offer.

In 1971, Wooden had just led his UCLA team to another outstanding season. So it was no surprise when the Los Angeles Lakers, the richest and most successful professional team in the National Basketball Association, offered the job of head coach to John Wooden.

As coach of the Lakers, he would be in a worldwide media spotlight. Not only would he make 10 times his college salary of $35,000, but he would coach some of the best players on the planet, including the legendary Wilt Chamberlain. John Wooden would be at the peak of his profession, the greatest coach of the greatest team in basketball.

What would you have done?

John Wooden turned it down.

He stayed true to what mattered most to him, which was preparing young people for the biggest game of all—the game called life. For Wooden, winning games was only part of his calling in life. "I have always tried to make it clear that basketball is not the ultimate. It is of small importance in comparison to the total life we live."

Wooden saw himself first as a teacher, and his subject was how to become a successful person. His main teaching tool was a chart he called the "Pyramid of Success"—a set of principles such as loyalty, friendship, cooperation, honesty, and integrity that are the building blocks to competitive greatness. "It was never about basketball," remembers one player, the remarkable Bill Walton. "It was about life."

> What will you do with the next 40 years of your life? Will you have the discipline to still be pursuing your dreams when you hit 80?

John Wooden, said to be the greatest basketball coach in history. Photo at UCLA: Southern Campus 1960

125

Think in terms of computer programming. Habit 1 says, "I am the programmer of my life," Habit 2 is writing the program, and Habit 3: Put First Things First is about executing your program.

When he died a few months short of his 100th birthday, John Robert Wooden was called the greatest coach of all time. To this day, UCLA basketball players wear the initials "JRW" on their uniforms.

Why did Wooden say no to 10 times the salary, fame, and fortune? As Stephen R. Covey put it, "He had a deeper yes burning inside him."

As I hinted, this story is not about sports; it's about you and what you are going to do with the next 40 or more years of your life. In the last chapter of Habit 2, you got to identify what matters most to you—your deeper yes. This chapter focuses on how to put those things first. It's Habit 3: Put First Things First. You'll start taking action every day to achieve your mission and goals, and to say no to anything that pulls you off course.

If you practice Habit 3, you plan your weeks and stay focused on your top priorities. That's why we call it the "habit of integrity." People with integrity do what they say they're going to do. I also call Habit 3 the habit of willpower—the strength to stay true to what's most important—and the habit of "won't power"—the courage to say no to less important things, to distractions or things society or our peers may pressure us to do but that don't really matter.

The basic concepts of Habit 3 are summarized by the See-Do-Get Cycle in the following way:

PEOPLE WHO PRACTICE HABIT 3:

INTEGRITY AND FOCUS

SEE

- Effectiveness first, then efficiency.
- Importance first, then urgency.
- Relationships first, then schedules.

DO

- Live in Quadrant 2.
- Plan weekly.
- Adapt daily.
- Organize your stuff.
- Dive into the courage zone.

GET

- More productivity.
- Less stress.
- Greater life balance.

PARADIGM OF PUTTING FIRST THINGS FIRST

One of the top challenges first-year students face in college is managing their time. Suddenly, there are so many things to do and so many deadlines. Trying to balance school with work, friends, family, and fun can be dizzying.

Most people think of time management with a paradigm of efficiency. Efficiency is doing more things faster. By contrast, the paradigm of Habit 3: Put First Things First is this:

- Effectiveness first, then efficiency
- Importance over urgency
- Relationships before schedules

Effectiveness First, Then Efficiency. Effectiveness is doing the right things. Efficiency is doing things right.

Imagine a large work crew building a road with bulldozers and dynamite. They're about to knock down a house to make way for the road. They've planned their approach to the house, got all the right equipment, and moved people to safety. They're ready to do an efficient job.

Now imagine their leader—the one with the vision and the blueprint—arriving on the scene with compass in hand. After a moment of gazing and calculating, he shouts to the crew: "That's the wrong house!"

Embarrassing, right? It doesn't make sense to do something efficiently that shouldn't be done at all.

Silly as it sounds, people do this sort of thing on college campuses every day. Take the example of a woman who chose a college major because her dad liked it, even though her internal voice kept telling her it was a mistake. She got so far into it, she decided it

WRONG HOUSE... MY BAD!

would be too expensive to start over, so she ended up graduating and getting a job in a profession she didn't like. Talk about "wrong house"!

Highly effective college students first make sure they've got the right house (effectiveness), then they figure out how to cut through it as fast and with as little cost as possible (efficiency). Efficiency doesn't matter unless you're effective first—if you care about time, money, and your sanity. It doesn't matter how fast you're going if you're headed in the wrong direction.

Importance Over Urgency. In today's busy world, it is easy to become addicted to urgency. We love our fast food, our crash courses, and our "buns of steel in seven days." Instant gratification isn't fast enough. A text comes and we have to answer it instantly. Somebody asks us to do something fun that we don't really have time for right now, but we just have to do it anyway. (Notice the reactive "have to"?)

Just because something is urgent doesn't make it important. In fact, a lot of texts, phone calls, TV shows, bar nights, and social media stuff really don't matter. These activities may feel urgent, but they're not important, and we end up wasting time.

The problem with living on impulse, jumping at every urgent thing, is that we end up shortchanging important things such as staying physically fit, building real friendships, and doing school work. As the philosopher Goethe said, "Things which matter most must never be at the mercy of things which matter least."

One nontraditional student named Rich tells his story:

I went back to the university when I was 33 years old. I felt like an antique. It took me four years to get my degree while working at the same time, but looking back on it now, it was the best thing I ever did. The whole thing was a Quadrant 2 experience. Before college, I was living totally in Quadrant 1, working 12-hour days, constantly feeling exhausted, and wondering why I could never get ahead. But in college, things were quieter. The classes made me think, and the younger students were really nice to me. I made friends. I did a lot of reading—a huge amount of reading—and I felt like my brain was growing muscles. It was like working out in a brain gym. I came out a different person with a different perspective. Since then I've tried to live a Quadrant 2 life because I got used to it during my four college years. It's a much better life than the life I had before. I feel sorry for people who never get to have those years.

Later on in this chapter, I'll explain what Rich means by Quadrants 1 and 2. But for now, just remember that Quadrant 1 represents urgency and Quadrant 2 represents importance.

"It is a mistake to think that moving fast is the same as actually going somewhere."

—Steve Goodier, author

Johann Wolfgang von Goethe

Campus Voices

When I asked some first-year students to identify their biggest time-management challenges, they said:

"Trying to work and go to school and have enough time in the day."
–Travis

"Not procrastinating to the last minute to begin projects."
-Ashley

"Caring for my children. They are my first priority and I have to take care of them when they are ill."
-Maria

"Trying to get two hours of study in for every hour of class."
–Jeanette

"Getting classes that would fit my work schedule."
–Ricardo

"Knowing what is most important and what to do first when it comes down to getting work done in a limited amount of time."
-Darby

"Finding time to do all the homework."
-Kevan

"Sticking to my study schedule."
-Kristin

"Finding time to sleep."
–David

"Having to turn down my friends to do school or work."
-Calvin

Relationships Before Schedules. I think most people would say relationships are the most important part of their lives. But when we get really busy, we tend to brush people off and focus instead on our to-do lists and schedules. We can get so caught up in doing things that we neglect the people that make life worth living.

Highly effective college students know better. They know there's a time for sticking to a calendar or schedule and a time for being with someone. For them, putting first things first means putting people first. Always think of being effective with people and efficient with things.

"Indifference and neglect often do much more damage than outright dislike."

—J.K. Rowling, *Harry Potter and the Order of the Phoenix*

WHAT STUDENTS *DO* WHO PUT FIRST THINGS FIRST

The three paradigms of Put First Things First will make even more sense as you get into what highly effective students Do, which is:
• Live in Quadrant 2.
• Plan weekly.
• Adapt daily.
• Organize their stuff.
• Dive into the courage zone.

Live in Quadrant 2

The key to putting first things first is to spend less time in Quadrant 1, more time in Quadrant 2, and no time in Quadrants 3 or 4. Let me explain.

Everything you do fits into four quadrants, divided up according to what is important and what is urgent. The four quadrants make up the Time Matrix.

The Time Matrix

Important: What matters most—your mission, goals, and the important people in your life.

Urgent: Things that scream for your immediate attention.

	URGENT	NOT URGENT
IMPORTANT	**1** • Crises • Deadlines (exam tomorrow, project due today, etc.) • Pressing problems • Call from a good friend who needs to talk • Late for work • Car breaks down • Need to eat • Some phone calls, texts, emails *The firefighter lives here.*	**2** • Planning • Proactive work • Paper due in a week • Exercise • Relationships • Relaxation and renewal • Advance studying for a test • Prevention of problems • Preparation • Proper sleep • Preventive car maintenance *The highly effective student lives here.*
NOT IMPORTANT	**3** • Unimportant texts, phone calls • Constant interruptions or tempting distractions • Other people's small problems • Negative peer pressure • Too many clubs, activities, hobbies • Addictions *The yes-man lives here.*	**4** • Too much TV • Endless phone chats • Mindless hanging out • Excessive computer games • Personal time-wasters • Stupid social media stuff • Binge drinking and hangovers *The slacker lives here.*

Quadrant 1 is filled with things that are both important and urgent. It's getting a critical phone call from a friend, rushing to be to work on time, or cramming at the last minute for a big exam. Many Quadrant 1 things are unforeseen and unavoidable. They can pop up at any time, like a bus that isn't on time and makes you late for class. But procrastination causes many Quadrant 1 activities. For example, that research paper that used to be due in a month is now due in two days and is screaming at you. Or you've been putting off talking to your friend who needs you and your relationship now needs CPR.

Some people get an absolute thrill out of living in Quadrant 1. I call them Quadrant 1 firefighters because they thrive on the rush they get when putting out fires. But at some point, they learn that a Quadrant 1 life inevitably leads to poor work, stress, and burnout.

My older brother Stephen is one of my heroes and is the author of *The New York Times* best-seller *The Speed of Trust*. But when he was in college, he was the ultimate firefighter. He'd skip class all semester, cram for the final the last few days, and somehow pull out a good grade. But finally, it caught up with him. He'd skipped calculus several times and then spent 48 hours straight studying for the test without sleep. He told me, "During the final, I thought I had it made. And then, my brain suddenly shut down completely. I couldn't remember a thing and I bombed the test." Years later, when he got into grad school, he told me how he regretted all those years of cramming because suddenly he was competing with students who had really paid the price to learn the stuff.

Stephen M. R. Covey

Quadrant 2 is filled with things that are important but not urgent. Take exercise, for example. Is exercise important? Yes. Is it urgent? No, not usually. So it belongs in Quadrant 2. What about a research paper that is due in a week? Is it important? Yes. Is it urgent? No, not yet. So it belongs in Quadrant 2. Regularly changing the oil on your car is another Quadrant 2 task. Is it urgent? No. Is it important? Yes.

Quadrant 2 is recreation, goal setting, planning, proactive work, relationship building, and proper rest. The interesting thing about Quadrant 2 is that you can usually get away with neglecting it for a while, but eventually it will bite you in a bad way and throw you into Quadrant 1. If you eat lousy food and don't exercise for months, you'll end up sick. Now you have a Quadrant 1 crisis on your hands. The same is true with putting off your research paper to the last minute. You'll just make a mess.

"As we all know, it's easier to do trivial things that are urgent than it is to do important things that are not urgent, like thinking. And it's also easier to do little things we know we can do than to start on big things that we're not so sure about."

—John Cleese, actor

This is why highly effective students live in Quadrant 2. It is the quadrant of preparing, planning, and preventing. It leads to better performance in school, greater balance, better friendships, less stress, and less time fighting fires.

Quadrant 3 is filled with things that seem urgent, but are not important, such as pointless phone calls and text messages, or other people's trivia (videos of their cat on YouTube™ or a selfie of their new haircut on Facebook™). Quadrant 3 deceives you. Things that pop up feel urgent, and urgent things tend to masquerade as important things that really aren't. Spending so much time reacting to stuff like social media leaves no room for a proactive life of your own. Because Quadrant 3 is urgent, it feels important. In reality, it's not important. Maybe it is to someone else, but not to you.

One big reason students end up in Quadrant 3 is peer pressure. They get talked into doing things they don't want to do, such as skipping class or doing something stupid they later regret. They just can't say no. That's why Quadrant 3 is the quadrant of the yes-man. If you live in Quadrant 3, you say yes to everything because you don't want to disappoint or get left out. So if somebody drops in for a minute while you're studying for a big test, and then that person talks to you about nothing for two hours, you have just said yes to Quadrant 3.

One student said, "I wish I'd known in my first year of college that there was no need to stay up all night yakking with my friends. After all, my friends were still there the next day."

Beware of Quadrant 3. It only leads to frustration.

Quadrant 4 is waste. It's the home of the slacker. It's too much of anything, including too much of a good thing, like too much sleep, too much TV, endless Internet sessions, mindless hanging out, or shopping marathons. You might start out in Quadrant 2, because you need time to kick back and relax, but when it becomes excessive, you fall into Quadrant 4. Watching a favorite TV show, for example, is a good Quadrant 2 activity, but watching hour after hour turns you into a slacker. Games can be Quadrant 2 stress relievers, but overdone they become addictive sinkholes. (How many hours can you play "Pop the Bubble Wrap"?) Afterward you want to slap yourself on the head: "Why did I just stay up until 3 a.m. watching *Star Trek* reruns?" Spending time in Quadrant 4 leads to feelings of low self-esteem and depression.

So those are the four quadrants of the Time Matrix. I hope you get the point that the more you say no to Quadrants 3 and 4 and yes to Quadrant 2, the less time you'll spend going crazy in Quadrant 1.

So how can you as a busy student spend more time in Quadrant 2? Try these two strategies:

Strategy 1: Live Above the Line

The best way to say yes to Quadrant 2 is to say no as much as possible to Quadrants 3 and 4. This is living above the line. It's not easy, but why not give it a try? For 30 days, stop excess TV, mindless Internet surfing, pointless hanging out, or other below-the-line activities. Stop answering every single text or social media update or phone call that comes your way. Try studying in the library instead of your dorm room so you won't be susceptible to interruptions. Try telling someone, "Let me think about that and get back to you," instead of saying "Yeah, I'll be there." You get my drift.

"An overindulgence of anything, even something as pure as water, can intoxicate."

—Criss Jami, poet

According to the A.C. Nielsen Co. the average American watches 3 hours and 46 minutes of TV each day. That's more than 52 days of TV watching per year.

Living Above the Line

	URGENT	NOT URGENT
IMPORTANT	**1** • Crises • Deadlines (exam tomorrow, project due today, etc.) • Pressing problems • Call from a good friend who needs to talk • Late for work • Car breaks down • Need to eat • Some phone calls, texts, emails *The firefighter lives here.*	**2** • Planning • Proactive work • Paper due in a week • Exercise • Relationships • Relaxation and renewal • Advance studying for a test • Prevention of problems • Preparation • Proper sleep • Preventive car maintenance *The highly effective student lives here.*
NOT IMPORTANT	**3** 🚫	**4** 🚫

LIVE ABOVE THE LINE.

Living above the line might be harder than it looks. Why? Two reasons. First, people are addicted to urgency. Second, many people lack a deeper yes. So staying above the line requires either (1) killing the urgency addiction or (2) finding a deeper yes—your Habit 2 mission and goals.

Killing the Urgency Addiction. Again, despite all the drawbacks, some people love the rush that comes from being firefighters. I know because I was one of them. They can't seem to work on a paper or study for a test until the night before. They like to push off things like caring for their health, their car, or their relationships until they break down.

Many students are urgency-addicted and don't know it. You may want to try the next activity to test if you're an urgency addict.

> "ADDICTION: When you can give up something anytime, as long as it's next Tuesday."
>
> —Nikki Sixx, American musician

133

Are You Urgency-Addicted?

YES	NO	
		I cram for tests the night before.
		I write papers the last minute before they are due.
		I'm late a lot.
		I take things as they come rather than plan ahead.
		I have a hard time getting motivated unless there's pressure.
		I answer text messages within seconds of receiving them.
		I hate to wait in lines or get behind slow people.
		I seem to always rush between places and events.
		I always wish I had done things sooner.
		I often do things I shouldn't have said yes to in the first place.

Yes scores: 8–10—You're an urgency addict; maybe even an urgency pusher; **5–7**—You're at risk of becoming an addict; **1–4**—You are free of an urgency addiction!

WELL, PERHAPS YOU COULD TEXT THEM BACK LATER.

According to Amy Bjork Harris and Thomas A. Harris, M.D., in their book *Staying OK*, with urgency addicts, entire "days can be wasted getting out of tasks we shouldn't have taken on in the first place. We know we don't have the time… but when asked, we still say yes." (Harris, 239)

As an experiment, some students at the University of Maryland decided to give up all their technology for one day. Listen to the voice of one urgency-addicted student:

Texting and IMing my friends gives me a constant feeling of comfort. When I did not have those two luxuries, I felt quite alone and secluded from my life. Although I go to a school with thousands of students, the fact that I was not able to communicate with anyone via technology was almost unbearable.

Honestly, this experience was probably the single worst experience I have ever had.

I got back from class around 5 p.m. frantically craving some technology and a look at my phone, so I cheated a little bit and checked my phone. From my phone, I accessed text messages, noticed close to a dozen missed calls, glanced at some emails, and acknowledged many twitter replies from followers wondering where I was and if I was ok. At that moment, I couldn't take it anymore being in my room… alone… with nothing to occupy my mind so I gave up shortly after 5 p.m. I think I had a good run for about 19 hours and even that was torture. My short attention span prevented me from accomplishing much, so I stared at the wall for a little bit. After doing some push-ups, I just decided to take a few Dramamine and go to sleep to put me out of my misery. (Moller, "A Day Without Media")

So how do you get over an urgency addiction? Practice saying no. You can do it. When people continually interrupt your life, you've got to say no at some point or you have no life. Harris and Harris suggest that "a helpful way to break the pattern is to decide never to make a decision on the spur of the moment. It takes a little time to say, 'I'll have to think about it and call you back,' but not nearly as much as muddling through a job we don't have the time to handle." (Harris, 240)

I think the best advice comes from Gandhi: "A 'no' uttered from the deepest conviction is better than a 'yes' uttered merely to please, or worse, to avoid trouble."

Finding a Deeper Yes. It's far easier to say no to Quadrants 3 and 4 if there is a deeper yes burning within you. If you're not committed to a clear mission or a set of goals, you'll hang out aimlessly in Quadrant 3 trying to please other people or in Quadrant 4 tossing your time in the garbage. This is why Habit 2, defining your mission and goals in life, precedes Habit 3. It's so much easier to say no to peer pressure or to drugs or to time-wasters if you've made up your mind that you're going to get good grades and find that perfect job someday.

"I'm tempted to type meaningless twaddle all the time on Twitter… with alliteration, no less!"

—E.A. Bucchianeri, author

Strategy 2: Stay Out of Quadrant 1

The second strategy for moving into Quadrant 2 is to minimize the time you spend in Quadrant 1. Ironically, the best way to do that is to spend more time in Quadrant 2. Time spent in Quadrant 2 shrinks time in Quadrant 1.

Realistically, you'll never stay completely out of Quadrant 1. Unexpected things happen. But you can reduce the amount of time you spend in Quadrant 1 with three P's—planning, preparation, and prevention—all of which are Quadrant 2 activities. Do your homework in advance, not the night before the test. Start your papers a week before they're due. Start looking for that summer job three months before school ends. Take time for yourself. Go for a walk with a friend. Listen to music. Write in your journal. Get out in nature. Work out. Eat right. Whatever renews you, do it often and you will find yourself spending less time in Quadrant 1.

135

Learning about the Time Matrix helped Kurt, a first-year student:

In high school, I was a good student, so I assumed I would do the same in college. Yet when tests came, I did poorly. I couldn't understand why. When I saw the Time Matrix, I realized I fit the label of a Quadrant 3 yes-man. When I was supposed to be studying, I would give in to constant interruptions that I thought were important, like a bunch of phone calls from friends. So I was easily distracted, and often ended up cramming the morning before a test. I have since learned to politely say no to friends' interruptions at times when I need to be saying yes to other priorities.

Like Kurt, you might want to track how much time you spend in each of the quadrants and to plan how to move into Quadrant 2. Try the next activity: "My Last Week."

My Last Week

Now that you're familiar with the Time Matrix, estimate what percentage of your time is spent in each of the quadrants. Estimate based on how you spent your time last week and yesterday. Think carefully. Be honest.

	URGENT	NOT URGENT
IMPORTANT	**1** Last 7 Days ___% Yesterday ___%	**2** Last 7 Days ___% Yesterday ___%
NOT IMPORTANT	**3** Last 7 Days ___% Yesterday ___%	**4** Last 7 Days ___% Yesterday ___%

If you spend less than 25 percent of your time below the line in Quadrants 3 or 4, way to go. If you spend more than that, how could you move more of your time above the line?

Plan Weekly

Strategies 1 and 2 are good, but the best way to get into Quadrant 2 is to spend 20 to 30 minutes planning your week.

Weekly planning involves two big steps: (1) reconnecting weekly with your mission and goals, and (2) scheduling your Big Rocks first.

Step 1: Reconnect Weekly With Your Mission and Goals. At the end of the week or the start of the upcoming week, find a time to review and think deeply about your mission and goals—the same time every week in a quiet place is best. Remind yourself why you are in college. Think about what you want to accomplish. Tap into your deepest motivations. Review the key roles you are fulfilling in your life, such as student, friend, or family member. Go back and look at the goals you came up with in Habit 2.

Now think about the upcoming week. What can you do this week to move your mission and goals forward?

Why plan your week? A week is the perfect unit of time for reconnecting and planning. Planning a whole month is a big job, while planning a day at a time is too short term to get anything meaningful done. A week's time is neither too close nor too far away. Within a week you can take steps toward achieving your goals. So the week is just right.

Step 2: Schedule Your Big Rocks. To do this step you'll need a calendar. I use my phone and my computer, but I also use a paper calendar because I like to see a whole month at a time. Do what's best for you.

So what do I mean by Big Rocks?

Imagine you have a bucket more than half filled with small rocks. Next to it is a pile of Big Rocks. Your job is to get all of the rocks, the big ones and the small ones, into the bucket under the rim.

Suppose you put the Big Rocks into the bucket of little rocks. Even using all your wiggle power, you'll never get more than half of the Big Rocks into the bucket, as pictured on the right.

> "Let's be reasonable and add an eighth day to the week that is devoted exclusively to reading."
>
> —Lena Dunham, actor and director

137

Now suppose that the bucket stands for your week, the Big Rocks are the goals that are most important to you, and the little rocks represent all the minor things you could do. For instance, the Big Rocks might have labels: Do research paper, call mom, take a big test, see friends, work, go on date, exercise, visit your professor, and eat right.

If the Big Rocks truly are the most important things in your life this week, you really need to fit them all in. You don't want to miss calling your Mom for the second week in a row and you really need to start on that research paper. The problem worsens when the same Big Rocks, like exercise, get left out of the bucket week after week after week.

If you want to get all of the Big Rocks into the bucket, you'll need to think differently—a different paradigm—based on Quadrant 2. Start with an empty bucket. Put your Big Rocks in first. They all fit! Then add small rocks to that bucket, if you want to. Most of the small rocks will fit in between the Big Rocks, but it really doesn't matter if they don't. After all, they aren't nearly as important. As the saying goes, the main thing is to make the main thing the main thing.

So start with an empty bucket when you plan your week. You might say, "No way, my week is already full." Maybe you're right. But be proactive and clear that calendar anyway—at least mentally.

Once your calendar is empty, do step 1. Revisit your mission, roles, and goals. Think about what is most important to you. Think about why you are going to school.

Next, do step 2. Schedule your Big Rocks for the week. For each role, ask yourself, "What is the most important thing I can do in this role this week?" Think deeply. Reflect. Listen to your conscience. It might go something like this:

- "As a student, the most important thing I can do this week is to prepare for the test on Friday."
- "As a friend, the most important thing I can do this week is to spend some quality time with my roommates."
- "As a construction worker, the most important thing I can do this week is to finish the sanding project."
- "For myself, the most important thing I can do this week is to eat well and exercise."

And so on. Once you've identified those Big Rocks, maybe three or five or eight, block out time for them before the week fills up with little rocks. Believe me, if you don't block out time in advance for your most important things, the little rocks will fill up your bucket, and you'll end the week feeling worn out yet frustrated that you never got the most important things done.

Finding space for the Big Rocks might require some maneuvering, but you can fit them in if you empty the little rocks first. This one idea, blocking out time in advance each week for your Big Rocks, is the single greatest time-management technique ever discovered. If you don't plan before you get into the rush of the week, you will be into urgency mode the rest of the week. And that's not very fun now, is it?

Here's the idea in a nutshell: Proactive people schedule their priorities; reactive people prioritize their schedules. Did you follow that? Reactive people take whatever comes and schedule it, whether it's a Big Rock or not. By contrast, proactive people schedule their Big Rocks first, and then let the little ones fall in around them. That's nifty.

> "The most important thing in life is knowing the most important things in life."
>
> —David F. Jakielo, business consultant

With a traditional, reactive approach to managing time, you start with a week filled with all kinds of events and tasks that may or may not be important or connected to your mission and goals. What results is that lots of little rocks fill in the week and a number of Big Rocks get neglected or forgotten.

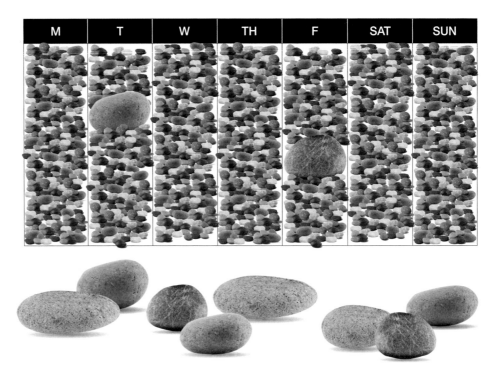

Quadrant 2 weekly planning is a proactive approach to managing time. You start out by first scheduling your Big Rocks into the week. Then the smaller rocks may fill in the gaps at other times during the week. A few of them may not fit into the week, but at least the Big Rocks are addressed.

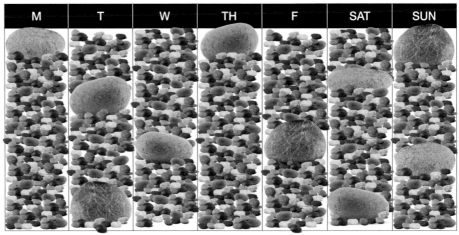

Be sure not to set too many Big Rocks. Usually one, maybe two, per role per week are more than enough. After you have done weekly planning a few times, you will notice that you're getting into good routines ("habits"): "I exercise first thing each morning," or "I call my mom every Saturday morning." You may block out Saturday nights for going out and having fun or Tuesday and Thursday afternoons for history homework. I like to block out Sundays completely for my family.

QUADRANT 2 PURCHASE

QUADRANT 1 PURCHASE

I take the day off from my job, my phone (mostly), my shopping, and my exercise. This ensures that I spend quality time with my family and it gives my brain and body a rest. You too will develop routines as you do weekly planning consistently. If you don't, just watch out—your schedule will take over your life. You will become the victim of your schedule instead of the creative force of your life.

Vett Vandiver is a graduate student with an incredibly busy life, and weekly planning is her lifesaver:

> The past few weeks, and this week, of grad school are what I call ridiculously BUSY. You know those weeks when you have something to do, some assignment due, some meeting scheduled, or some obligation on every single day of the week! That's how it's been recently.
>
> Currently, I'm taking 12 hours of classes, working part-time off campus, participating in a nonprofit organization, supporting a few campus organizations, working for my own company, blogging, and maintaining a healthy social and eating lifestyle.
>
> This is how I handle a ridiculously busy week during the school year.
>
> At the start of the week, I look at my planner/agenda and see what I have to do for the week. I use the week view for homework assignments and events/places I need to be. Whether you use a paper agenda or your phone, if you're in college, you should have some method for organizing your time and keeping up with your schedule. During busy weeks, I schedule my tasks by the hour.
>
> Then I categorize and prioritize the things I have to do in three ways (must-dos, should-dos, and could-dos). You can call them whatever you'd like, but this is how I cut down on my list of things to do. If I can move the could-dos to another week, I move them back and lessen my load for the week.
>
> These are the weeks when I want to spend hours on Facebook or Instagram, ignoring reality... but I can't. I limit my social-media time during busy weeks to 30 minutes to 1 hour a day and use this as a break or combine it with my eating time. (Vandiver, "How to Plan")

In the next activity: "Weekly Planning," try planning your upcoming week.

"Spontaneity is one of the joys of existence, especially if you prepare for it in advance."

—Alan Dean Foster, author

Vett Vandiver

Photo courtesy of Vett Vendiver.

141

ACTIVITY 28

Weekly Planning

Apply the steps to weekly planning by filling in the following calendar for your next week. The Tips on the next page will show you how to do it.

	ROLES	WEEKLY GOALS (BIG ROCKS)	MONDAY	TUESDAY
8 a.m.				
10 a.m.				
Noon				
2 p.m.				
4 p.m.				
6 p.m.				
8 p.m.				
10 p.m.				
Midnight				

Tip 1: Set aside time to plan your week.

Tip 2: Review your mission and long-term goals.

Tip 3: Identify a Big Rock for each role.

Tip 4: Review what is already scheduled for your week, then eliminate any tasks that are not important.

Tip 5: Schedule Big Rocks around fixed items on your schedule.

WEDNESDAY	THURSDAY	FRIDAY	SATURDAY	SUNDAY

YOU CAN USE THE BIG ROCKS TOOL IN THE *LIVING THE 7 HABITS* APP FOR DAILY AND WEEKLY PLANNING.

Adapt Daily

Planning your week gives you perspective and balance. A week is a short enough time to be realistic; it gives a good perspective. A week is also enough time to schedule Big Rocks for each of your roles, which brings balance to your life.

Of course, you can't foresee everything; stuff happens. "Everyone has a plan," said former heavyweight champion Mike Tyson, "until they get hit." For example, you can't schedule getting the flu. Old friends may show up out of nowhere with front-row seats to the big championship game. Your computer might crash. The research paper may take twice as long as you thought it would.

Such things are bound to happen. That's not only life, it's also okay. Just adapt your plan for the week to the stuff that happens each day.

Start the minute you wake up and think through your schedule for the day. You might need to shift unfinished business from the previous day into the new day. You might recognize that you overestimated what you could do that day, and you now need to simplify. An appointment might cancel. Again, adapting is okay, as long as you do it proactively, where possible. What is not okay is reacting to every trivial little interruption that comes along.

You adapt proactively by choosing to replace one important activity with a higher or more pressing important activity connected to what matters most to you. It's saying, "I know my goal was to exercise at noon today, but my mother needs to go to the doctor, so I will swap my Quadrant 2 exercise with a Quadrant 1 trip to the doctor." It needs to be done.

If you're not sure what to do, ask yourself, "What is the best use of my time right now?" And then follow your instincts. You might think, "I'm on a roll writing this paper right now, so I'm going to keep writing and skip lunch with my friends." Such proactive adaptations are logical, as long as you don't make it a habit to ignore your friends.

> "Expect trouble as an inevitable part of life, and when it comes, hold your head high. Look it squarely in the eye, and say, 'I will be bigger than you. You cannot defeat me.'"
>
> —Ann Landers, advice columnist

LESSON ON LEADERSHIP: Steven J. Ross

Steven J. Ross was a corporate executive and a visionary for his time. He was a pioneer in the video-gaming industry, and helped make soccer popular in the United States. As a teenager, he was summoned to his father's deathbed to learn that his sole inheritance consisted of this advice:

"Steven, there are those who work all day, those who dream all day, and those who spend an hour dreaming before setting to work to fulfill those dreams. Go into the third category because there's virtually no competition." (Roger Cohen, "The Creator of Time Warner, Steven J. Ross, Is Dead at 65," *The New York Times*, December 21, 1992.)

His father's advice is a great recipe for adapting daily. Start out each day reconnecting with your vision and then go to work to make it happen. Incidentally, Ross took his father's advice and carried with him a small card he looked at every day. The card contained a quote from Ralph Waldo Emerson, and Ross used it like a mission statement:

To laugh often and much, to win the respect of intelligent people and the affection of children; to earn the appreciation of honest critics and endure the betrayal of false friends; to appreciate beauty, to find the best in others; to leave the world a bit better, whether by a healthy child, a garden patch or a redeemed social condition; to know even one life has breathed easier because you lived. This is to have succeeded.

Ralph Waldo Emerson

When Ross died in 1992, his friends took out a full-page ad in *The New York Times* to thank him for his legacy. What would your friends say about your legacy if they took out a full-page ad to describe you? Do you start out each day with a little bit of dreaming and reflecting on your mission and vision?

Realize that Habit 3: Put First Things First accomplishes nothing without the discipline to carry out your plan. Up to this point you've only done "mental creation." In other words, you've been setting goals, prioritizing, planning the week, and scheduling tasks, which are all mental creations. In the end, though, Habit 3 is about doing—the physical creation.

Reflect back on John Wooden. He didn't just write down his goals. Nor did he say no to millions of dollars just to do nothing. He spent his life—well into his nineties—bringing his dreams and goals to life by befriending, mentoring, challenging, comforting, complimenting, and preparing young people for life. Now that's putting first things first.

"Life's a fragile thing Harry.... One minute you're chewin' on a burger, the next minute you're dead meat."

—Lloyd, from *Dumb and Dumber*, 1994

145

Here are four ideas to keep in mind while you're acting on your plans:

1. The Enemy of the Best Is the Good. Stupid things don't usually keep you from achieving your goals. Good things usually keep you away from doing the best things. For example, your goal might be to get a 3.7 GPA so you can keep your scholarship. But you might overbook yourself with so many good extracurricular activities that you end up with a 3.5 and lose your scholarship. As William James once said, "The art of being wise is the art of knowing what to overlook."

One student shared this experience about chasing the good instead of the best:

I was so excited when I went head-to-head against some of my more senior peers in competing for a summer internship and I was selected. It was a prestigious internship that paid well. I had fought hard to get it.

But as the excitement began to settle, I was in bed one night and the thought came to me, "So what?"

As I thought about it, I realized that I had been so caught up in the hype of the competitive situation that I had ignored the fact that the type of work I would be doing was not what I needed for my career. I would be spending an entire summer doing work that was good work, but that was not closely tied to my career pursuits.

I felt kind of dumb that I had even applied. Yet, how could I call and say I was not really interested? They had spent money flying me out for interviews and on hotels, food, etc.

What would you do in this situation? How would you recommend this student handle similar situations differently in the future?

2. Go for Two Marshmallows. Be patient. Be willing to wait. Be willing to sacrifice what you want now for what you want later.

Years ago, psychologist Walter Mischel conducted an experiment at a preschool on the Stanford University campus. He gathered a group of four-year-old children around a table and placed an assortment of marshmallows in the middle. Mischel told them he was going to leave the room for a few minutes. If they could wait until he got back, he would give them two of the marshmallows. If they couldn't wait, then they could have one marshmallow right then. That was the deal: one marshmallow now, or two later. He then exited the room.

A few of the kids could not resist and ate a marshmallow the second he left. Some waited a few minutes before devouring one. One kid picked up a marshmallow and began licking it. Some covered their eyes, trying to resist. Only a few resisted entirely.

> "The best day for doing your best is the one that comes seven times a week."
>
> —Vikrant Parsai, author

When Mischel returned, he gave those who held out their well-earned extra marshmallow. He then followed the lives of each of the children through high school. Remarkably, those who had resisted eating the marshmallow did far better in life than those who couldn't wait. They were better adjusted, more confident, more popular, and more dependable. They also did much better in school.

For some, quitting college is like eating the marshmallow now. Dropping out of school may taste good at first, since you can immediately start making more money to afford things like a car or your own apartment. But by dropping out now, you may be sacrificing two marshmallows later. The two marshmallows later show up down the road in the form of stronger skills, a better-paying job, a nicer car, and more career opportunities.

Marshmallow Test

DID YOU KNOW?
It Pays to Finish College

Do you realize that finishing college pays? Dropping out to make $8 to $15 an hour may seem like good money right now, but compare it to how much more you might make if you complete college.

It is estimated that a person with a bachelor's degree will earn twice as much over a lifetime of work (ages 25–65) than a person with a high school diploma.

Check it out:
- Those with a high school diploma: $1.3 million over a lifetime (one marshmallow).
- Those with a bachelor's degree: $2.27 million over a lifetime. (two marshmallows).

Furthermore, on average, a person with a master's degree earns $31,900 more per year than a high school graduate. It all adds up. So by dropping out of college, you may literally be saying no to a million dollars. Ouch!

Patience in pursuing what matters most is a proactive choice.

(Georgetown University, *The College Payoff*, 2011)

   3. Say No With a Smile. Throughout this chapter we've talked about saying no, sometimes even to good things. It can be hard to say no to someone you like and respect. But there are diplomatic ways to say no:
- **Be direct.** People appreciate honesty. They prefer it over a person who beats around the bush or flat out lies. They often wish they could be so direct. In fact, often when one student stands up and says, "I can't go to the movie; I've got to study for a test," or "I can't go out of town this weekend," others in the group say, "Yeah, me too," or later say, "I wish I had been strong enough to do that."
- **Use humor.** "I'm sorry. I can't go with you to the bar tonight. My brain cells and I have an agreement."

"Say no to everything so you can say yes to the one thing."

—Richie Norton, author

147

- **Suggest an alternative.** "I think you're fun and would like to go out with you, but I've got to study tonight. How about sometime next week?"
- **Get up and leave.** One first-year college student set a curfew for himself at 11 p.m. because he wanted to be alert for his daily 8 a.m. class. When he's with friends, even if the movie is only half over, he just gets up, says "See ya," and goes. Okay. This may be a bit abrupt and not so diplomatic, but it works for him.

ACTIVITY 29

Testing Your Fortitude

Wouldn't it be great to have a 25-hour day? Think about what you could do with that extra seven hours a week.

Well, chances are you waste at least 10 hours each week and scarcely realize it. To test my point, try recording how much time you've spent the past seven days in four specific areas.

ACTIVITY	TIME SPENT THE PAST 7 DAYS
Excess TV/movies	
Excess social-media time	
Excess gaming	
Excess texting and phone conversations	
Excess time-wasters (such as shopping, loafing around, oversleeping, doing nothing, etc.)	
Total Hours	

Did you reach 10 hours? If not, you are the exception. What can you say no to this week to cut your number in half? What would you do with an extra 10 hours each week?

4. Use Moderation in All Things. Decide in advance how much of a good thing is enough, then stop when you reach that point. When John F. Kennedy was president of the United States, he used to golf for an hour and then stop, regardless of how he was doing or how many holes were left.

Even studying and education can be taken too far. I remember reading of a young man in his twenties who inherited a large sum of money. He decided to go to college and get a degree. That went well, so he went for a graduate degree at a prestigious university. That went well, so he went for another degree. The pattern continued into his sixties. He just kept getting more degrees. It wasn't long before people began to see him as some type of freak. He couldn't deal with people, just books and taking tests. His world was no bigger than his college's campus.

I know of another student who felt exercise was good, so he exercised for hour upon hour every day. It took him 11 years to graduate.

Decide how much studying, sleep, fun, work, exercise, and socializing is enough, then stop and move on.

President John F. Kennedy

Photo from Library of Congress archive.

Organize Your Stuff

Stuff may not be a great academic word, but do you ever feel like a walking magnet? Stuff just somehow sticks to you.

Weekly planning involves two big steps: (1) reconnecting weekly with your mission and goals, and (2) scheduling your Big Rocks first.

Many first-year students leave home for college with everything they own tucked snugly into the back seat of a car. When graduation comes, Dad shows up with a moving truck: "Here, Son, let me help you with that weight-lifting set your roommate gave you and that slow cooker your ex-girlfriend never came back for. Maybe we need two trucks."

Stuff can collect anywhere and rapidly: under the bed, in your backpack, in the back seat, and on the refrigerator. It shows up on desktops, on bookshelves, on toilet tanks, on dressers, and occasionally in closets and drawers. It can take the form of neat piles or a pigsty.

The question is, how much time do you spend every day looking for lost keys, hunting down misplaced assignments, or trying to find your socks? How often do you hear yourself saying things like, "Where did that syllabus go? I know I put it right here."

You could do what Marcus did.

"The less we have, the more we win."

—Anthony Liccione, author

SURE, I CAN DO THAT. I HAVE SOME ROOM IN MY SCHEDULE RIGHT HERE.

149

> "Blessed are the organized, for they will gain everything that they'll never lose."
>
> —Jarod Kintz, humorist

My most important possession is a big box of trash bags. My half of the dorm room is so tiny. How tiny is it? Well. There's more stuff than storage, so I use my bags. I can't live without my bags. Where to put laundry? In a bag. Shoes? In a bag. I keep old papers and handouts and pencils and printer cartridges and cards and stuff in one bag—I can stick my hand in it and pull out what I need. I even keep my clothes in a bag. Nobody cares about wrinkles, least of all me.

Oh, I also use my trash bags for trash. A lot of disasters happen in dorm rooms, so you need a bag for broken glass, old food, spilled smoothies, and other stuff you don't want to pick up with your fingers.

All my bags are piled in one corner of the room. Nothing is left out. My tiny little half of the room is totally un-junky. The other half, well… Not my problem.

Marcus has an ingenious solution that works for him. Here are some more quick tips on organizing stuff.

1. Organize by Role. Organize your handouts, notes, and assignments according to your roles. Create a separate folder, binder, binder tab, cardboard box, or space on your computer for each of your major roles. Math 101 might have its own folder, for example, as might Geography 201 and Psychology 220. A separate binder or folder could be set up for family or work or other key roles. Everything that is associated with those roles is then kept in that binder, folder, or box, or placed on that shelf. Then, when you need something related to that role, you know exactly where to find it.

2. Have a Place for Everything. Some things might not fit into roles. "Where did I put my keys?" (People lose their keys an average of 12 times a year.) "Has anyone seen my shoes?" Most people know where their clothes go. But where do the car keys go? They should go in one place every time. The same is true for the phone, the tablet, the tools, the dirty clothes, the remote, the purse, the laptop, and the blow dryer. I used to lose my wallet and my keys all the time until I followed this simple rule. Consider buying yourself a label maker so that you can name the places where things go. As the old adage states, "A place for everything, and everything in its place."

3. Shed Frequently. There are two kinds of people in the world: keepers and shedders. Organizing expert Julie Morgenstern says if you want to get organized, you've got to shed. Throwing out stuff you don't really need creates not only physical space but also psychological space. Your mind will feel lighter. Don't keep those old notes you will never look at again. Sell that old textbook. If you haven't worn that top in the last year, you're not likely to wear it again. Toss it. Shovel out the junk mail. You don't need 30 pairs of shoes. You don't need four staplers. Eliminate the clutter, the garbage, the old magazines, and all the stuff you think you may need someday but don't need now. And see how good it will make you feel. Wendell Berry said it best, "Don't own so much clutter that you will be relieved to see your house catch fire."

Dive Into the Courage Zone

A final item I like to place on the Do list for students trying to Put First Things First is to devote a small amount of time each week to their courage zone. To do this requires moving outside of their comfort zone.

Your comfort zone represents all of the people, places, and things you are comfortable with. Hanging out in this zone is safe and secure and free of risk. On the other hand, the courage zone represents new and different and maybe even hard things. There is risk here and a chance you might fail. But as my dad used to tell me, the risk of riskless living is the greatest risk of all.

We all need to regularly dive into our courage zone in order to stretch ourselves, build new skills, and grow. This may mean you have to make a new friend, sign up for a class that scares the heck out of you, or apply for that job you've always wanted but never dared try for. It might include attending a campus lecture on an unfamiliar topic, going to an opera for the first time, trying out for a sport, eating a foreign food, volunteering at the hospital, or admitting you have a problem and seeking help.

One student said that when he first met his wife, he took one look at her and thought, "She'll never go out with me." His next thought was, "Why not try? All she can do is say no." So he took the risk, asked her out, and now they're married. All because he dared to enter his courage zone.

While in college, I decided to take a singing class because I couldn't sing and wanted to stretch myself. As part of my final grade, I had to sing a solo from the play *Les Misérables* in front of a panel of judges. When my time came to perform, I was so scared I wanted to throw up. And I bombed. One of the judges told me, "Geez, Sean, all those muscles sure don't help you sing, do they?" But do you know what? I was really proud of myself that day for trying something way outside my comfort zone and I am a stronger person today because of it, even though my voice still sucks!

Good things happen when you do hard things. You discover new sides of yourself, you challenge your paradigms, and you open up your life to serendipity. Who knows where it may lead? So block out a time in your weekly plan for doing some things you don't normally do. Make room for a weekly or daily walk in your courage zone.

"We forget that stepping out of our comfort zone also happens in the mundane. You don't need to swim the English Channel to challenge yourself. It's also going to the gym after a hard day."

—Jonathan Precel, fitness coach

THE REWARDS OF PUTTING FIRST THINGS FIRST

In general, students who consistently Put First Things First feel less stress, find more free time to relax and have fun, enjoy stronger relationships, have greater life balance, and produce more. Not a bad list, wouldn't you say?

Of course, putting first things first doesn't guarantee a stress-free life. Everyone has stress. And, in fact, some stress—called eustress—is actually good for you. Hans Selye, a foremost expert on stress, discovered that eustress is a natural part of facing and overcoming challenges. Without eustress, life is not nearly as interesting or rewarding.

But when challenges become more than we can handle, eustress turns into just plain old bad stress. And that's not good.

A big reward of Habit 3 is shedding the bad stress that comes from wasting time and at the same time feeling the good stress that comes from doing the things that matter. You'd think people would want to Put First Things First, and they do.

"People, here's something that you should be considerin':

Things could turn bitter when you don't use discipline."

—GangStarr, "Discipline"

Check Out Your Stress Level

Take a free stress assessment. Go to Franklincovey.com/tc/resources and click on "Stress Assessment."

However, at FranklinCovey, we have surveyed over a million people about how they apply the 7 Habits. We have collected data from their bosses and their peers. Habit 3: Put First Things First scores the lowest across the board, but particularly when people rate themselves, it appears to be the hardest habit to live. But when we ask people after training which habit has helped them most, they usually say Habit 3. "I am so much more organized," they say. "I've learned to say no." "I know what my priorities are." "I use my time so much better." Of the 7 Habits, maybe Habit 3 is the one that can make the biggest difference in your college experience.

Now pause for a few minutes and complete the next activity: "It's About Time."

It's About Time

Think back on the principles of Habit 3 and the activities you have completed in this chapter. Identify one or two actions that would help you most. What results do you hope to Get as a result of doing these things?

	ACTIONS I WANT TO TAKE	WHAT I HOPE TO GET
ACTION 1		
ACTION 2		

IN SUMMARY

Putting first things first is not for wimps or weaklings. It takes focus and discipline. Research indicates that the problem with most leaders today is not that they lack good planning, but rather that they lack the discipline to stick to their plans and carry them out.

Putting first things first requires planning your time so you take care of what's most important, saying no to distractions, and saying yes to hard things. It requires sacrificing something good for something better.

Your success as a student will depend, in large part, on how you See, Do, and Get Habit 3: Put First Things First.

Here's a summary:

> Remember, the key is not to prioritize your schedule, but to schedule your priorities.

Habit 3: Put First Things First
Principles: Integrity and Focus

	REACTIVE PEOPLE	PROACTIVE PEOPLE
What They *See*	• Everything urgent is important. • They thrive on crises and putting out fires.	• They focus on the important, not the urgent. • They schedule their priorities. • They keep relationships first, then schedules.
What They *Do*	• Prioritize their schedule. • Devote much of their time to Quadrants 1 and 2; they're slaves to the urgent. • Respond to every urgent request. • Avoid planning.	• Live in Quadrant 2. • Plan weekly. • Adapt daily. • Organize their stuff. • Dive into the courage zone.
What They *Get*	• Neglected important things. • Stress, burnout. • Less effectiveness, less efficiency.	• Sense of meaning and purpose. • More time and space. • Better life balance. • Higher productivity.

Habit 3: Put First Things First is the summit of the Private Victory. It is the final step toward independence on the 7 Habits Leadership Continuum. By being proactive, beginning with the end in mind, and putting first things first, you put yourself in a strong position to do well in school and in life. You take enormous steps toward being self-reliant and being able to thrive on your own.

The remaining chapters will focus on moving toward interdependence and the quest to achieve the Public Victory. While it is good to be independent and self-reliant, to be most effective in college and life, it is necessary to learn to work well with others—not only to get along with them, but to combine their strengths with yours so everyone can win.

COMING ATTRACTIONS

Coming up next, you'll discover the secrets to building great relationships and friendships. So don't stop now.

Baby Steps

1. Teach to Learn. Using the summary chart on page 154, teach the key concepts of Habit 3 to a friend, classmate, or family member within the next 48 hours.

2. Take the week-long screen-free challenge. Go for seven days without TV, movies, games, social networks, and so on, and see how much time you save. You can use the phone for important calls and vital information and the computer for homework, but that's it.

3. Get outside your comfort zone and get to know a professor. Say hello, ask questions, be friendly, and pay a compliment.

4. The next time you're in a car or a bus, turn off the radio or headset and think about your life goals. Shut out the noise so you can think about what's important and how you are doing in meeting your goals.

5. At the end of the week, sit down and take 20 minutes to plan your next week. Block out time for your Big Rocks, one for each role.

6. Stop losing your keys. Designate the place you will always put your keys at home and when you're moving around.

7. Today or tomorrow, say no to something or someone that will take you off your top priorities. Use one of the "no" techniques, such as Be direct, Use humor, Suggest an alternative, or just Get up and leave.

8. Shock yourself today and start working on an assignment that isn't due for some time.

9. Try to make one new friend today. Say hi to someone you don't know. Don't wait until someone approaches you. Go out of your way to make the effort first.

10. Write down what you believe your biggest time-waster is: _____.
Now make up your mind to cut it in half this week.

11. Write down the first things in your life right now and put them in order of importance:

    1. _____

    2. _____

    3. _____

    4. _____

    5. _____

Academic Protip

In high school, I was good at test taking. I could go into a test with very little preparation and figure it out pretty easily. So much of it was common sense. I had also learned to write, and could put down a persuasive answer to most any question I knew even a little about. The teacher would go for it. The A's rolled in.

And then I hit college. Tests were different there. Professors did not give me points for writing fancy but empty stuff or for being creative on science tests. The multiple-choice questions were not so easy to figure out. Ouch!

Fortunately, we've asked for advice from Professor Laurie Rozakis, a world-class expert on how to ace college tests. She has wonderful insights, and it turns out that the key to success is Habit 3 after all—planning and preparation!

How to Study for a Test

By Dr. Laurie Rozakis, Farmingdale State College, State University of New York

If you really want to do well on your college tests, these tips will help you do your best:

Set up a study schedule. Cramming doesn't work. Start studying at least a week ahead of time and then study 10 or 15 minutes at a time until you know the content. I see a lot of students who just don't know the stuff. If I ask on a test, "When did Shakespeare live?" or "What is hubris?" you either know it or you don't. You can't dance around it.

Learn the test format. Ask the professor, "What is the format of the test—multiple choice, fill-in-the-blank, short answer, essay, or hybrid?" Ask the professor to go over the format so you can avoid that moment of panic when you're facing something you didn't expect. If it's an essay test, practice writing essays. If it's a multiple-choice test, memorize key facts. And so on...

Make a reference sheet. Pretend that the professor is going to let you bring one page of notes to the test. Create a handwritten cram sheet,

writing on both sides of the page, single-spaced. The act of hand-writing the notes brings together all the key information you need to know for the test—the order of the planets, the quadratic equation formula, whatever. It forces you to go through the text, to go through your notes, and to make sense of what you've learned. Don't keyboard it: hand-write it. If you can't make that sheet, you're not ready. If you can't do it, take the notes you do have to the professor and say, "I don't understand what this or that means. Can you help me?"

Eat breakfast. It's not okay to skip it. Maybe you've had an energy drink and a pack of potato chips—you're still starving. You can't do your best if you haven't eaten real food.

Come prepared. Bring the supplies you need for the test: a pen, a No. 2 pencil, your calculator, etc. Don't show up and say, "I don't have a pen, or I don't have a flash drive," or whatever. That doesn't cut it with a college professor.

Bring a watch. You probably won't be allowed to use your phone clock to pace yourself, so get a cheap watch.

If there are 60 questions on an hour-long test, you have one minute per question, so you have to pace yourself. You're seriously harming

Dr. Laurie Rozakis, Farmingdale State College, State University of New York

your chance to do well if you don't pace yourself and spend too much time on a handful of questions.

Work steadily. You've got your watch; figure out how much time you've got and keep going. You're a sled dog in a Jack London novel. Leave yourself a few minutes to check your work.

Don't cheat. Any college's policy is "you cheat: you fail." Cheating just isn't worth it. You're better off failing than getting kicked out for cheating. There's an enormous amount of cheating. I've seen students taking photos of somebody else's test. Just don't do it.

Work carefully. Be careful to fill in the test correctly. Don't miss filling in a bubble. Proofread your essays. Be sure to check that you've read the entire test: I know students who have missed the last page!

Work to impress. Try to show the professor you know something; you're better off putting down a partial answer than no answer. The professor sees it and thinks, "The student missed this point but got that." As a professor, these partial answers help me realize what information I have to reteach, so your writing down even partial answers helps me as much as it helps you.

TIPS FOR ACING ESSAY TESTS

Start by brainstorming ideas. You can draw a circle on paper and write your main idea in it. Then draw spokes out from the circle and list supporting ideas on them. Another way to brainstorm is to list three to five big ideas. Suppose my essay question is: "Lawyers are expected to give free legal advice at some point in their careers. Should doctors also

be expected to give free medical care?" I might write down ideas like "cost, liability, and time." Now I look back at my list. What do I want to say about each idea?

Another way to brainstorm is to answer the 5 W's and an H—who, what, when, where, why, and how. Suppose you're writing about a leader such as Nelson Mandela or Martin Luther King, Jr. Brainstorm answers to the 5 W's and an H to make sure you have the facts you need.

Make a quick outline. Use the classic five-paragraph college-essay format: An introduction with a thesis; points 1, 2, and 3; and a conclusion. Here's a quick outline: "Standardized tests should be abolished: (1) Intro, (2) They're costly, (3) They're time-consuming, (4) They're not reliable, (5) Conclusion." Here's another: "*The Big Bang Theory* is the funniest show on TV: (1) Intro, (2) Characters, (3) Plot, (4) Dialog, (5) Conclusion." This format helps you organize your ideas in a logical manner.

If it's a comparison-contrast essay question, do four paragraphs instead of five: (1) Introduction and thesis, (2) Similarities, (3) Differences, (4) Conclusion.

Start writing. You don't have to start at the beginning. You might start with paragraph 2, for instance. Figure on writing about 350 to 500 words in an hour. If you write fewer words, you're probably not answering the question with sufficient detail.

Make sure you're answering the question. Essays often get poor grades because they go off course. If you're supposed to be writing about doctors giving free care, don't take a long detour into the whole issue of health care.

Make a good case. Come up with good reasons for your point of view. I'm the justice for the college traffic court. Most of the students who come before me with a traffic citation have no argument to make. They just say, "It's not fair," "I can't afford it," or "You're mean to me." I say, "Sorry. Life is tough." But if they bring me logical explanations, relevant photos of the scene, and reliable-witness statements, they most likely will make their point and avoid a fine. One student got cited for having a clear plastic cover on his license plate, which is against the law in our state but is not part of our campus regulations. He made that point effectively, and the ticket was dismissed. Give me information that's specific enough to convince me. Muster quotes, statistics, photos, references that are relevant and persuasive.

Use specific examples to make your case. "Unlike lawyers, doctors should not be expected to provide free medical care because they have to go to school for 12 years, while lawyers go for only 7 years. Medical school costs far more than law school," and so forth.

Draft for about 35 to 40 minutes if you have an hour. Spend the rest of the hour editing, revising, and correcting. If you're on a computer, use the spell check and grammar check—the squiggle isn't there for decoration. If you can't figure out what the problem is, scrap the sentence and start again. If you're handwriting, be aware of the problems you have as you write. For instance, people tend to misspell the same words. If that's your

issue (there/their/they're), focus on getting it right. If you know you have a tendency to write run-ons and fragments, focus on that. Watch out for things you know you have a problem with.

Proofread. It might take you from a D to a B. You'll smack your forehead later when you see the mistakes you could and should have fixed. Never leave an essay test early. You think you're done? Guess again. When you finish drafting, look up for a minute or two, then look back at your paper. You'll see things you didn't see before.

So brainstorm, outline, draft, revise, and proofread. Use all of your time.

After the test, don't beat yourself up. If you didn't do well, go to the professor and say, "What do you suggest so I can do better next time?" Most professors will help you if you ask for it, or they can direct you to a resource center to get help. Almost every college has free resources for students—a writing center, a tutoring center, a testing center. They're there. Use them!

Dr. Laurie Rozakis earned her Ph.D. in English and American literature from Stony Brook University. A full professor of English at Farmingdale State College of the State University of New York, Dr. Rozakis has published over 100 books and scores of articles. She's appeared on the *CBS Morning Show*, *Live with Regis and Kelly!*, National Public Radio's *Morning Edition*, and Cablevision News. *The New York Times* describes Dr. Rozakis as "an incredible researcher and an amazing writer."

References

Harris, Amy Bjork and Thomas A. Harris, M.D., *Staying OK: How to Maximize Good Feelings and Minimize Bad Ones*, Harper & Row, 2011.

Mischel, Walter, *The Marshmallow Test: Mastering Self Control*, Little, Brown & Company, 2014.

Moller, Susan D., "A Day Without Media," Phillips Merrill College of Journalism, University of Maryland, 2010. http://withoutmedia. wordpress.com/study-conclusions/ emotional-reactions/

Vandiver, Vett, "How to Plan for a Busy Week (College Students)," *Real College Student of Atlanta*, blog, March 3, 2014. http://www.rcsoatl. com/2014/03/how-to-plan-for-busy-week-college.html

Think Win-Win

The Habit of Mutual Benefit

4

> "What do we live for, if it is not to make life less difficult for each other?"
>
> –GEORGE ELIOT

IN THIS CHAPTER, YOU WILL DISCOVER WAYS TO:

- Balance courage with consideration.
- Be happy for the successes of others.
- Share credit and recognition.
- Make deposits in other people's Emotional Bank Accounts.

Also, look for the Academic Protip...

- How to Think Critically

Habit 4:
Think Win-Win

is the habit of seeking mutual benefit.

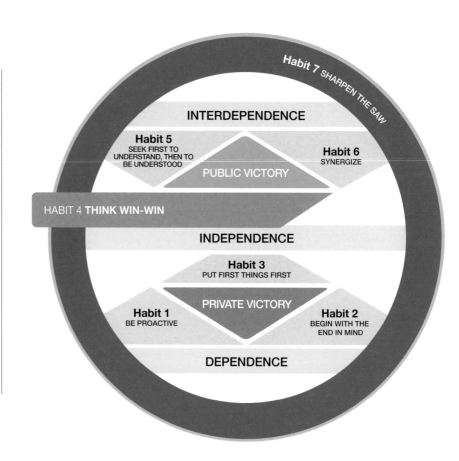

What I Wish
I'd Known in College

"I wish I'd known that I could make my own career, and that I could leverage my strengths and interests to do something unique that is both financially rewarding and makes a contribution, even if it doesn't fit into the tidy career categories in a university course catalog."
–Aaron, Brigham Young University

"I wish I'd known how important scholarships and grants would be to funding my education and to take advantage of professor office/available hours."
–Kerry, Portland State University

"I wish I'd known how important it is to establish the ground rules with roommates early on, and be sure you build in the consequences."
–Dayna, Texas Tech

"Yes, it's college and it's an investment but it's not worth it to go into major debt to get your undergrad. You can find a less expensive community or state college and graduate almost debt-free."
–Leisy, University of Toledo

REAL CHOICES:
Designing a Win-Win Solution

Wendy Kopp was like so many college students. "In October of my senior year at Princeton, I realized I needed a plan. What was I going to do after graduation? I had no idea of what I wanted to do. I felt uninspired. I wanted to do something that would make a real difference in the world. I just didn't know what that was."

Most of her fellow students were headed for corporate jobs, but Wendy wasn't sure she could make a difference there. She kept thinking about her roommate, who had attended a low-performing public school. "She was smart and creative. She was a brilliant poet. Still, she struggled under the academic demands of Princeton."

It disturbed Wendy that so many kids lacked the preparation they needed for college and had to struggle so hard once they got to college. While attending an on-campus conference of students and businesspeople, Wendy noticed that a lot of her classmates had the same concerns she did. They wanted to do something meaningful once they got out of college.

Somebody asked the question: "How many of you would choose teaching if you could?"

Wendy was startled when nearly all her fellow students raised their hands. As Princeton students, they "had been chosen through a rigorous application process and were certainly among the nation's more talented students." They had unlimited options, but most of them would like to be teachers.

"I had a sudden idea: Why didn't this country have a national teacher corps of top recent college graduates who would commit two years to teach?" All at once Wendy envisioned thousands of the most talented young people working with the most impoverished and underserved children.

All at once she had a meaningful mission, and Wendy started making her vision a reality. It was a struggle getting corporate funding and buy-in from schools, but within a few years her organization, Teach for America, was making a serious difference in the struggling schools of 25 states. Now more 11,000 of the brightest graduates in the country devote at least two years to teaching 750,000 children each year.

In a country where only 8 percent of poor children graduate from college, these graduates are making a serious impact.

"We give the kids with the greatest challenges the crummiest education," says Joel Klein, former chancellor of New York schools. So he welcomes the infusion of bright college graduates from Wendy's organization, and studies show they perform as well or better than professional teachers.

It's a classic win-win situation. Millions of impoverished children have benefited. Schools get bright young teachers without having to pay for them. Thousands of graduates have gained meaningful experience, and about two-thirds of them stay connected to education even after their two-year commitment is up.

Wendy is totally energized by her vision for the future. "We must unleash the energy of our most promising future leaders against the problem [of poor schools]. Fortunately, they don't need any convincing—top college graduates all over the world are already clamoring to rise to this challenge." (Kopp, *One Day All Children*)

Habit 4: Think Win–Win is essential to your meaningful life. It's a basic principle of successful living: You can't win unless other people win too. What you do with your life is up to you, but please know that helping others to win is just as important as you winning.

For Wendy Kopp, winning means helping poor children win. What does winning mean to you? You don't have to start a worldwide movement to be a winner, but how will you lead a win-win life?

Habit 4 is also the key to getting along with other people. It's not "you win or I win" or "let's compromise"—it's "we both win." As you build a life for yourself, you're also building the lives of others, including co-workers, friends, spouse, children—all the people who are important to your future.

What about your situation right now? What if your roommate:

- Falls asleep listening to *The Lord of the Rings* soundtrack on her speakers?
- Duct-tapes your stuff to your door if you leave anything out of place—like your pen, your textbook, your bowl of cereal you forgot in the sink?
- Says he's a communist and refuses to pay his share of the bills because that would be "propping up the system"?
- Screams at you for opening the potato-chip bag the wrong way?
- Ties bundles of herbs to the doorknobs for unexplained reasons?
- Has a pet crab that keeps escaping?
- Won't wash her towel, which after a couple of months smells like a fungus factory?
- Gets obsessed with body building and shaves his entire body with your razor?
- Keeps a stuffed raccoon that stinks up the room?
  (Lewis, "Flatmate Horror Stories")

How do you Think Win–Win in *those* relationships?

College is about relationships—with roommates, friends (some of them really *close* friends), teachers, study-group members, and a spouse if you're married. For some, it's the first time they're away from family, and lots of new people enter their lives.

This chapter is about how to succeed with all those relationships.

Too many students (and people in general) get into "me" mode in their relationships, always thinking, "What's in it for me?" Some take it so far as to cheat on a test or plagiarize other people's work when writing a paper, as long as they don't get caught. In study groups, they do the least work possible while leaning on others to carry the load. They don't mind undermining others if it helps them get ahead.

By contrast, students who practice Habit 4: Think Win–Win have the courage to stand up for themselves but also respect others. They know it's better if everybody wins. They do their share of the work, and help others with their work too.

> "EGOTIST: A person of low taste, more interested in himself than in me."
>
> –Ambrose Bierce, humorist

PEOPLE WHO PRACTICE HABIT 4:

SEE

COURAGE AND CONSIDERATION

GET

DO

GET

- More wins.
- Faster, better solutions to problems.
- Richer, more lasting relationships.

SEE

- There is plenty for everyone.
- It's possible to win in a way that others win too.
- No one has to lose.

DO

- Balance courage with consideration.
- Be happy for the successes of others.
- Share credit and recognition.
- Make deposits in other people's Emotional Bank Accounts.

FIVE PARADIGMS OF HUMAN INTERACTION

It's easier to describe the paradigm of Habit 4 by describing what it isn't:

1. Win-Lose: *"I'm going to beat you no matter what."* You're always trying to get ahead of others or be better than other people. You're proud. You can't win unless other people lose. I like how C.S. Lewis, author of *The Chronicles of Narnia*, said it, "Pride gets no pleasure out of having something, only having more of it than the next man…. It is the comparison that makes you proud: the pleasure of being above the rest." It's like the story about two friends being chased by a bear in a forest, when one turned to the other and said, "Hey buddy, I just realized something. I don't need to outrun the bear. I just need to outrun you." This thinking doesn't work, as the actor Lily Tomlin pointed out: "The trouble with the rat race is that even if you win, you're still a rat."

A student named Chris had this paradigm. "I was playing soccer, and I was very upset that we lost. I took it out on the guy at Walmart. I complained to my wife about it for hours. My wife, who is seven months pregnant, told me that I need to change before my son is born. I want him to see me as a happy and proactive person. I don't want him to trash-talk other people the way I do. I realize now that games aren't just about winning or losing—they're about having fun and doing what I like and being with people I love."

2. Lose-Win: *"I always get stepped on."* You're insecure. You're not brave enough to stick up for yourself. You're saying, "Have your way with me—everybody else does." You say yes too fast, are easily taken advantage of, and bury a lot of feelings. You have a permanent-victim mentality (Poor me!), and you're always looking for sympathy. One coed complained that she and her boyfriend always did what he wanted to do, never what she wanted to do.

OKAY, I THINK I SEE THE PROBLEM IN YOUR RELATIONSHIP

"He always gets his way," she complained, not realizing that she had unconsciously trapped herself in a lose-win situation.

Lots of people just take it if a roommate or friend wins at their expense. But you don't have to lose. If your roommate falls asleep listening to loud music, won't pay her share of the bills, won't wash her towel—talk straight with her. Be courteous, but make it clear that you need quiet at bedtime, a fair sharing of costs, and a clean place to live. You can be kind and patient and still stand up for yourself.

3. Lose-Lose: *"If I'm going down, you're going down with me."* If you can't win, nobody wins. You get revenge. "If I can't have Justin, I'm sure as heck not going to let Samantha have him." You envy and criticize others. You put other people down (and often yourself too).

Are You a Doormat?

What's a doormat for? For wiping your feet. The doormat gets nothing out of this except being walked all over.

If you consistently think lose-win, you choose to be a doormat for others. While losing now and then is a *part* of life, it's not a *way* of life. Consider the following relationships. Have you ever thought lose-win in these relationships? What might you have done differently?

RELATIONSHIP	A TIME WHEN I THOUGHT LOSE-WIN	WHAT COULD I HAVE DONE DIFFERENTLY?
With a boyfriend or girlfriend		
With a parent		
With a close friend		
With a boss		
With a professor		
With a roommate		

Once there was a news story about a man who burned his house down in a divorce so his wife would have no place to live—even though he also lost the value of the house. Lose-lose causes many quarrels and sibling rivalries. "I don't care what happens to me as long as my brother fails." With lose-lose thinking, there is no winning, only degrees of losing.

Listen to this student who has a lose-lose mentality and doesn't quite realize it yet:

> *My roommate stole my jewelry, clothes, and even my underwear. When confronted, she refused to look at me. She also told me I was the one who violated her privacy (true), but she had been stealing from me all year (she also ate my food ALL THE TIME and lied about it), so I did the same to her.*
>
> *I was technically taking back what was mine. She also told me that I was selfish for not allowing her to just take whatever clothes she wanted because she would "give someone the clothes off her back" and she, unlike me, was a really unselfish person!* (North, "Top Ten Worst Roommate Stories")

Obviously, both roommates were stealing from each other. Both were selfish. This was a lose-lose relationship.

4. Win: *"As long as I win, I don't care if you win or lose."* Students with this paradigm think only of themselves and not others. As long as they get their "A" grade, make the team, get the attention they crave, or get whatever they happen to be seeking, they don't care how others do. "You do your thing and I'll do mine." "You leave me alone and I'll leave you alone." It's a common paradigm and seems okay on the surface, but it ignores the fact that life is a team sport. Remember from the 7 Habits Leadership Continuum that being independent is good, but being interdependent is better. In fact, in today's world, you won't survive in the long run if you're just in it for you. The world is increasingly becoming more interdependent.

"What does it mean to be the best? It means you have to be better than the number-two guy. But what gratification is there in that? He's a loser."

—Jarod Kintz, humorist

"One of the major reasons for the downfall in many relationships is too much 'me' in 'we.'"

—Vikrant Parsai, author

King Pyrrhus of Epirus

LESSON ON LEADERSHIP: Pyrrhic Victories

A Pyrrhic victory is a victory where the winner turns out to also be a loser. It's named after King Pyrrhus of Epirus, who defeated the Romans in the Battle of Asculum in 279 BCE.

According to the ancient historian Plutarch, King Pyrrhus said after the battle, "Another such victory, and we are undone." Even though he had won the battle, he had lost most of his army, including his best friends and chief commanders. Even worse, he knew it would be hard to find more recruits, and the Romans were gathering forces for revenge.

Do you know anybody who has won an argument, but lost a friend in the process? Do you know anybody who cheats and gets good grades, but loses out as a person?

When the final score is settled, people who go for win-lose often end up with lose-lose outcomes. They might win the battle but lose the war.

BEFORE YOU MARK MY TEST, PLEASE CONSIDER WHAT YOUR GRADE COULD DO FOR MY SELF ESTEEM.

> "Not what we have, but what we enjoy constitutes our abundance."
>
> —Epicurus, ancient Greek philosopher

Scarcity vs. Abundance

Each of the above paradigms—win-lose, lose-win, lose-lose, and win—are basically flawed. None are based on correct principles, yet all are very common. From time to time, most of us have these paradigms. I think I've tried most of them myself. Why?

In our society we constantly compare ourselves to each other. Young children are generally content with simple fairness, which is a low form of win-win. But as they get older and see a sibling or friend getting more than their share of ice cream, they find out that life isn't fair. Then they see other kids get higher scores on tests or art projects. They get involved in sports and winning becomes everything. At games, they see adults argue with officials as if the fate of the world hung on the outcome. After years of this, it's inscribed into the brain: "If they win, I lose. So I had better do all I can to win, or I'll lose."

This competitive scripting leads to a Scarcity Mentality, the belief that the world is like a pie and there is only so much of it to go around: "Every piece you take means less for me, so I'd better take the biggest piece before you get it." Scarcity thinking continues into college with grading curves and into the workplace with competitive pay scales and advancement opportunities. Only one person gets the highest grade, the biggest raise, or the top promotion. One person is the winner; everyone else is a loser.

The biggest losers base their self-worth on how they stack up next to others. Your self-worth is about who you are in your heart. It's about your unique talents and potential. It's about improving the hand life has dealt you. It has nothing to do with anybody else. Still, too many people beat themselves up: "I'm not as popular as Sarah" or "If only I were as smart as Jesse." If you base your self-worth on things outside yourself like a GPA, popularity, or other people's opinions of you, you'll avoid risks because you don't want to "look bad." You'll chase grades instead of learning, and you'll be more likely to cheat to get ahead.

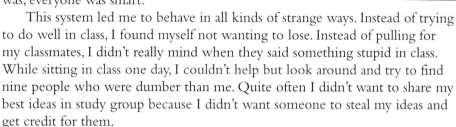

When I hit MBA school, I got caught up in a Scarcity Mentality for a while. Students were graded on the infamous forced curve. There were 90 students in each class, and 10 percent, or 9 people, automatically failed. The problem was, everyone was smart.

This system led me to behave in all kinds of strange ways. Instead of trying to do well in class, I found myself not wanting to lose. Instead of pulling for my classmates, I didn't really mind when they said something stupid in class. While sitting in class one day, I couldn't help but look around and try to find nine people who were dumber than me. Quite often I didn't want to share my best ideas in study group because I didn't want someone to steal my ideas and get credit for them.

All of these feelings were eating me up inside and making me feel small. The problem was, I was thinking scarcity when I should have been thinking abundance. It took me a while to finally figure out what I was doing and to start thinking differently.

What do I mean by an Abundance Mentality? A person with an Abundance Mentality believes there is plenty to go around for everybody. That person believes the "pie" can grow and grow forever.

If you go back to the very early days of computers, they were extremely expensive and mountainous in size, taking up entire rooms. The paradigm then was that the world's market for computers would always be very limited, with competition restricted to a small group of suppliers. It was a scarcity paradigm. Today we know that the market for computers is huge—abundant—with new devices developed daily, and that much of the world's market is still untouched. Now demand seems endless and insatiable. While competition remains stiff, many former competitors are now finding ways to partner. They recognize that there is a bigger world out there than they can handle on their own, and they now see that they're better off working together than against each other.

The ENIAC (Electronic Numerical Integrator and Computer) built in 1946. National Archives

One thing is for sure. It takes an independent person who is winning a Private Victory to have an Abundance Mentality. Without Habits 1, 2, and 3, people are reactive. They don't know what their win is. They don't have their own plans. They're insecure and feel threatened by the successes of others, while an independent person is secure enough to go for a win-win with everyone.

Win-Win or No Deal

Now we know what win-win thinking isn't. So what is it?

5. Win-Win or No Deal: *"Let's find a solution that works for both of us, or let's not play."* "I want everyone to win. There's enough to go around for everybody. If you can't win or I can't win, then let's forget it. I'd like to win, but not unless you win too."

The following are all examples of a win-win attitude:

- Your roommate likes to watch movies on the big-screen TV late at night, but you want to sleep. You mutually decide to designate some nights for movies and some nights for sleeping.
- You share your best ideas with your study-group partners, believing that they will share their best ideas in return.
- You recently got a promotion at the fast-food joint you work at. You work hard to champion others you work with so they, too, can get promoted.
- Your best friend just got the scholarship you also applied for but didn't get. Although you feel bad about your own situation, you're genuinely happy for your friend.

You might be thinking, "Come on, Sean. It's a competitive world. Get with it. Much of life is a win-lose game. What's with this win-win stuff? This is a dog-eat-dog world, and you can bet I'm going to compete. What about your business? Don't tell me you don't compete in business. Get real, Sean."

Of course, you're right. There is a time and a place for healthy competition—in sports and in business. If you don't compete there, you may always be a loser. I have nothing against healthy competition. In fact, it can lift us to better performance. So if you're competing as an independent individual, go for it. Compete with all your heart and energy, and do it with class and dignity.

But in most of life, you can't declare yourself independent of everyone else. We live in an interdependent world, especially when it comes to relationships and partnerships. "So who's winning in your relationship, you or your mom?" Or "Who's winning in your marriage, you or your spouse?" Or "Who's winning in your math class, you or your professor?" In meaningful relationships, if both parties are not winning, in the end, both will lose.

So there are times for healthy competition, but when it comes to living and working with others, win-win or no deal is the only effective way to go.

LISTEN, I'LL BET WE CAN COME UP WITH A WIN-WIN...

WHAT PEOPLE *DO* WHO THINK WIN-WIN

My experience is that most people want win-win relationships, but for some, it's so strange to think that way, they don't even know where to start. So here's what win-win thinkers Do:

- Balance courage with consideration.
- Be happy for the successes of others.
- Share credit and recognition.
- Make deposits in other people's Emotional Bank Accounts.

Balance Courage With Consideration

People who think win-win or no deal live by two principles: courage and consideration. Here's how these two principles work.

COURAGE AND CONSIDERATION MATRIX

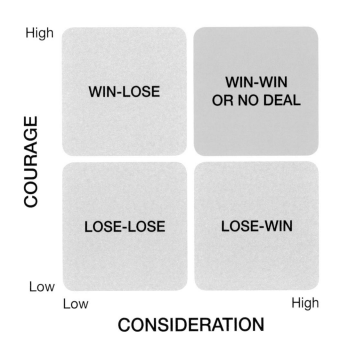

How would you describe the behavior of people who go for lose-lose? What advice would you give them?

Consideration

If you're in the bottom-right corner, you're high in consideration but low in courage. You're eager to please and reluctant to stand up for yourself; therefore, you often end up in lose-win situations. Your roommate makes all the decisions and treats you like a doormat. You don't dare say anything because you want to be liked and you don't want trouble.

When I was in college, I went with some friends one weekend to Lake Powell, a beautiful blue lake surrounded by high red sandstone cliffs. We decided to cliff-jump.

"How high are we?" I shouted to the boat below.

"About 70 feet," they yelled back. "Let's see you jump."

"I don't know about this," I hollered. "It looks pretty high from up here."

We had started at about 30 feet but kept challenging each other to go higher and higher. The peer pressure was intense.

"C'mon! Jump!"

I gave in and made the leap.

On the way down I kept thinking, "I'm such an idiot!"

When I hit, the water felt like concrete and my whole body shook violently. I clawed to the surface and gasped for air. I quickly checked and was relieved to find that all my body parts were still intact.

Peers can pressure you to do stupid things—things you wouldn't normally do. As Professor Dumbledore told Harry Potter, "It takes a great deal of courage to stand up to your enemies, but a great deal more to stand up to your friends." If you're not willing to stand up for what you think best, you'll probably end up losing.

Saying No to Peer Pressure

What would you do to show courage in the following situations?

TOUGH SITUATION	HOW YOU WOULD SHOW COURAGE
A friend wants to buy your laptop for half the price you listed it for.	
A classmate you don't know well wants to copy the paper you got an "A" on last term.	
A good friend really wants to copy the paper you got an "A" on last term.	
A boyfriend or girlfriend starts pressuring you to get more physical than you would like.	
Someone you're trying to impress invites you to go out late, but you have a serious test to take the next morning.	

If you're in the bottom-left corner, you're low in both courage and consideration. You don't care if other people lose, nor do you have the courage to stand up for yourself.

How often does this happen? A guy asks a girl out. The girl is not interested, but tries to be considerate and says yes. The guy spends big bucks trying to impress, but from the moment he picks her up, he can tell she has no interest. He breaks his piggy-bank, she doesn't enjoy herself, and both go home wishing it had never happened. She might not have intended a lose-lose, but that was the outcome because she wasn't courageous enough to say, politely, "No, thank you. I'm flattered, but I'm not interested." In the end, she isn't considerate either.

If you're in the upper-left corner, you're low in consideration and high in courage. You go for win-lose every time. You're bold but cold—unsympathetic, inconsiderate, unkind. You want to get ahead, be the best, rise above, even if it means stepping on someone else to get there. "It's not enough to succeed. Others must fail," as one snarky author put it. You might be subtle about it, but you ultimately see life as a competition, and you want to make sure you're taken care of first.

> "Being considerate of others will take your children further in life than any college degree."
>
> —Marian Wright Edelman, educator and activist

173

DID YOU KNOW?
The Abilene Paradox

When discussing how to get along with others, Professor Jerry B. Harvey of George Washington University likes to tell this story.

It's a hot summer's day in a small Texas town. Family members are gathered on the porch trying to catch some air. No one is saying much when the father-in-law suggests they drive 50 miles to Abilene for dinner. Everyone either agrees or remains silent. The trip turns out to be miserable and dusty, and the food lacking in savor.

On the return trip, someone, trying to be polite, suggests what a great idea it was. That's when the mother-in-law lets out that she didn't think it had been such a great trip, and that she would have preferred to stay home. She had only gone along because everyone else seemed to think it was a good idea.

At that point, there's a flurry of confessions. No one, including the father-in-law, wanted to make the trip. They were all only trying to satisfy the others, thinking they were the only ones who didn't want to go.

So everyone turned out to be Texas-sized losers on that hot, dusty afternoon. The trip wasn't a win for anyone.

How might the afternoon have turned out differently if anyone had said what he or she really thought? Have you ever been in a situation like this? Are you likely to be? Do you really want to stay up all night because everybody else is? Do you want to get drunk or high just because that's what everybody does? Or are you fooling yourself?

Don't say yes when you mean no.

> **THE ABILENE PARADOX**
> "[People] taking actions in contradiction to the data they have for dealing with problems and, as a result, compounding the problems rather than solving them."
>
> —B.J. Rakow, author

Ultimately, it's the upper-right corner where you want to be—high in both courage and consideration. You go for win-win or no deal. You're ready to walk away before someone loses—including yourself. Balancing courage *and* consideration takes proactive patience, so don't give up too soon.

Speaking of being patient, some things just aren't worth bothering about. If your roommate hangs bunches of herbs on the doorknobs, who cares? Maybe she's a witch, and that just makes her more interesting. If your roommate likes to sit on top of the fridge and meditate, so what? We all have our little obsessions.

But dangerous behavior is a different matter. It's not win-win if others are threatening to hurt you or themselves. Then you need to act.

Gerardo González was an immigrant kid who worked in a shop. After a friend talked him into taking a class at the local community college, he got really interested in school and eventually went to the University of Florida.

When he got there, he and his classmates got wildly drunk on the weekends. After car crashes, alcohol poisoning, and assaults, the bad stuff scared him and he swore off all of it.

But Gerardo still worried about his friends. He knew most of the heavier partiers were depressed and failing in school, so he was courageous and started talking straight with them. Surprisingly, they listened to him because he was one of them. When the college authorities preached against binge drinking, they didn't hear, but when a fellow student showed concern for them, that made a difference.

Eventually, Gerardo and his friends formed a group to stop the binges. The group called itself BACCHUS—Boosting Alcohol Consciousness Concerning the Health of University Students. BACCHUS was a stunning success and spread to other campuses. What started as a win-win for Gerardo and his friends is now "the largest active student organization in higher education today." Incidentally, Dr. Gerardo M. González became a college professor and dean of education in one of America's great universities.

Some people see going for win-win as wimpy or unrealistic. But going for win-win takes courage—sometimes a lot of courage. It takes courage to stand up for your own interests as well as the interests of other people. Going for win-win is a sign of toughness and wisdom, not weakness.

Gerardo González

Photo provided courtesy of Dr. González.

Be Happy for the Successes of Others

A person with a win-win mentality is genuinely glad to see other people succeed. One student told us this story about his co-worker:

A guy named Marshall whom I worked with on campus started dating a girl who was bright and talented, and who brought out the best in him. One night I invited the two of them to a party my roommates and I had at our place. Everyone had a great time.

From there, things seemed to start progressing between the two of them. Then he left on a two-week trip to California to visit some old friends. I knew he would miss the girl, but I didn't think much of it until I ran into her when he was about a week into his trip. To my shock, she was all cuddly with some other guy.

The fact that she was attached to some other guy wasn't the shock. The shock was that the guy she was with was one of my best friends. They had noticed each other at our party, and coincidentally had a class together. They began sitting together in class and things took off from there… in a very rapid fashion.

I, of course, worried what my traveling friend would say upon his return. The next time I saw him at work, he had already found out what was going on. I was a bit surprised by his attitude about it.

First he laughed. Then he looked really disappointed. Then he laughed again. It was clear he was frustrated and a little hurt because mixed feelings were all over his face. But what I remember most is what he said: "Hey, I can tell she is happy. So I'm happy for her. If I had a little part in bringing them together, then that is a good thing. I'm glad I had a part in it."

The two lovebirds did get married. I was the best man. But I'll always remember my stranded friend's attitude. Instead of being mad, he was genuinely happy for her. In losing a girl, he definitely won my respect.

How would you respond if your heartthrob deserted you while you were away? Would you be happy for him or her?

"Your most precious, valued possessions and your greatest powers are invisible and intangible. No one can take them. You, and you alone, can give them. You will receive abundance for your giving."

—W. Clement Stone, businessman and philanthropist

People with a Scarcity Mentality are threatened by other people's successes, especially those closest to them, such as friends or siblings. They don't want others to succeed because they feel it takes something away from them. In contrast, people with the win-win Abundance Mentality are genuinely happy for the accomplishments and successes of others. They know there is more than enough success to go around.

> "We win justice quickest by rendering justice to the other party."
>
> —Gandhi

Share Credit and Recognition

People with a Scarcity Mentality try to take all the credit for successes. They use "I" language—"I did this," or "I did that," or "Look what I did"—and want all the recognition. They may even try to take credit for things they had no part in. They are not the best people to have in a study group.

In contrast, people with an Abundance Mentality prefer to share recognition and to place credit where credit is due. They use "we" language, ensuring that everyone is credited for their part in an accomplishment.

Imagine being 200 yards from the finish line of a half-marathon. Sweat is dripping all over your body. Muscles are pounding. And victory is guaranteed to be yours. How would it feel?

That was the exact situation Paul Petersen found himself in. But then he did a strange thing. He stopped. He waited for the runner behind him to pass by, and then he settled in for a second-place finish.

"What is he doing?" the crowd called.

When asked, Petersen didn't hesitate in responding, "There was no way I wanted to be on the podium above him. It wouldn't have been right."

According to Petersen, he and the other runner had been well ahead of the rest of the runners for some time. As they neared the finish line, however, Petersen was a good 100 meters behind the other runner. He knew there was no way he could make up the difference. But then the runner ahead of him made a nightmare mistake—he missed the final turn.

Paul Petersen, championship runner. Photo provided courtesy of Paul Petersen.

The race official who was supposed to point the way was out of position. Without that guidance, the lead runner kept on going straight when he should have turned. It all happened just out of sight of the finish line.

Oddly enough, Petersen had actually won such a race once before. In that race, the leader had also missed a turn, leaving Petersen the victor. Petersen later said, "It was an empty win. I didn't want to do that again."

So rather than let it happen again, Petersen called out to the lead runner. It took a few good yells to catch his attention, but he did. Petersen then stopped, waited for the leader to get back on track, allowed him to pass, and then followed him across the finish line.

"In my mind, he had won the race," said Petersen. "He had broken me. There was no way I was going to outkick him the last 100 meters. He did the work to win and he deserved to win, especially since [the failure to turn] wasn't his fault. The course wasn't marked."

If you were in Petersen's place, how would you have responded? Would you have received the winner's trophy, or settled for second place?

At the finish line, the winner thanked Petersen several times. It was the first time the two had met. (Robinson, "Runner Makes Wrong Turn Right")

Isn't that a great story? I find it uncanny that Petersen had twice been in the position to win a race because the leader went off track. Both times, he knew someone else deserved the victory.

People who think win-win don't feel threatened when someone else wins. Their feelings of self-worth don't come from being better than someone else. They prefer to give credit where it's due.

Make Deposits in Other People's Emotional Bank Accounts

When you start college, you're surrounded by strangers. Making new friends can be scary and complicated. Also, you risk getting distant from your family and your old friends.

If you're trying to make a new friend or keep an old one, think about your relationship as a bank account in which you can make deposits and withdrawals, but in this case the deposits and withdrawals are emotional. When you do something that helps the relationship, that's a deposit. When you do something that hurts the relationship, that's a withdrawal. Here are eight deposits you can make.

1. Find Out What a Deposit Is for the Other Person. What you think is a deposit for the other person may in fact be a withdrawal in his or her mind. You won't know unless you find out.

I knew guys in college, for example, who would set their eye on some girl and want to take her out. Their goal was to impress, so they would dream up the grandest date imaginable. For instance, one would ask her out to the big game and pay sometimes far more than he could afford to get the best seats. He would take her to the game, and then drag her afterward to some popular hangout to eat. Never once would he think that the girl didn't care for sports, or might prefer to go to a quiet place to eat afterward so they could actually talk and get to know each other. It never crossed his mind that the girl might be stressed out about a test the next day and would prefer a short date over giving up an entire afternoon and evening. Some of those guys could have saved a lot of money in their financial bank accounts had they first found out how to make a deposit in the girl's Emotional Bank Account.

A Deposit or a Withdrawal?

Think of a person with whom you have regular contact. Then put an "X" in the box (Withdrawal, Neutral, or Deposit) that best indicates how you would perceive the other's behavior if he or she…

	WITHDRAWAL	NEUTRAL	DEPOSIT
Took you to lunch at a fast-food restaurant so you could talk about a school project you were working on.			
Asked you to attend a class and take notes while he or she went away on a pleasure trip.			
Noticed you were having problems on a math assignment and pointed out what you were doing wrong.			
Gave you opera tickets for your birthday.			
Gave you a late birthday card.			

> "If you want others to be happy, practice compassion. If you want to be happy, practice compassion."
>
> —Dalai Lama

2. Do Small Acts of Kindness. A second deposit is to treat people with kindness. The opposite—the withdrawal—is to be unkind, discourteous, and disrespectful. On campuses these days, many people won't even smile at each other. You walk past others without seeing them or flop down in a seat next to people without even a hello. Maybe you worry that they might take a smile or a greeting as being too forward or manipulative, so you hold back on being nice. Clearly, there are times to hold back, but if you want to make friends, do the little kindnesses. In relationships, the little things are the big things. Simple compliments can go a long way. As Mark Twain put it, "I can live three months on a good compliment." And as Ken Blanchard said in his book *The One Minute Manager*, "Unexpressed good thoughts aren't worth squat." So don't wait until people are dead to send flowers.

LESSON ON LEADERSHIP:
Going to the Dogs

In his classic success guide *How to Win Friends and Influence People*, Dale Carnegie notes that some of the best tips for making friends come from dogs, otherwise known as "man's best friend." Have you ever noticed, for example, how when a dog's owner comes home, the dog wags his tail, pants, and gets all excited? Have you ever wondered why more people don't act like that? Consider this student's story.

In college, I had a good friend. Better yet, he had a good-looking sister. I couldn't see our personalities together in a dating relationship, but she was a lot of fun, quite intelligent, and caring, and I thought she would make a good friend.

I attempted to get to know her, but every time I bumped into her on campus or tried to say as much as hello, she threw up huge STOP signs. Seriously, she gave me such a cold shoulder. She treated me like I was some creep trying to make a big move on her. It made me feel bad. I wanted to stop her and say, "Look, I'm not interested in dating you, so relax!" But I decided just to give her space.

This went on for months before a friend stopped me outside a party and said, "Hey, why don't you ever take Jake's sister out?" I asked why. He said, "Can't you tell she's got the biggest crush on you? She about dies every time she sees you."

I had to make sure he and I were talking about the same sister. He assured me that she had confided in him. I never, never would have had a clue. She never gave me the slightest hint of interest.

Are you more like a dog showing excitement when seeing friends, or do you shyly try to hide your thoughts and feelings? If you are trying to make new friends, it might pay to openly make a few deposits. Show them a kindness, a courtesy, or some act of respect, albeit moderate—after all, you don't want to get giddy, wag your tail, or act like a raving dog.

Preserve the cold-shouldered withdrawals for the true creeps.

Little kindnesses don't need to cost money. In fact, withholding judgment, paying a compliment, or including someone doesn't cost a penny.

3. Keep Promises. Nothing bankrupts the Emotional Bank Account faster—even if the account has a huge balance—than to break a serious promise. That's why it's so important to make good on your word and be very careful before using the words "I promise" or "I commit."

I remember asking my dad to borrow his car for a date. He said no, since it was a loaner a friend had arranged. I said okay.

But when it came time for the date, I found myself in a jam. The other cars were all gone, and so was my dad. So I quietly took the car anyway, sure he would never notice.

My date and I had a great time until I accidentally rammed into the back of another car. I'll never forget that most miserable phone call of my life.

"Dad."

"What?"

"I had an accident."

"YOU WHAT? ARE YOU OKAY?"

"I got into a wreck. No one's hurt."

"IN WHICH CAR?"

"Your car."

"NOOOOOOOOOOOO!!!"

For the next few weeks, I lived in the dog house. It wasn't the crash that he was mad about. It was that I had said I would not take his car, and then I did. It was a huge withdrawal.

With big withdrawals like lies or broken promises, it takes a long time to rebuild an Emotional Bank Account. You can't talk yourself out of problems you behave yourself into. People must see it to believe it. That's why you do what you say you're going to do.

4. Be Loyal. Keep confidences. When someone shares something with you in confidence, keep it that way. Be loyal to the absent. Avoid gossiping or backbiting. If you bad-mouth someone, the people listening to you will wonder if you're doing the same to them behind their backs. Stick up for people. If you hear someone bad-mouthing a friend, step up.

5. Set Clear Expectations. Don't leave things fuzzy, especially with roommates: "I'll make dinner this week if you'll clean the kitchen." Or with a study group: "We all need to read 100 pages by the next time we get together." Or at work: "I just want to be clear about the job you're asking me to do." Then follow through on what's expected.

6. Apologize. If you're in the wrong, admit it: "That was unkind of me, I apologize." Don't wait. Some people refuse to say they're sorry until the other person apologizes, or they make up excuses for their behavior. Making excuses instead of making things better turns into an even bigger withdrawal.

One student went online for help with a messy situation with his professor:

For my seminar class, I chose Professor Kim [not his real name] for my advisor. He asked us to make an outline and then report on our paper to the class using a presentation.

I presented my paper and outline without consulting the professor or asking for his advice because I thought I should do it on my own, but Professor Kim was angry that I was not taking his course seriously and never consulted him for anything. He told me if I'm going to have this kind of attitude, don't bother returning for the next semester. I was stressed and taking a lot of courses that semester, and snapped back with this response, "Well I thought this course was to develop independence! And I thought I wasn't supposed to cling to you all day and night asking, 'Oh professor, how do I do this or that?' And I didn't consult you because I thought I should do it on my own so not to annoy you!"

And the professor just stormed out very angry. A couple of other teachers overheard and said I should apologize (which I really should because I didn't mean it) or else I will fail the course. I want to do everything to make it up to him and propose a compromise that could leave both of us satisfied.

Any idea how? I don't know where or how to start. What should I do? What would you do if you were in my shoes?

> "An apology is the superglue of life. It can repair just about anything."
>
> —Lynn Johnston, cartoonist

What would you do? If you want to turn this losing situation into a win, follow the advice another professor gave the student:

Just apologize. Explain, calmly, that you have been stressed over your classes, and that you misinterpreted what you were supposed to do for the class and that in the future you will ask the advice of the professor, and that you wanted to apologize for not doing so before, and for snapping at him.

That is it. If he is like most people in the world, he will accept your apology. Oh, and you can do this privately before or after class.

("*How Should I Apologize?*" answers.yahoo.com)

7. Give Feedback. Sincere, honest feedback is a deposit if it's done with tact, so let people know how you feel and what a win is for you. It's a withdrawal to hide things from people, to keep them in the dark, or to pretend everything is okay when it isn't.

8. Forgive. Learn to forgive and forget so that you don't keep hurting yourself the way you were hurt. Don't let yesterday hold your tomorrow hostage. Getting even or talking about other people's failings won't help you.

DID YOU KNOW?
Rules for Making Deposits

Two rules to remember for making deposits in the Emotional Bank Account:

1. A deposit is only a deposit if the other person sees it as a deposit.

2. An already-satisfied need is not a big motivator.

So these are eight ways to make a deposit in someone's Emotional Bank Account. Obviously there are dozens of others, but these are the basics. How are you doing with these? What's the balance in your Emotional Bank Account with the people who are most important to you? Do you need to make some deposits and avoid some withdrawals?

DEPOSITS	WITHDRAWALS
Seek first to understand what is a deposit/withdrawal to others.	Assume you understand what is a deposit/withdrawal to others.
Show kindness, courtesy, and respect.	Be mean, rude, or disrespectful.
Keep promises.	Break promises.
Be loyal to the absent.	Bad-mouth people behind their backs.
Set clear expectations.	Expect people to read your mind.
Apologize.	Be arrogant, and make excuses.
Give feedback tactfully.	Don't tell people what they need to hear.
Forgive.	Hold grudges; get even.

LET'S FIND A WIN-WIN SOLUTION, DAD.

Don't forget your family's Emotional Bank Account. Unlike many of your friendships, your family lasts for a lifetime. But a lot of first-year students struggle with family. You want to be independent, but you still rely on your parents for a lot of help. You might be trying to mend ties after some rough teen years. You might need their financial help but resist the conditions that come with it. The point is that family relationships can be tough to manage. What deposits should you make? What withdrawals should you make up for?

LESSON ON LEADERSHIP: Making Friends

A hero of our time was Mother Teresa, a small, frail woman who devoted her life to helping the poorest of the poor. Her influence radiates from her work in India clear around the world, even after her passing. She owned nothing, had no formal titles, and sought no fame. Yet she inspired millions. On a wall in her room she hung the following poem. I like to think of it as a set of rules for making and keeping friends:

Mother Teresa

Photo courtesy of Mother Teresa Center.

People are often unreasonable, illogical, and self-centered;
Forgive them anyway.
If you are kind, people may accuse you of selfish, ulterior motives;
Be kind anyway.
If you are successful, you will win some false friends and some true enemies;
Succeed anyway.
If you are honest and frank, people may cheat you;
Be honest and frank anyway.
What you spend years building, someone could destroy overnight;
Build anyway.
If you find serenity and happiness, they may be jealous;
Be happy anyway.
The good you do today, people will often forget tomorrow;
Do good anyway.
Give the world the best you have, and it may never be enough;
Give the world the best you've got anyway.
You see, in the final analysis, it is between you and God;
It was never between you and them anyway.

WHAT YOU GET: THE PAYOFFS OF WIN-WIN THINKING

So does going for win-win really pay?

Years ago, FranklinCovey was working with a telecommunications company. It was during the onset of the cable-television industry. The company was busy laying cable in cities across the U.S. In most cases, cities were eager to have the cable laid, in spite of the temporary disruptions it caused.

One major city, however, was not keen on the idea. They knew that if they allowed one cable company to tear up their city, they would have to allow the same for every cable company that followed them. They did not want their city repeatedly torn up.

Negotiations ultimately came to a standstill. The city was not willing to proceed unless the company paid a large fee, and the company was not willing to pay the fee. It was headed for a "no deal." The result would be no cable access for the citizens (a lose for the city), and no access to thousands of customers (a lose for the company); both would lose. So in essence, they were headed for lose-lose.

One of the negotiators for the telecommunications company had recently been through *7 Habits* training and began thinking, "How can we turn this into a win-win?"

Under his leadership, the company went back to the city and said, "What if when we lay our cable, we were to also lay cable for two or three other potential cable providers? Then when they come to you, you send them to us and we will agree to turn over the cable access to them for less cost than they would typically incur. In that way, the city will only be torn up once."

The city loved the idea. The cable was laid. When the competitors arrived, they were delighted to learn that the cable was already in the ground and at a much-reduced cost. So the city and its citizens won because their streets were not constantly torn up and they got their cable, and the competition won because they got their cable laid at lower rates. But the biggest win was for the initial company: The two competitors paid them more than the installation had cost! They had laid their cable for free and picked up some spending money on the side.

In this case, all it took was one person to start thinking win-win for everyone to ultimately win. Yes, thinking win-win does pay.

And just think about the costs of not thinking win-win.

Martin Seligman, an expert on human happiness, pointed out that lawyers are consistently among the highest-paid professionals, even surpassing medical doctors, yet they are also among the saddest. Citing a poll, Seligman indicated that 52 percent of lawyers described themselves as dissatisfied with their career. Furthermore, Johns Hopkins University research puts them at a rate 3.6 times higher for depression than the general population. Their divorce rates are also higher than the general population's.

What's most interesting is what Seligman identifies as the primary reason for these ailments: "The deepest of all the psychological factors making lawyers unhappy is that U.S. law has become increasingly a win-loss game." He goes on to add that U.S. law has "migrated from being a practice in which good counsel about justice and fairness was the primary good to being a big business in which billable hours, take-no-prisoners victories, and the bottom line are now the principal ends." (Seligman, 179–180)

That's what you get with win-lose.

Some people will say, "That win-win stuff is soft. You try going for win-win in business, and people will eat your lunch." But that has not been my experience. People who go for win-win and are tough enough to say no deal usually do pretty well. They have the best friendships and, in business, are the ones with the diehard suppliers and customers.

Now pause for a few minutes and complete the next activity: "What I Want to Get."

What I Want to Get

Think back on the principles of Habit 4 and the activities you have completed in this chapter. Identify one or two actions that would help you most as a first-year student. What results do you hope to Get as a result of doing these things?

What I Am Doing Well

What I Hope to Do Better

What I Hope to Get by Doing Better

IN SUMMARY

Some situations lend themselves to healthy competition, such as sports and many aspects of business. And even there, if winning is the only thing that matters, the results can be disastrous.

But in your most important relationships—such as a marriage, a friendship, or a working partnership—thinking win-win is the only way to succeed.

To go for win-win, you must win the Private Victory and be sufficiently independent so that you have the emotional maturity to be both considerate and courageous. If not, you'll go for win-lose or lose-win. You'll take advantage of people, or people will take advantage of you. That's why the Private Victory must precede the Public Victory.

Your success as a student will depend in large part on how you See, Do, and Get Habit 4: Think Win-Win.

Here's a summary:

Habit 4: Think Win-Win

Principles: Mutual Benefit, Courage, and Consideration

	INEFFECTIVE STUDENTS	EFFECTIVE STUDENTS
What They *See*	• Win-lose • Lose-lose • Lose-win • Scarcity (The pie is only so big.)	• Win-Win or no deal • Abundance (There is plenty for everyone.)
What They *Do*	• Think of me first, or play the role of victim or martyr. • Get jealous and frustrated when others do well. • Hog all the credit when things go well. • Make more withdrawals than deposits.	• Balance courage with consideration. • Are happy for the successes of others. • Share credit and recognition. • Make deposits in other people's Emotional Bank Accounts.
What They *Get*	• Victories at the cost of integrity and personal contribution. • Loss of the friendship and respect of others.	• More life satisfaction. • Less personal stress. • Lasting relationships.

In conclusion, Habit 4: Think Win-Win is the key to succeeding in all your relationships with people—friends, wives, husbands, family members, teachers, study-group members, roommates, landlords—you name it.

Try some of the Baby Steps on the next page. I also recommend carefully studying and applying the tips found in the Academic Protip: "How to Think Critically."

COMING ATTRACTIONS

Do you wish other people understood you better? Don't we all? Strange as it may seem, the key to being understood by others is to understand them first. This seems like a paradox, but it works every time. We call it Habit 5. Read on and discover for yourself why it works.

Baby Steps

1. Teach to Learn. Using the summary chart on the prior page, teach the key concepts of Habit 4 to a friend, classmate, or family member within the next 48 hours.

2. The next time someone very close to you (like a best friend or sibling) succeeds in a big way, instead of feeling threatened, feel genuinely happy for that person and go out of your way to compliment him or her.

3. Think through all of your key relationships at school, at work, and at home. Are you thinking lose-win or win-lose in any of them? If so, what must you change?

    Situation/Relationship:_____

    What am I thinking? Win-lose or lose-win? _____

    What must I change? _____

4. Think of a person you know who has an Abundance Mentality. Write down three things that person does that others do not.

    Person with an Abundance Mentality: _____

    The three things: _____

    _____

    _____

5. Consider a tough situation you are currently facing that involves another person. Quickly fill out the T-chart to see if you can find a solution.

What are the wins for them?	What are the wins for me?

6. Be nice to everyone you meet for one whole day. No gossiping, ignoring, excluding, scoffing, criticizing, sneering, sulking, snickering, or backbiting allowed. Sign your name and date only after you do it perfectly. Record how you felt at the end of that day.

    Signature _____ Date _____

    How I felt: _____

7. Write down a key deposit you can make into another person's Emotional Bank Account. Record when you do it.

    Person: _____

    Deposit I can make: _____

    When done: _____

Baby Steps (Continued)

8. What are the top three things you could change that would make you a more likeable friend? Ask someone you trust for feedback on the kind of friend you are.

    1. _____

    2. _____

    3. _____

9. Has someone offended you? Sometime this week, shock them by treating unkindness with kindness.

10. Do you have a friend or friends who are bringing you down? If so, figure out how you can gracefully exit the relationship or group.

    My exit plan: _____

    _____

Academic Protip

I believe a main reason for going to college is to learn to think critically—to develop the skill to do clear, reasonable thinking based on evidence. The opposite is shoddy thinking, which is unclear, unreasonable, and based on ignorance or prejudice. In a world of shoddy thinking, everybody loses—time, money, and quality of life.

The great skill in life is to learn to think critically without becoming a critical person. The people I most admire can think critically, scrutinizing and considering differing points of view, but they're not cynics or skeptics you hate to be around because they critique everything and never seem to trust anyone.

Good critical thinking is also win-win thinking. Everybody wins when people make decisions and solve problems based on facts instead of unsupported opinions or prejudice. Professor Diane Halpern's key focus is to help college students understand how to think well and live better lives. You now get her expertise.

How to Think Critically

By Diane F. Halpern, Minerva Schools at Keck Graduate Institute and Claremont McKenna College

So you've got people wearing silicon wristbands that supposedly give them super athletic powers. They're everywhere. My students wear them because some pro athletes on TV say the wristbands make them faster and stronger. But ask scientists and they'll tell you as politely as they can that the product simply doesn't work.

Except it does work—on your brain. It works well enough to separate you from $30 or so. And if your athletic powers do improve, it's because of the placebo effect—you believe it will help you and your belief makes it so. But it's still a scam, and an expensive one.

We're flooded with pseudo-science, especially on the Internet. Billions of dollars are wasted on products based on bogus claims that can't possibly be true: "Lose weight without cutting calories! Learn without studying! Stay up all night and still feel fresh! Miracle eye cream takes years off your face!"

Too many unscrupulous people are winning at the expense of others.

Not long ago a major shoe manufacturer had to give hundreds of millions of dollars back to customers because they'd been promoting an athletic shoe that made you "faster and stronger." When somebody questioned their claims, it turned out that the shoe didn't do anything for you that an ordinary shoe wouldn't do.

So why did millions of young people shell out $425 a pair for these "miracle" shoes?

Because so many haven't developed the critical-thinking skills you go to college for. And that's the great thing about college—if you study hard and take the right mix of classes, you can learn to think critically. Critical thinkers don't fall for the fake and the phony. They spend their money, time, and energy on things that do work.

Critical thinking means seeing both sides of an issue. If you're a critical thinker, you want evidence for a claim, and when the evidence doesn't clearly favor one side or the other, you keep an open mind.

So when you see a TV offer for a diet pill and hear all those testimonials from people who say it really worked for them, you don't just go online and pay $49.99 for a bottle. First, you go online and check out the claim. You look at more than one site.

Diane F. Halpern, Minerva Schools at Keck Graduate Institute and Claremont McKenna College

You read what scientists have to say about it. Then decide for yourself what you really want—to lose your hard-earned money on a scam or to lose weight the way your doctor says, by exercising and watching calories. Don't think lose-win—allowing other people to win at your expense.

In the end, critical thinking is about discovering truth, and that's a big reason for going to college in the first place. When the truth wins, everybody wins.

But how can you know what's true? How can you tell a fact from fiction?

Critical thinkers have a toolbox they use to decide what's a fact and what isn't. Here are some of the tools they use:

Appeal to Authority. How do you know the breakfast cereal Gravel-O's has 100 percent of your daily requirement for iron? You'd have to go to the chemistry lab and use complex equipment to find out. Or you could rely on a trustworthy authority to tell you, such as the U.S. Food and Drug Administration, which checks out claims like that. But how do you know the authority is trustworthy? Usually, you consider track record and appropriate expertise. Because of her training, experience, and long relationship with you, your doctor is usually a better authority than a salesman who is trying to sell you pills for losing weight. Your doctor has your interests in mind—the salesman has his wallet in mind.

So "consider the source," as they say. Politicians, the talking heads on radio, Internet bloggers, salespeople, marketers, lawyers, even some professors are often biased. The word "bias" literally means "slanted to one side." Of course everyone is entitled to an opinion, but not all opinions are equal. You might believe that it's okay for pregnant women to smoke; my opinion is that it's not, and I can give you evidence and data that back up my opinion.

We all like to hear from people who support what we believe is true, but critical thinkers are always on the alert for bias.

Cause and Effect. "When I wear this wristband, I can jump higher." A critical thinker immediately thinks, "Well, that's interesting. How do you know you jump higher? Have you actually measured it? How many times? And if so, how do you know the wristband is causing you to jump higher? Could it be something else?"

Just because "A" happened before "B" doesn't mean that "A" caused "B." There's one pro athlete who never calls his mother on game day because his team lost a couple of games on days when he did call his mother. But is there any way to prove that the one event caused the other? Not likely.

Scientists will test a new drug for years in the laboratory to make sure it's safe and actually helps people. You wouldn't want them to do any less, or you might end up taking medicine that doesn't work or—even worse—poisons you.

Probability. This is a tricky one. "I won't vaccinate my child because a friend got her child vaccinated and he had a bad reaction." This means the parent is willing to take a much bigger risk that the child will get a serious disease than the incredibly small risk of a bad reaction. Simple math shows that this parent is not thinking critically. The number of unvaccinated children who get deadly, damaging diseases is far higher than the number of vaccinated children who react badly. All life is a gamble—would you rather take a small risk or a big risk with your child's life? Critical thinkers prefer the small risk.

False Analogy. If you say something is like something else, you're using an analogy. If you say "my girlfriend is like a rose," you're not saying that she is literally a woody flowering plant with thorns. That's why you can't use an analogy to prove anything. An analogy is not a fact.

But that doesn't stop people from trying to use an analogy to prove something. "College can't prepare you for life any more than you can learn to swim without going into the water." This is a false analogy because college and swimming are not at all the same thing. (It also overlooks the fact that you can learn quite a bit about swimming before you go into the water.)

These are just a few of the tools in the critical thinker's toolbox, and they're especially important in doing college work.

Suppose you're asked to write a paper. What's your conclusion? What evidence and reasons do you have to support that conclusion? Are your evidence and reasons any good? If you learn to use the tools of critical thinking, you can see the difference between a fact and an opinion or between a reasonable argument and a weak argument.

Suppose a professor asks you a question in class. Will you just throw out your opinion and say, "That's what I think," or will you be ready to give good reasons and evidence for your opinion? Most real-life questions don't have a single, correct answer, and opinions will differ. So pause; think about what you know about the topic; state your opinion; and give facts, reasons, and evidence. Try to avoid the errors we've talked about, such as false analogies or appeals to weak authorities.

Critical thinking won't make you negative or cynical, just skeptical—in a healthy way. And you don't have to be the smartest person in the room to think critically. In fact, reasonable thinking is not the same thing as "high IQ." Anyone, including you, can learn to think better and make better decisions for better outcomes in life. And that's a good reason for going to college.

Dr. Diane F. Halpern is a psychologist and past president of the American Psychological Association (APA). She is Dean of Social Science at the Minerva Schools at Keck Graduate Institute and also the McElwee Family Professor of Psychology at Claremont McKenna College. She has taught in colleges in Portugal, Hong Kong, Turkey, Mexico, Canada, and Russia. Dr. Halpern's *Thought and Knowledge: An Introduction to Critical Thinking* has gone through many editions and is one of the most respected books on the subject.

References

Harvey, Jerry B. *The Abilene Paradox*. San Francisco: Jossey-Bass, 1996.

"How Should I Apologize to My Professor?" *Answers.Yahoo.com*. https://answers.yahoo.com/question/index?qid=20091020033956AAlF8ny

Kopp, Wendy, *One Day, All Children…: The Unlikely Triumph of Teach for America*, Public Affairs, 2003, 3–6; Wendy Kopp, "Five Things I've Learned," FiveThings.org, Pearson Foundation. http://www.thefivethings.org/wendy-kopp/

Lewis, Luke, "16 Flatmate Horror Stories," Buzzfeed.com, Oct. 21, 2013. http://www.buzzfeed.com/lukelewis/16-flatmate-horror-stories

North, Anna, "Top Ten Worst Roommate Stories," *Jezebel.com*, Nov. 10, 2010. http://jezebel.com/5686643/the-top-ten-worst-roommate-stories/all

Robinson, Doug "Runner Makes Wrong Turn Right," *Deseret News*, June 23, 2010.

Seligman, Martin, *Authentic Happiness*, Simon & Schuster, 2002.

5

Seek First to Understand, Then to Be Understood

The Habit of Personal Vision

"Listen, or thy tongue will make thee deaf."

-NATIVE AMERICAN PROVERB

IN THIS CHAPTER, YOU WILL DISCOVER WAYS TO:

- Avoid poor listening habits.
- Practice empathy by listening for content and feeling.
- Present ideas from other people's point of view as well as your own.
- Give and receive helpful feedback.

Also, look for the Academic Protip...

- How to Make a Presentation

Habit 5:
Seek First to Understand, Then to Be Understood

is the habit of good communication—first, listening with empathy to others and second, making yourself clearly understood.

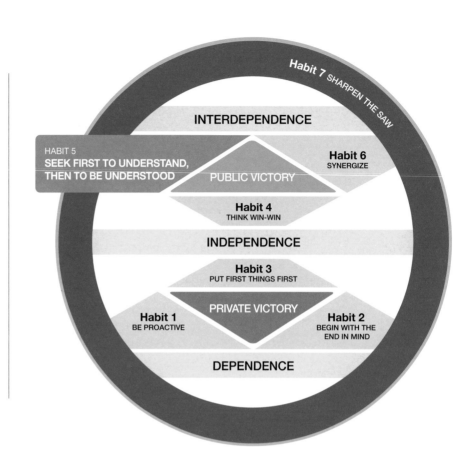

What I Wish
I'd Known in College

"I wish I'd known to seek first to understand my roommates before insisting they understand me. Life would have been easier for all of us."
–Bendi, University of Idaho

"Make sure your professors know who you are. Take the time to stop by their office once or twice to ask a question. The more interest you show in understanding the subject, the more likely the professor will be able to put a name to your face. Come grading time, the more likely you will be to get a higher mark."
–Jordan, University of Utah

"The courses you select are less important than the communication skills you learn. The ability to write and speak effectively are vital social and professional skills that will sink or propel your career."
–Scott, Rollins College

"It was in college I really learned to listen. I had to. Some of the professors, every word they said was important and I was responsible for it on tests. At the time it was hard to focus and concentrate, but it was a really important skill. I think I learned more by just keeping my ears and brain open for what the professor thought was important than I did from all the reading I did. "
–Bridget, University of Washington

"That all college professors are NOT created equal. Check out your professor before signing up for a class."
–Taylor, SUNY Buffalo

REAL CHOICES:
Getting to Understanding

Have you ever felt that someone you cared about didn't understand you?

Kelsey, a community-college student, felt that way.

My mother and I spent most of my high-school years arguing about everything from the friends I had, to the clothes I wore, to the classes I took. She didn't understand my world. So graduation from high school was going to mean finally being independent and making my own decisions without my mother's unwanted intrusions and rules.

I had received a scholarship offer to the four-year college that my closest friends were attending and had a great dorm room lined up. I would not be too far away from home but not too close either. But then, just weeks after graduation, the unexpected happened. I found out I was pregnant.

I was scared to tell my mother because I knew how excited she was for me to attend college. When I broke the news, she was devastated, but she listened. We agreed that we would somehow find a way for me to attend college. And so, instead of living on campus at my dream school, I lived at home and went to the nearby community college. To balance motherhood and school, I took some online classes, which was torture for a social person like me. All my friends were out on their own enjoying college life, and I was living in my mother's house coping with pregnancy.

In high school, I had been so into myself that I had never thought about how my mother felt. I had blown off everything she had to say and never really listened to her. I felt she never really heard what I had to say, nor did I believe she even cared about what was going on in my life. Our inability to communicate harmed our relationship. It resulted in rebellion on my end and frustration on hers.

But then I had my baby and for the first time, as the proud mother of a little boy, I could feel empathy for my mom. I knew how much she cared about me. I understood why she worried so much. If only we had

> How could Kelsey and her mother have understood each other's feelings more effectively? What emotions may have blocked their understanding?

taken the time to listen to what each other was saying earlier, we would have had such a better relationship.

Having my son was a blessing in disguise because by being a mother, I learned the reasons for my mother's concern, rules, and standards. I now know how important such understanding is. I just wish I'd discovered this when I was a teenager. My mom and I have a lot of catching up to do. But I'm really looking forward to it.

Kelsey's situation is more common than we like to think. Most emotional misunderstandings happen with the people we care about most: parents, friends, siblings, spouses, and other loved ones.

Such moments call for our best communication skills, but during these very moments our skills often come up short. We care so much about being heard that we don't hear the other person. Sometimes tempers or egos get in the way and we say things we wish we hadn't, or we give people the silent treatment and relationships get broken.

The secret of good communication is in this simple phrase: Seek First to Understand, Then to Be Understood. In other words, listen before you talk. You have two ears and one mouth—use them accordingly.

You might be dealing with a tough situation at home, a difficult roommate, a demanding professor, an emotional breakup, or a dysfunctional study group. You might have to make a class presentation, and you really want to succeed. You might have an important job interview coming up. Habit 5: Seek First to Understand, Then to Be Understood is all about communicating successfully.

PEOPLE WHO PRACTICE HABIT 5:

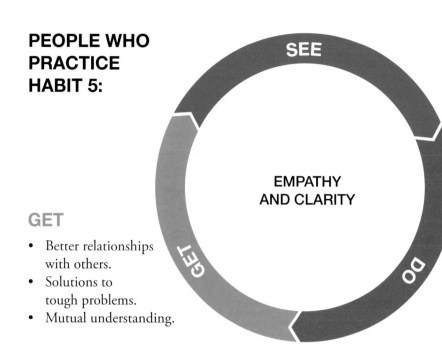

EMPATHY AND CLARITY

SEE

- Listening first allows you to understand the problem.
- My own opinion is important too, and worth sharing.

DO

- Avoid poor listening habits.
- Practice empathy by listening for content and feeling.
- Present ideas from other people's point of view as well as their own.
- Give and receive helpful feedback.

GET

- Better relationships with others.
- Solutions to tough problems.
- Mutual understanding.

THE PARADIGMS OF HABIT 5

Some time ago, I took my 10-year-old son Nathan to see a doctor about the pain he was having in his ankles. It was a complex, quirky issue that had been going on for over a year. Unless we could solve it, he wouldn't be able to play football, which meant everything to Nathan. The doctor didn't ask a lot of questions and made a quick diagnosis. After the appointment, Nathan said to me, "Dad, that doctor didn't listen to one thing I said. I don't think what he told me to do is going to work."

Nathan turned out to be right on both counts. The doctor hadn't listened, and his prescriptions didn't help at all. Later, we found another doctor who listened intently, asked a lot of questions, and really sought to understand Nathan. "That doctor knows what he's talking about, Dad," said Nathan afterward. And he was right again. His prescription turned out to be the perfect solution, and Nathan was able to play football that year. Nathan and I were both happy about that.

Unfortunately, like Nathan's first doctor, most people don't know how to listen or don't care to listen. Or they know how to listen but get in a rush and don't do it. They leave behind a pool of broken relationships and misunderstandings that could fill the Indian Ocean. Businesses lose billions of dollars each year because they don't listen to customers. Marriages are destroyed because couples won't hear each other out. Students flounder on exams because they can't focus and listen to the instructor.

There are two paradigms at work in Habit 5. First, you won't have influence with other people until you understand them first. Another way of saying this is "Diagnose before you prescribe"—what my son's first doctor didn't do.

You assume you already know it all: "I know exactly how you feel, Jenny. I went through the exact same thing." You think you know what the other person is feeling and experiencing, but you don't because you didn't really listen to him or her. It's like assuming that your own glasses will help your friend see better.

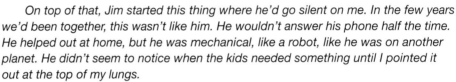

Wrong assumptions set off wars, lawsuits, divorces, and fact-starved gossip sessions.

The main principle of Habit 5 is empathy. Empathy is seeing things from the point of view of another person—feeling what he or she feels and knowing what that person knows.

Gina was studying to be a therapist for troubled youth. She had just started her program at the community college, in addition to the pressures of two small children at home and an internship at a local school. It was almost too much for her.

On top of that, Jim started this thing where he'd go silent on me. In the few years we'd been together, this wasn't like him. He wouldn't answer his phone half the time. He helped out at home, but he was mechanical, like a robot, like he was on another planet. He didn't seem to notice when the kids needed something until I pointed it out at the top of my lungs.

This went on for weeks until finally I shouted at him, "What's wrong with you anyway? Why can't you see I need you to hold up your end? I can't handle all this plus your moping around all the time."

Then he just blurted it out: "My mom has cancer. She's only got a few weeks."

It was like getting hit by a bus. "Why didn't you tell me?"

"I didn't want you to worry about it with everything else you've got going."

Needless to say, I felt awful. He'd been bottling this up trying to spare me. And here I was in college supposedly learning how to have empathy for emotionally troubled people. It was time I learned it.

Diagnose Before You Prescribe

Most people don't know how to listen. They're full of advice, but they don't really help much.

1. Describe a time when someone—a parent, friend, teacher, or boss—just didn't listen to you. How did you feel?

2. Now describe a situation when you didn't listen to someone. What was the result?

3. With hindsight, what would you do differently? What would be the result?

The second paradigm of Habit 5 is the courage to speak up and make yourself understood. The ability to communicate effectively is one of the most important skills you will develop in college, whether you're talking to a friend or giving a formal presentation in class. Oddly enough, the first step in making yourself understood is to understand the other person. In other words, the key to influencing others is to be influenced by them *first*. We'll see how this concept works a little later.

Before moving on, let's see how Habits 4, 5, and 6 work together. Think of Habit 4 as the attitude of good communication, Habit 5 as the skill of good communication, and Habit 6 as the fruit of good communication.

This sequence is important. Habit 4 is the attitude of wanting everyone to win. You don't want to step on someone (win-lose), but you don't want to get stepped on either (lose-win). You see yourself as an equal—not better than or less than, but just as good as the other person. With this attitude in place, you'll truly desire to understand the hearts and minds of other people and you'll want them to understand you as well (Habit 5). This kind of genuine, deep communication enables creative problem solving and generates all kinds of new ideas. We call this synergy. As you'll see, you never get to synergy (Habit 6) without first practicing Habits 4 and 5. There really is magic in the sequence.

> "Two monologues do not make a dialogue."
>
> —Jeff Daly, Chief Designer of the Metropolitan Museum

WHAT STUDENTS *DO* WHEN THEY SEEK FIRST TO UNDERSTAND

My experience is that most people want to be good communicators, but nobody has ever taught them how to do it. Good communicators:

- Avoid poor listening habits.
- Practice empathy by listening for content and feeling.
- Present ideas from other people's point of view as well as their own.
- Give and receive helpful feedback.

Avoid Poor Listening Habits

I found it interesting just how quickly my young son could tell the doctor wasn't listening to him. Yet, I think most of us can tell when someone is not truly listening. We sense it by their eye contact, body language, and tone of voice.

Most of us are guilty of some or all of these five poor listening styles:

- Spacing out
- Pretend listening
- Selective listening
- Word listening
- Self-centered listening

Spacing Out. This can happen when we try to multitask, like talking to your mom on the phone while you're watching TV or texting a friend while you're writing a paper. Sometimes we ignore others because we are stressed, in a hurry, or caught up in a daydream

199

about the Bahamas. We "check out" during lectures. Just ask any professor how offensive that is. And sometimes people intentionally ignore you. Kelsey ignored her mother because she assumed her mother was "out of it" and didn't care.

Pretend Listening. Not wanting to be totally rude, we nod occasionally and say "uh-huh" once or twice, but our heads are elsewhere.

Speaker: "And then that professor went on to embarrass me in front of the whole class."

Listener: "Uh-huh. Nice. What are we going to do this weekend?"

Selective Listening. Sometimes we hear only what matters to us, not to the other person.

Speaker: "I've been taking a lot of math classes, but I'm not sure what I should major in at this point. What do you think?"

Listener: "Speaking of math, I've got to study for my test. Thanks for reminding me."

Word Listening. This happens when we listen to the words we hear but not the feelings behind them.

Speaker: "I'm supposed to write a paper on China. I just found this paper on College-Papers-R-Us.com. I don't know why I shouldn't be allowed to use it."

Listener: "Yeah, I don't either."

If the listener were more sensitive to body language and tone of voice, he would hear what the speaker is really asking: "Do you think I ought to cheat and pretend this paper is my own work?" The speaker is feeling unsure, hesitant, and maybe guilty. But the listener is hearing only words, not emotions.

Self-Centered Listening. "I know exactly how you feel." "You think *you* had a bad day." "The same thing happened to me." As far as this listener is concerned, "It's all about me." This is the guy who thinks you like his awful music because he likes it.

Not listening shows a lack of respect and a sort of selfishness. We're so into our own heads that we can't focus on somebody else even for a minute. Yet the deepest need of the human heart is to be understood.

If I were to suck all of the air out of the room you're in right now, what would happen? Obviously, you'd panic. You wouldn't think about anything but getting air. So it is with people. Not feeling understood is like not having psychological air, and people become desperate for it. They'll go somewhere else to get it if they have to. This short poem captures how badly people just want to be heard:

Please Listen
When I ask you to listen to me
and you start giving me advice,
you have not done what I asked.
When I ask you to listen to me
and you begin to tell me why
I shouldn't feel that way,
you are trampling on my feelings.
When I ask you to listen to me

> "You know, it's at times like this when I'm trapped in a Vogon airlock with a man from Betelgeuse and about to die of asphyxiation in deep space that I really wish I'd listened to what my mother told me when I was young!"
>
> "Why, what did she tell you?"
>
> "I don't know. I wasn't listening."
>
> —Douglas Adams, *A Hitchhiker's Guide to the Galaxy*

and you feel you have to do something
to solve my problem,
you have failed me,
strange as that may seem.
Listen! All I ask is that you listen.
Don't talk or do—just hear me.
-Anonymous

If we care about others, we listen to them with empathy. That means really listening—focusing—and hearing not only what they are saying but how they are feeling.

A friend of mine was in class listening to the professor give an important lecture. Another student a few seats away propped his feet on the desk in front of him and started reading the school newspaper. My friend could tell that this really bothered the professor, who finally lost it. "Put that newspaper away!" he snapped. "Why are you so rude?" The student slowly put the paper down and sat up, but he didn't apologize. The whole class was jumpy from then on.

How would you feel if you were the professor and your students sat in front of you texting, tweeting, and surfing social media? Teachers are people with feelings, but many students don't treat them that way.

So make an effort to listen, not just because you've paid for a seat in a class, but also because the teacher is like you—a human being who deserves respect.

The same is true of your friends and your family, especially when emotions are running high—sadness, excitement, anger, passion, jealousy. This is the time to listen with empathy. Your brain needs to change its address and move out of itself into the minds and hearts of other people.

Ordinarily, we think of listening as hearing what other people say. But Empathic Listening is more than that—it's hearing and seeing and sensing what they feel too.

Empathy is not sympathy. Sympathy is feeling sorry for someone. Empathy might lead to sympathy, but there's no judgment in empathy—no criticism or agreement, no "for" or "against." You're just trying to understand what other people think and feel by putting yourself in their position. Kelsey, for instance, started to listen empathically to her mother only after she became a mother herself.

To pick up feelings, you need to use your eyes and heart as well as your ears. The ears pick up words and tone of voice, the eyes see the body language, and the heart picks up deeper feelings. The Chinese wisely write the word "listen" with this character:

> "If there's a thing unsuccessful people have in common it's that they talk about themselves all the time."
>
> —Stephen Fry, comedian

EYES

EARS

HEART

201

Empathic Listening isn't easy for most of us because we tend to listen *autobiographically*—that is, we listen more to our own thoughts than to other people. When listening to others, we start thinking about how to advise them; or we probe them, interpret what they say, or judge their ideas.

> "Of course, there's something fishy about describing people's feelings. You try hard to be accurate, but as soon as you start to define such and such a feeling, language lets you down."
>
> —Iris Murdoch, author and philosopher

ADVISING	Trying to solve other people's problems based on your own experiences.	"Let me tell you what I did when the same thing happened to me…"
PROBING	Asking questions from within your frame of reference.	"I get along fine with Tim. Why can't you?"
INTERPRETING	Trying to figure people out in terms of what you think or believe.	"You don't mean that. You mean this…"
JUDGING	Either agreeing or disagreeing according to your logic and values.	"You're crazy. Tim is the best thing that ever happened to you…"

To see how a poor listener is no help, imagine this: You've made real sacrifices to go to college, but after a month, you feel overwhelmed. (If you're like me, that's easy to imagine.) You've just flunked a test. But your real problem is that you have no idea what to major in. You're studying all this stuff, but you don't know what to do when you grow up. One night you're on the phone talking to a friend about it, but the friend isn't very empathic.

	WHAT YOU SAY	HOW YOUR FRIEND RESPONDS
	Hi.	So how's it going?
ADVISING	Oh… (audible sigh) I just flunked a test.	Oh, no. That's too bad. I remember my first term. I cratered on two or three tests too. What you need to do is get off the video games and hit the books. Put in a couple of hours of study a day. That's what I had to do.
PROBING	Actually, I haven't been playing games. I've been trying to study hard, but I'm feeling a little confused about what I want to do in the future, you know?	(Interrupting) Yeah, I know. So, is everything okay in your life? How about all those hotties? Are they getting in the way?
INTERPRETING	Well, I haven't connected with any of those hotties…	(Interrupting again) That's your problem. You need to get out. College is for hanging out. You'll never have this chance again.
JUDGING	It's not that. Like I said, I just don't know about college anymore. What I mean is…	(Interrupting one last time) I think I know what you mean. But hey, you know as well as I do: no degree, no job. So you really ought to rethink this. Remember that time in high school when you weren't thinking clearly either? But yeah, I know you'll figure it out. You always do.
	Yeah, right.	Hey, I've got to run… got another call coming in. You remember what I said. (Click)

So how do you feel? Your friend interrupted you again and again with his stories, assumptions, and judgments. Do you feel understood?

You probably feel frustrated, to say the least.

Practice Empathy by Listening for Content and Feeling

> "To my mind, empathy is in itself a healing agent…because it releases, it confirms, it brings even the most frightened person into the human race. If a person feels understood, he or she belongs."
>
> —Carl Rogers, psychologist

Empathy means you listen first, not only for content but for feelings. You "diagnose before you prescribe." Now call up a friend who knows how to listen, and see how it goes:

WHAT YOU SAY	HOW YOUR FRIEND RESPONDS
Hi.	Hey, how's it going?
Oh… (audible sigh) I just flunked a test.	Oh, no. That must be hard.
It was hard. I've gotten okay grades on all my other tests so far, so it was a shock.	You must have felt like you were on top of it all, then suddenly, it wasn't so easy.
Well, I thought my answers were good. The instructor didn't think so.	So that's frustrating.
I'm just feeling really… well, frustrated is a good word for it. I can't seem to focus. I just wish I could figure out what I want to do when I graduate.	You're worried about life after college.
Yeah, that's just it. I really am learning a lot about random stuff. It's just that I don't know what my major should be, so I don't know if any of this stuff is any use.	So you're feeling kind of aimless and you're not even sure what you should be studying.
That's exactly how I feel. And that's why I called. I know you had the same problem your first year, but you eventually chose a major. So I'm calling for your advice. How did you do it?	Well, you're right. My first year I didn't know what to do either, and it was a real problem. If I were in your shoes, this is what I would do…

Can you feel the difference? By the end of this conversation, you're open to advice because your friend properly listened and diagnosed your problem.

So, what made the difference? Here are some highlights:

- Your friend didn't advise, probe, interpret, or judge. Instead, he reflected feelings and content in his own words.
- The listener never offered any thoughts until asked.
- You both got to the real issue fast. Empathic Listening is much faster than ineffective listening. Nobody wasted time talking about video games, study habits, or hotties.

- The listener never interrupted you.
- Once you got to the real issue, you were able to ask for advice. The diagnosis was correct, so it was time for the prescription. In the first scenario, the diagnosis was premature, so the prescription was incorrect. In the medical field, that's called malpractice. In relationships, it's a withdrawal from the Emotional Bank Account.

Empathic Listening has a calming effect on people. It allows their emotions to settle and their thoughts to clear. They are getting psychological air.

"I'm hearing voices all around

I'm hearing voices making sounds

What would they take?

What would they say to me

If only I was listening?"

—OneRepublic, "Hearing Voices"

Often the best response for an empathic listener is to say nothing. A pause encourages the other person to talk, and you can't understand people if they don't get to talk. But if you feel you need to say something, try reflecting the feeling first and then the content. It looks like this:

"You seem to feel _____ about _____."

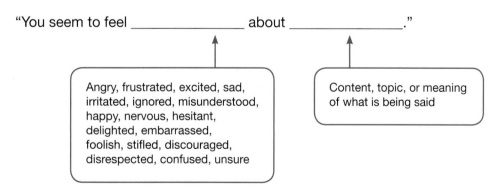

So you might say:
- "I can see you feel really angry about what I said to you."
- "I sense you're a little freaked out about this guy I'm dating, Mom."
- "I can tell you feel very strongly about getting a different work schedule."

Try phrases like these:

- "As I get it, you feel…"
- "So as you see it…"
- "You must have felt…"
- "What I am hearing is…"
- "Now you're feeling…"

Lauren, a psychology major, roomed with her best friend, Anya. They were very different from each other: Anya came from a well-off family who paid for everything, while Lauren had to work a couple of part-time jobs just to stay in school. But they both loved the same music and movies, and they both loved animals—they even smuggled a pair of guinea pigs into their apartment and took turns hiding and feeding them. Lauren remembers when things went wrong:

Have you ever noticed that "listen" and "silent" are made up of the same letters?

Anya complained a lot about school. She just didn't like it. Her teachers were boring, her books were too hard to understand, and she was always putting off homework. She kept saying she was going to quit and save herself the agony.

One day at the end of the term, she breezed in and announced that she'd flunked out and wouldn't be graduating. I said, "Congratulations!"

She turned and looked at me. "How can you say that?" And then she went into her room and didn't come out that night. The next day she was gone before I got up, and I didn't see her slink back into her room that night. For days she wouldn't talk to me.

I couldn't figure it out. Had I done something wrong? She hated school and I thought she'd be happy to get out of it. That's why I congratulated her. School wasn't even necessary to her; her parents were loaded, so she wasn't going to suffer.

Then she told me she was moving back home. She was polite about it, but she was cold, and after that, we were never close again.

A year later I was taking a Human Behavior class and we were talking about empathy, so I told my story about Anya. And it hit me what I had done—or hadn't done, actually. How did I not see it? I'd shown no empathy at all. Anya was struggling. She had plenty of financial support but no moral support when it came to school. And flunking out just reinforced that she was a failure in life.

And here I had congratulated her for failing. I couldn't believe it.

So I phoned her that night and told her how sorry I was about it all, that I had made a mistake and thought she would be happy to get school out of her life.

She was really gracious and told me what a good friend I'd been. I asked her how her life was going, and this time I had the good sense to just listen. It was good to hear her laugh again.

Try out your Empathic Listening skills by doing the next activity.

Empathic Language

Read the scenarios below and come up with an empathic response for each.

1. A 21-year-old student gets a call from his mom to make sure he is getting in on time at night and making it to class in the morning. The student wants to say, "Hey, I'm 21 years old and have been out on my own for three years, so don't you think I can…?" Instead, his empathic reply might be:

2. All semester, Mary has been talkative. Almost overnight, however, she goes silent on her roommates, including you. It's been going on for days and no one knows why. As you head out the door to grocery-shop, Mary yells angrily to the other roommates, "Don't anyone touch my food in the refrigerator!" Your empathic response to Mary's outburst might be:

3. You've become a shift manager at work. One of the long-time employees comes to you and says, shaking his head, "I can't work here any longer. I'm treated like a second-class citizen and I don't know what I'm doing wrong." Your empathic response is:

The single guideline that helps me most to listen empathically is this: *Simply restate what the other person is feeling and saying in your own words.* Here are some other tips:

*   Focus on what speakers are feeling and saying, not on yourself. You don't need to solve their problems; you're just there to understand them.
*   Don't be afraid of a little silence. Give others space to share more of what's going on in their heads.
*   Know when and when not to listen empathically. You don't need to listen empathically if the situation isn't emotional ("I can see that you really want those french fries"), or if the situation is already clearly understood ("What I hear you saying is that you really need to use the restroom").

"Before you criticize someone, you should walk a mile in their shoes. Then, if you do, you're a mile away—and you've got their shoes."

—Jack Handey, comedian

- Delay listening empathically if you are highly emotional yourself. It's always wise to calm down and get clear about your own feelings before getting into an emotional conversation. Don't start an important conversation when you're angry, because you'll always regret it later.
- Don't force the issue. If someone doesn't want to talk, give that person space. Wait until he or she is ready to open up.

Now try Empathic Listening for real.

ACTIVITY 37

Empathic Listening
Practice

Try listening empathically by following these steps:

1. Get together with two friends and teach them about Empathic Listening, including the basic paradigms and the skills.

2. Once you all understand how to listen empathically, each of you identify a situation in your personal, school, or work life that you feel strongly about—one you wouldn't mind sharing.

3. Take turns. Let one partner go first in describing his or her situation, while you practice giving empathic responses.

4. Have the third person play the role of observer and coach. That person can suggest other phrasing that could have been used, or point out feelings that were missed.

5. Rotate so that each person gets a turn to listen empathically.

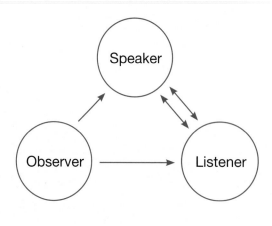

You can also use Empathic Listening to get to know other people better. What do they feel most strongly about in life? How do they feel about college, certain types of movies, or politics?

Now try using your Empathic Listening skills.

Getting to Know You

You might think you know a parent, sibling, roommate, work colleague, close friend, or girlfriend or boyfriend, but just how well do you really know that person? Choose one of these people and ask the questions below. Use your Empathic Listening skills to delve a little deeper into that person's responses so you get a richer understanding of him or her.

What is his or her...
- Favorite hobby?
- Thought on the nicest thing you could do for her/him?
- Worst experience in school?
- Dream job, if time and money were no factor?
- View on the value of college?
- Greatest unfulfilled dream?
- Warmest memory of childhood?
- Favorite hero?
- Ideal vacation spot?
- Preference: watch a good TV show, see a movie, go to dinner with friends, read a book, or something else?
- Biggest regret in life?
- Greatest strength?

ACTIVITY 38

If you chose someone you already knew, how well did you really know him or her? How effective were you in bringing out that person's feelings? How hard was it not to interrupt when listening? Did you use any autobiographical responses?

Present Ideas From Other People's Points of View as Well as Your Own

In some conversations, your role is to simply listen—to seek to understand. Plenty of other times, however, you need to express your thoughts and feelings—to seek to be understood. Sometimes you'll be assigned to do it in class. When you do, you want to be clear, confident, and persuasive.

Seeking to be understood is a balancing act between doing too little or too much. You probably know someone who never says a word in class, stays quiet at parties, and sits back and lets others do the talking. Or you might know someone who does all the talking, dominates conversations, and constantly interrupts.

I have a neighbor who always shares too much information. Frequently, in group settings, he will let everyone know that he used to be rich but has since been humbled and lost all of his money. It makes everyone feel uncomfortable because he is revealing personal info that he should share only with close friends. As a result, he has alienated most of his neighbors. Similarly, I used to work with a friend who talked so much that people would hide in their offices when they saw her coming. Every conversation was at least 10 minutes long, and you had to interrupt her to get out of it. Sometimes it's best to be quiet. It's polite to give somebody else the stage. On the other hand, silence can be a sign of a lose-win mentality, of a person who doesn't have the courage to be heard. Communication is an art—a balancing act.

Communicating requires more than a slick style or a strong voice. Your character—who you are and what you do—communicates before you ever open your mouth. Emerson said, "What you do speaks so loudly that I cannot hear what you say."

A friend told me this story: "My co-worker complained that his girlfriend was always checking up on him. I asked him why. He said she didn't trust him because he had dumped another girl to hook up with her."

You can't talk yourself out of a problem you have behaved yourself into. You communicate through actions, not fancy words or hollow promises. Actions speak louder than words.

At times you'll need to make a persuasive presentation—to get up in front of people and clearly present ideas. Later in the chapter, an expert will give you a lot of information on this, so I won't. But I do want to mention a couple of things that have worked for me.

First of all—like it or not—to succeed in college and life, you need to learn to speak up. Looking back to your teens, you might remember a few family conversations like this one:

"So, how was the dance?"

"Fine."

"What'd ya do?"

"Nothing."

"Where'd you go?"

"I don't know."

"Well, you must have done something. You've been gone since 6 o'clock."

"We just kind of hung out."

"With who?"

"Friends."

"C'mon. Talk to me. Open up a little."

"What do you want me to say? I've told you everything."

That sort of thing may have worked for you as a teen, but people expect more of an adult.

I dated girls in college who were so quiet and unexpressive that I never knew what they were thinking.

"So where would you like to eat tonight?"

"I don't care."

"Would you like to go to a movie or a play?"

"Whatever you think…"

I always want to say back, "Oh, please care. Pretty please. I really want your opinion!"

In school, professors will ask you questions and expect you to speak up. I like how Kristin of Winnipeg, Canada, took control of her fear of speaking up in front of people. She says:

WOULD YOU EXPOUND?

SHEESH! I *TOLD* YOU, OUR SECOND QUARTER NUMBERS ARE *FINE!* WHY ARE YOU ALWAYS ON MY CASE?

COMMUNICATION STYLES THAT DON'T WORK IN ADULTHOOD.

I came from a small private school, which I attended from kindergarten to Grade 12. I was one of a graduating class of 12 students. Talking in front of those classmates was no big deal since most of us had been friends our whole life.

After a couple years in the workforce, I decided to go to college. There the class sizes were far greater. The first day, each student took turns going to the front of the class to tell everyone a little about themselves. When it was my turn, I could feel my face turn red as I stumbled over my words. It was a disaster.

At that moment, I decided to do something to improve my public-speaking skills. Every opportunity there was to speak, I signed up. Whether it was for a group project or to promote a school function, I was there speaking.

I'm happy to say that I no longer have a fear of public speaking. In fact, it's one of my strengths.

Kristin could have said, "I don't do public speaking. I prefer to remain silent and blend in with the walls." But she knew it was important and took proactive steps to learn how to do it.

I was much like Kristin when I was a teenager. I hated to speak or even read in public. I wanted to die each time I had to do it. I wanted to run for class office in high school, but then it dawned on me that I would have to give a speech to the whole school, so I chickened out. My fear was especially hard to deal with because my father was an internationally renowned public speaker.

Eventually, I faced my fear and took opportunities to speak again and again. As a college quarterback, I was often asked to speak to groups of teenagers. I was supposed to be the confident role model, but I was nervous as could be—teens can be frightening audiences. Despite the discomfort, over the years and in many countries I've gotten to the point where I don't mind it so much and have become pretty decent at it. I still get nervous and it still isn't my favorite thing, but I've learned ways to channel my nervousness into positive energy.

I once asked my father, Stephen R. Covey, how to make a persuasive presentation. He was the best in the world at it. Here are a few of his tips.

Sean Covey as a college quarterback

- Make eye contact with people. Connect with them one by one. Look around so that you're making regular eye contact with everyone.
- Speak clearly. Enunciate. Err on the side of talking slowly.
- Be genuine. Speak from the heart. Don't pretend to be something you're not. Once you have been dishonest with people, they will always question your credibility and intentions.
- Know your audience. Get out of your own head and into their heads. Ask yourself, "What's in it for them?" Too often we are caught up in our own selves and problems. Instead, try to understand your audience's issues and problems. Before giving the presentation, walk around and talk with people so you can get a feel for what's on their minds. This one needs a little more explaining.

"The most courageous act is still to think for yourself. Aloud."

—Coco Chanel, French fashion designer

Here's the basic idea, and it's somewhat ironic: *The key to being understood is to seek first to understand.* That's right. If you want other people to understand you and buy in to what you say, you must first understand them. Know their needs, feelings, priorities, backgrounds, aspirations, likes, and dislikes. Know their language. Understand what motivates them, what worries them, and what it is like to be in their shoes.

How do you find out these things? Ask. If you're going to present to a class, know exactly what the professor wants you to do. If you're going into a job interview, do your research; go online and find out everything you can about the interviewer and the company. What are their problems, plans, strategies, values, and vision as a company? How can you help?

Knowing your audience enables you to present your ideas from their frame of reference, not your own. To illustrate, compare these two presentations. On the left, the speaker talks mostly about himself; on the right, he talks about the audience. Notice how he shifts from using "I" messages to "You" messages.

> "When I was 14 years old, I made this PowerPoint presentation, and I invited my parents into my room and I gave them popcorn. It was called 'Project Hollywood 2004.' And it worked! I moved to L.A. in January 2004."
>
> —Emma Stone, actor

FROM THE SPEAKER'S PERSPECTIVE ("I")	FROM THE LISTENER'S PERSPECTIVE ("YOU")
I'm Gilberto Marron, and I'm applying for the job to design ski-racing suits. I have the background and expertise for this job.	I'm Gilberto Marron, and I'm applying for the job to design ski-racing suits. Let me make sure I understand your priorities for this job.
I intend to cover the material I have in about 10 minutes and then open it up for questions.	You've said that your customers are national ski teams. They're all looking for a suit that can shave a few seconds off a downhill racer's time.
I recently completed my degree in chemistry with an emphasis on aerodynamics and materials design. In my internship, I conducted hundreds of fabric tests, including a study of their air-flow properties. I have also finished a study-abroad program in Switzerland, where I studied wind-tunnel mechanics…	You need an expert in fabrics that cut air resistance. In my internship, I tested more than 100 of the most advanced fabrics, so I know their properties. You also need a suit that's fast but not too hot. In school, I took an advanced class in Switzerland on air flow and how it relates to different kinds of materials…

Can you feel the difference between these two presentations? The "I" perspective is "I have something to say and I would like you to sit and listen while I say it," while the "You" perspective says, "I have listened to you, I understand your needs, and I'm here to help you." Which speaker would you rather listen to?

It pays to know your audience and put their needs first.

LESSON ON LEADERSHIP: Getting the Job

It can literally pay to seek first to understand before trying to be understood. Check out Brian's experience:

When I was growing up, one of my father's friends told me how he had applied for a job during the Great Depression. There were 400 applicants and one opening. He decided to research the company thoroughly before going to the interview. When they asked why he wanted to work for the company, he handed them a 20-page report about all the good qualities of the company and why he wanted to work for them. He got the job and later became the CEO.

So when I neared graduation, I had the opportunity to interview for a job I really wanted. The company handed out copies of their philosophies and annual report to the various applicants. I decided to follow the lead of my dad's friend. I condensed the key points of the materials and put them in writing in the form of an executive summary. When asked during my interview if I'd had a chance to read the report, I handed them my summary. They liked it so much they asked if they could use it for internal purposes. And, yes, I did get the job.

Becoming a good presenter involves a lot of things, but unless people feel you're honest and have their interests in mind, nothing else matters much. All your other persuasive-speaking techniques will offer little value or impact. Presenting is a vital skill in the 21st century, in school, and at work, so you'll want to get as good as you can at it.

"Everyone has an invisible sign hanging from their neck saying 'Make me feel important.' Never forget this message when working with people."

—Mary Kay Ash, Founder of Mary Kay cosmetics

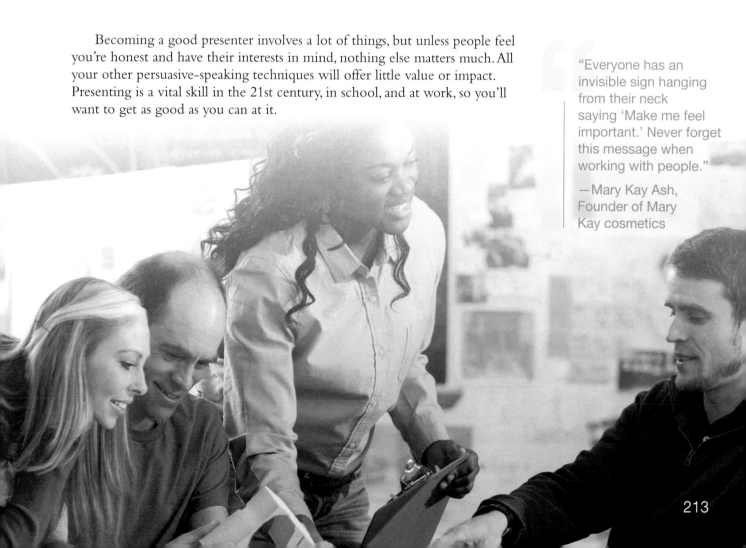

213

Give Helpful Feedback

The toughest part of communicating may be telling people bad news they need to hear.

A student named Jolene was at a party when her good friend Marianna did something to embarrass Jolene's boyfriend. Jolene held back. She said nothing. She stewed in her anger overnight.

But when she saw Marianna the next morning, her feelings erupted:

"Marianna, last night you were such a jerk. You really ticked me off. How dare you have the gall to make fun of my boyfriend—to make him feel small in front of all our friends? You have absolutely no social skills! It's no wonder more guys don't ask you out."

Well, that was the end of a friendship.

How would you have handled this situation?

Jolene was probably right about Marianna's behavior, and maybe Marianna needed to know she was out of line. But you don't have to wreck a relationship to give good feedback to someone.

DID YOU KNOW?
Some Greek Advice

Early Greeks had a formula for persuasive speaking: ethos + pathos + logos.

Ethos has to do with personal credibility. Are you believable? Two things make you believable: your character (honesty, integrity, good motives) and competence (your knowledge and skills). Show you're credible by sharing your background and your intent.

Pathos has to do with emotions. Do you care about your message? Do you care about your audience? Emotions are influenced by examples, music, pictures, and especially stories. Your listeners need to know you care about them—that you're real, not some mechanical robot.

Logos has to do with logic and reason. Do you have good evidence for your point of view? Do you have your facts straight? Does your argument make sense? Is it organized logically? Tell them early on what you're going to be talking about, then tell them, and then review what you told them. That is a good outline for any speech.

The next time you make a presentation, think of this sequence. First, establish your credibility (ethos) by making clear who you are and what you know. Second, connect with your audience's emotions and show that you're human (pathos). Third, have a simple, well-planned outline (logos).

Avoid "You" Messages. The key to giving helpful feedback is to use "I" messages instead of "You" messages. (Oddly enough, this is the opposite of what you should do in giving a presentation.) In giving feedback, "You" messages typically attack the person: "You're so rude." "You're never on time." "You're a lazy bum." "You" messages usually attack character, but can also attack competence: "You're so stupid." "You don't have what it takes to graduate."

Notice that Jolene fired "You" messages at Marianna, shooting down her character and competence; the tirade destroyed a friendship. Guess who regretted it most? Jolene. Marianna only said, "I'm sorry. I didn't mean to embarrass him." She looked hurt and from then on had something else to do when Jolene tried to get together with her. Jolene grieved at losing a good friend.

As Jolene learned, "You" messages are big emotional withdrawals. "You're so mean," "You're so selfish…" "You're so bratty, you never think about anybody but yourself." Wouldn't these messages put you on the defensive?

Use "I" Messages. In contrast, "I" messages describe your feelings—your concerns, perceptions, or frustrations: "The other day when you came and talked to us, I felt…" or "My perception was…" or "My concern was…" Then, once you have expressed your feelings, you describe what the person is doing to cause those feelings. An "I" message isn't an attack. You emphasize the behavior instead of the person's character or competence.

What if Jolene had given feedback using "I" messages instead?

"Marianna, something is bothering me that I want to clear up. Last night, I felt hurt. When you made that joke about my boyfriend's shirt in front of everyone, I was really embarrassed, and I felt hurt."

"I" messages are candid, honest deposits in people's Emotional Bank Accounts. If you're considerate, an "I" message can build the friendship. Had Jolene sent "I" messages, Marianna might have apologized, thought about it, and continued the relationship.

It's not easy to give feedback, especially if you're hurt or angry. If your intent is to hurt someone in return or get even, you're better off giving no feedback at all. But if you're proactive and patient, and you really want to help, then you should share your feedback.

Here are some other tips for sharing feedback:

- Be specific and factual. Don't generalize. Instead of saying, "Why are you so cheap?" you could say, "Three times this month I've had to pay for your pizza."
- Focus on things the person can control. "You need to do something about your height if you want more guys to go out with you." This kind of feedback doesn't help.
- Focus on one or two issues. Don't unload a barrelful of bad news all at once.
- Be timely. Don't wait for months to give feedback. It should happen soon.
- Allow for a response. Seek to understand.
- Give more positive feedback than negative. As management expert Ken Blanchard says, "Catch people doing things right," then let them know about it.

> "Working with people inevitably generates feelings…. While experiencing such feelings is not unhealthy, repressing them is."
>
> —Dr. Thomas Gordon, psychologist

215

Sharing Feelings

Giving feedback is hard for some people. Create helpful feedback for each person.

1. A teacher returns your research paper and says it was so good that he suspects you plagiarized it. You worked hard on it, even skipped going out so you could do your best—and you get accused of cheating. You're hurt and ticked off.
    Your feedback:

2. You are a supervisor in the campus copy center. You notice that a lot more copies are made than are paid for. You expect some extras due to mistakes and paper jams, but this is ridiculous. One day you see your favorite employee handing over copies to her friend, and the friend walks away without paying.
    Your feedback:

3. Your friend was rushing to class when she caught you out of the corner of her eye. You could see she was late, but she stopped to see how you were doing. You call her that evening to say thanks.
    Your feedback:

WHAT YOU GET BY SEEKING FIRST TO UNDERSTAND

So, what's in it for you to be an empathic, two-way communicator? Your college success and happiness might depend on how well you communicate with teachers, recruiters, and other students. And you'll build lasting family relationships and best friends forever.

My older sister, Maria, is a great example. She takes genuine interest in people and is always asking, "So how are things going? What is happening in your life? Tell me about your work," and so on. She always makes you feel so good about yourself. If you're not careful, you'll have long conversations with her that are entirely about yourself. It isn't a put-on. She really cares and enjoys it. As a result, she has a boatload of friends.

I contrast Maria with other people I know who seem to talk only about themselves; you end conversations noticing that you never once mentioned anything about your own life. It's sad. It reminds me of the guy who said, "We've talked enough about me. Now let's talk about you. What do you think about me?"

"Only one thing is more frightening than speaking your truth. And that is not speaking."

—Audre Lord, civil rights activist

Without good communication, relationships are one-sided, feelings get hurt, family relationships grow cold, we don't learn nearly as much, we never fully understand other people, and we never feel fully understood ourselves. These are not the outcomes we want.

Calculating the financial and emotional costs of poor communication is impossible, but we know they are big. My brother Stephen, in his best-selling book *The Speed of Trust*, compares mistrust to a tax burden. Whenever a relationship or business lacks trust, two things happen: cost goes up and speed goes down. It is like a great big tax that mires everything down.

But the opposite is true as well. Whenever you practice Habit 5 and have high trust, cost goes down and speed goes up. By seeking first to understand, you get to the root of issues faster, you build lasting friendships, your Circle of Influence expands, and you feel understood more often. Empathic communication is powerful.

What I Want to Get

Think back on the principles of Habit 5 and the activities you have completed in this chapter. Identify one or two actions that would help you most as a first-year student. What results do you hope to Get as a result of doing these things?

WHAT I DO WELL	
WHAT I HOPE TO DO BETTER	
WHAT I HOPE TO GET BY DOING BETTER	

IN SUMMARY

In an interdependent world, good two-way communication skills are vital—particularly in emotional situations. Whether you are listening or sharing your ideas, the best tip is the same: Seek First to Understand, Then to Be Understood.

Your success as a student depends in large part on how you See, Do, and Get Habit 5.

Habit 5: Seek First to Understand, Then to Be Understood
Principles: Empathy and Clarity

	INEFFECTIVE STUDENTS	EFFECTIVE STUDENTS
What They *See*	• I want to seek first to be understood; if there's time I will seek to understand. • I will prescribe before I diagnose.	• I must seek first to understand before trying to be understood. • I need to diagnose before I prescribe.
What They *Do*	• Listen with the intent to reply. • Present ideas only from their own viewpoint. • Give insensitive feedback.	• Avoid poor listening habits. • Practice empathy by listening to content and feeling. • Present ideas from other people's points of view as well as their own. • Give and receive helpful feedback.
What They *Get*	• Emotionally draining relationships. • Surface-only solutions. • Long delays in getting to issues. • Misdiagnoses.	• Greater influence with others. • Understanding of complex, emotional problems. • Faster problem solving. • Strong relationships.

In conclusion, Habit 5: Seek First to Understand, Then to Be Understood is the key to learning, whether in school or in life. It's also the key to making meaningful connections to other people. Without Habit 5, you'll struggle to build friendships and family relationships, and you'll be ineffective in your career.

To begin improving your Habit 5 skills, try a few of the following Baby Steps. Then take a look at applying Habit 5 to the Academic Protip: "How to Make a Presentation."

COMING ATTRACTIONS

When you meet people who are vastly different from you, do you find them weird and threatening, or do the differences interest you? Up next, you'll discover ways to turn differences into advantages and conflicts into solutions. Flip ahead to learn more.

Baby Steps

1. Teach to Learn. Using the summary chart on page 218, teach the key concepts of Habit 5 to a friend, classmate, or family member within the next 48 hours.

2. If you don't see one of your parents often, visit or call and ask a few empathic questions: "What is the best thing going on in your life right now, Mom?" "Dad, tell me how your week went." Then listen and get to know your parent better.

3. Ask a few friends to explain their political views to you. Listen empathically, then restate their opinions to them. This exercise will help you truly understand different points of view. (Don't argue—just listen.)

4. Now, try sharing your political views, but take the other person's views into account first. See how it goes.

5. See how long you can hold eye contact with someone while he or she is talking to you.

6. The next time you attend a lecture, discipline yourself to listen for understanding. Note the key points your professor is trying to make. Afterwards, summarize the lecture to a friend or classmate. You'll listen more closely if you know you'll have to summarize it later.

7. Tell a friend you have an assignment to ask him or her, "What's on your mind these days?" (It's true; this is your assignment.) Then just listen. See how much you can learn about your friend's foremost concerns.

8. The next time you want to bury your feelings and not express how you feel because you're afraid you might offend someone, change tactics and express yourself in a responsible way. Use "I" messages instead of "You" messages.

9. Write a letter (or a long email) to someone you'd like to express yourself to. Use "I" messages. Respectfully make yourself understood.

10. Think of a person who would benefit if you were to share constructive feedback with him or her. Share it when the time is right.

    Name of person who could be helped by feedback: _____

Academic Protip

Many college classes require you to give some kind of presentation. I had to do a few presentations in college, and getting up in front of people was not my favorite thing. But you stand and deliver, and you learn how to get over yourself. Sometimes it's an informal presentation where you just report on something; other presentations are formal, with slides and a song-and-dance routine. In all these situations, the secret of success is to make a human connection with your audience. So we found someone who can do that. Professor Craig Escamilla from Texas is not only an oral-communication expert, but also a concert musician, so he knows all about audiences.

Craig Escamilla,
Lamar University

How to Make a Presentation

By Craig Escamilla,
Lamar University

Who loves to get up in front of everybody to make a big presentation?

Not many of us, I suspect.

But we do it all the time in college. Part of the college experience is helping others learn by presenting what you know—and the cool thing is, by presenting what you know, you learn it better. So a college presentation is not just repeating someone else's information. It's also contributing to learning.

Look at a presentation as an opportunity. Chances are you'll be giving presentations of one kind or another in your job, so now is a good time to learn how to do them well.

Most college students have the same questions about classroom presentations:

- What do I say?
- How do I get over feeling nervous?

Here are some tips that will help you with these questions.

What Do I Say?

Excite us from the beginning. A good presentation is actually a good discussion. You know how to start a discussion—with something new and interesting: a challenging question, a startling fact, a story we've never heard before.

Nearly all of the best presentations we see start with explaining the "gap" between how things are now and how they could be in the future.

Sometimes it helps to start with a picture—a photo, a graph, a chart. The best pictures surprise people with new information. If you're reporting on a chemistry experiment, start with before-and-after photos. If you're reporting on a new and better technology, put up a graph that shows how much better it is. Choose an image that tells the whole story of your presentation.

Make sure your purpose is clear—to you and to us. If you've been assigned to make a presentation, make sure you know exactly what the assignment is. Ask the instructor questions if you're not clear: "Why are we doing this? What do you expect from this? How will it be graded? How long do we have? Can we use slides and audio?"

When you present, tell us your purpose right up front. Why are you here? What do you want to accomplish? What do you want us to do with your information, if anything?

Preview coming attractions. Before a movie starts, you see trailers of upcoming movies. Do the same for us. Give us a preview at the beginning of the main points you're going to cover. If you have a three-part presentation, tell us what the three parts are before launching into them. It helps us stay with you if we know where you're going.

Tell a story. We're all wired to love stories. Good stories have a plot, and the most intriguing stories are mysteries. What's the "plot" of your presentation? What mystery are you cracking open for us? What problem are you solving?

And tell it like a story. Give it a setting ("Once upon a time…"): "Last month we were experimenting with…" "This week a question occurred to us…" "Yesterday we found that the world was not the way we thought it was…" You'll hook people right away, and help them see the "gap."

Be information-rich. Collect lots of interesting data, stories, and examples, then choose the best ones to present to us. Google is your best friend here. You'll find tons of material for your presentation. Just make sure it's accurate.

Stay simple. Follow a simple outline of introduction, body, and conclusion: "Here's what I think. Here are my three reasons for thinking this way. In summary, you can see why I think what I think."

If you use slides, keep them simple. A good rule of thumb is one idea per slide. Don't fill the screen with spreadsheets and huge blocks of text. A simple picture, a few key words, a short list—this is all you need. Try not to use any bullet points.

Involve us. The average attention span today is just a few seconds. You know how you fall asleep when your professors just lecture? Don't do that to your audience either.

Instead, ask a lot of questions and wait for us to answer you. When you put up a picture, ask us what we think about it before you tell us. When you

tell a story, don't just explain it—ask us what we get from it. When you give us a startling fact, ask what it means to us. Talk with us instead of at us.

Remember, a good presentation is a good discussion.

How Do I Get Over Feeling Nervous?

It's good to feel a little nervous when you're making a presentation. The adrenaline in your system wakes you up, makes you talk a little faster than usual, and generally fills you with energy. These are good things.

Obviously, you can also be too nervous. Your mouth dries up, you tremble, your skin flushes, and your mind can go blank. So how do you avoid freaking out when you give a presentation? Here are a few tips:

Prepare well. There's no substitute for knowing your stuff. If you don't do the upfront work to get ready, you'll have a well-deserved attack of nerves. Rehearse the presentation with a friend and get input. Rehearse it again. Rehearse it with your dog, or just talk to the wall if you have to.

Video yourself. Make a video of your rehearsal and you'll see how you come across. You might be surprised that you don't look as nervous as you think you do; this is a common reaction. Watch for distracting things like looking away from the audience, fidgeting with your hands, talking too fast, or dancing around aimlessly. Practice looking at us and keeping your movements under control.

Use notes. Even if you're well prepared, you might still feel jumpy. If referring to a few note cards will help, use them. Don't put your notes on your slides, but you can put notes under your slides and refer to them. (Try PowerPoint's Speaker View setting.) Just be careful not to read to your audience.

221

Handle questions calmly.
Sometimes someone asks a question that throws you. Stay calm and repeat the question. Pause and frame your answer. (Pauses are often dramatic.) Then give it your best shot. Ask if your answer satisfies us. If not, or if you just don't know how to answer, say so. Tell us you'll get back to us after you've done some research. Then do it.

Don't let questions scare you. Nobody expects you to know everything, and often a question is helpful if it leads you to more thinking and new ways of looking at the problem.

Be empathic. In the end, the key to presentation success is Habit 5: Seek First to Understand, Then to Be Understood. Ironically, the best presenters are often the best listeners. If you're an empathic presenter, you work at understanding what we, the audience, need from you. You ask questions, listen closely, and do your best to see the world as we see it, especially in your preparation.

Strangely enough, if you see things from our perspective, you'll be better at helping us see things from your perspective. Ask yourself, "What do these people need from me? How can I help them succeed? What kind of presentation will give them the most value?"

If you practice a little empathy and think about your audience a little more and about yourself a little less, you might find your nervousness slipping away. And we'll be a lot more interested in what you have to say.

Craig Escamilla is a management instructor in the College of Business at 15,000-student Lamar University, located in Beaumont, Texas. Craig has done executive coaching and strategic-planning work for a number of clients and, interestingly, served for several years as executive director of The Symphony of Southeast Texas.

6

Synergize
The Habit of Creative Cooperation

"Alone we can do so little; together we can do so much."

–HELEN KELLER

IN THIS CHAPTER, YOU WILL DISCOVER WAYS TO:

- Value differences.
- Build complementary teams.
- Go for the 3rd Alternative.
- Remove barriers to synergy.

Also, look for the Academic Protip...

- How to Read College Textbooks

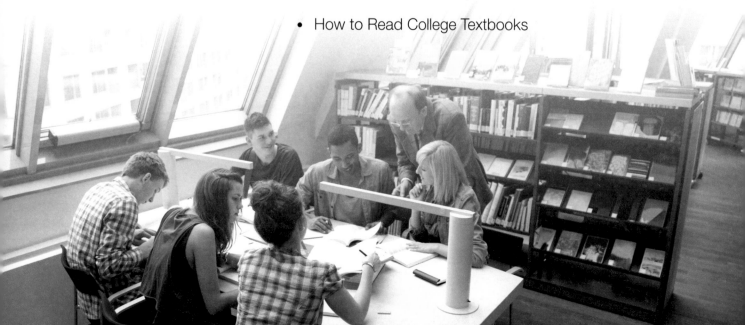

Habit 6:
Synergize

is the habit of working with others to create new and better solutions.

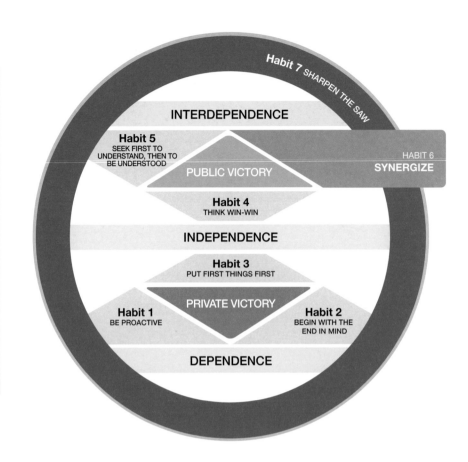

What I Wish
I'd Known in College

"Professors and their teaching assistants are there to help you get through the class and perhaps even love it. Take advantage of the TAs and any extra study sessions that the TA may oversee."
-Gina, San Jose City College

"I used my do-it-yourself-all-the-time attitude that I developed in high school for my first semester in college. It wasn't until the end of my freshman year that I realized... my peers were my 'go-to' resource for joint learning."
-Cathy, Cornell

"The importance of seeking out advice from experienced practitioners in their field of study and learning how they got where they are."
-Aaron, Weber State

"My college education has been crucial to living an examined life, and as such, has meant a great deal to me. Not only did I learn marketable job skills, but life skills as well, shaping and opening my mind. Under the guidance of amazing professors that really became mentors, my mind grew not only in knowledge, but also in a greater awareness of the world around me. I would not trade my years in college for anything. I am still well connected there and volunteer."
-Andrea, Utah State University

REAL CHOICES:
Going for Synergy

Sergey had been studying computer science at Stanford University for two years when he was assigned to help new students at spring orientation. That morning he was supposed to show a guy named Larry around the campus.

They did not hit it off. "We were both obnoxious," Sergey recalled later. Whatever Sergey said, Larry would make some snarky comment, and Sergey gave it right back to him. After a while they decided to make it a game: Each one would say something, and the other would automatically disagree.

"The sky sure is blue today."

"That's not blue. That's an illusion caused by the scattering of sunlight in the atmosphere." And so forth.

They had so much fun contradicting each other on everything that they became close friends. Both liked computers, but really they were opposites. Sergey was a party guy; Larry was "shy, private, and reserved." Sergey couldn't sit still. Larry was a patient nerd who had once built a printer out of LEGOS.

Sergey was also wildly curious and ambitious. He wanted to download the whole Internet to his brain so he would know everything—and then make a fortune from it. Larry, on the other hand, was kind of a math guy.

Thrown together that fall on a class project, they experimented with a new way to search the Internet. Up till then, you'd type in a word on a computer, and the Internet would report how many times that word showed up and where.

Larry's idea was to search not for words but for links. He figured the more often a website was linked to other websites, the more important it was. Using his approach, you could do a search and everything would come up on your screen in order of importance.

Sergey and Larry called their new program "BackRub" because it counted the number of links back to an original website. To run the program, they filled Larry's room with so many cheap computers that the university's network nearly shut down. So they moved into a girlfriend's garage.

Larry Page, left, and Sergey Brin, founders of Google.
Picture used with permission from Google, Inc.

Today only a few years later, more than a billion people each day use BackRub—now called Google®, the company Larry Page and Sergey Brin started in a dorm room. Millions of students now use Google to do their homework, find an apartment, buy a bike, or do research.

In college, you interact with a lot of people, many of them very different from you. You do projects together in study groups. You hear lots of different ideas and opinions in your classes. You're involved in class discussions. Like Sergey and Larry, you might get annoyed with each other.

Of course, you can isolate yourself—sit in the back of the classroom, avoid dealing with anyone at all, and get your diploma in the mail—some people do.

But if you practice Habit 6: Synergize, you learn to appreciate the people around you *because* they are different.

The term *synergize* comes from the Greek *syn-ergos*, meaning "working together." In a nutshell, Habit 6: Synergize is all about learning to value and work well with other people. Synergy is achieved when two or more people work together to create a better solution than either could have come up with alone. It's not "your way" or "my way" but a better way, a higher way. The whole is greater than the sum of its parts.

The two college guys who founded Google rarely agreed on anything. What would have happened if they always saw eye to eye on everything? What if they had exactly the same talents?

And they had opposite personalities. What if they had been alike—both introverts or both extroverts? Both nerds or both party guys?

They *needed* each other's strengths to build one of the world's greatest companies. Neither could have done it alone.

In this chapter, you'll learn how to Synergize in study groups, at work, at home, with roommates, in class settings, and in friendships.

Photo by Faine Greenwood.

PEOPLE WHO PRACTICE HABIT 6:

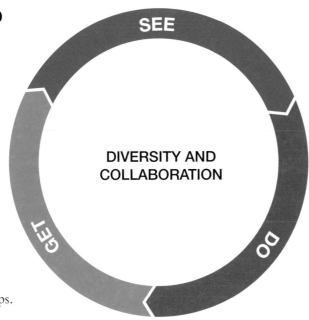

DIVERSITY AND COLLABORATION

SEE

- Together is better.
- Differences create opportunities.
- We can create a higher way that is better than your way or my way.

GET

- New and better ideas.
- Less to do "on your own."
- Better relationships.
- Greater learning.

DO

- Value differences.
- Build complementary teams.
- Go for the 3rd Alternative.
- Remove barriers to synergy.

PARADIGM OF SYNERGIZING

Habits 1 through 5 have prepared you for Habit 6: Synergize. Once you win the Private Victory, you have the direction and self-esteem you need to work well with others. And because you think win-win and seek to understand, you're ready to listen and do what's best for everyone.

The Habit 6 paradigm is simple: "Together is better." You know that life is a team sport. Interdependence is better than independence. If you have the Habit 6 paradigm, you believe that:

- You can do better in college working with others than working alone.
- You don't always need to have the best ideas.
- Other people's strengths can make up for your weaknesses, and vice versa.
- Working with others takes time but saves time in the long run.
- The best way is not "my way" or "your way," but a higher way we create together.

Or you can try to push your way through college on your own. You want to be alone or your ego gets in the way. You believe that:

- You can do it on your own—you don't need anyone.
- Your ideas are always better anyhow.
- People who think differently from you are weird.
- Involving others takes too much time; it gets too political.
- You want it one way, others want it another way, so you'll compromise—or just forget it.

Of course, some teams aren't helpful. For example, some athletic teams are stacked with individual talent, yet they lose regularly as a team. We say they "lack chemistry." We see couples who are great people individually, but together they bring out the worst in each other. In both cases, the whole is less than the sum of its parts. We call that negative synergy.

"Nobody ever achieved anything worthwhile alone."
—Jim Stuart, business consultant

I STILL THINK THERE'S A WAY WE CAN SYNERGIZE HERE.

227

On the other hand, positive synergy happens too. When have you been with a team or group that really clicked? It's a great feeling, isn't it? You've seen an underdog team pull together and win a championship. You've seen actors in a play or heard a singing group where they're just amazing together. In such cases, the whole is greater than the sum of its parts.

Synergy is a principle, a natural law. Two trees resist wind better if they mingle their roots. You can pick a lot more apples off high branches if you work with someone who sits on your shoulders. Just try tying your shoes with one hand, and you'll appreciate having *two* hands.

Here's the difference between negative and positive synergy:

NEGATIVE SYNERGY		POSITIVE SYNERGY
Hostility	$1 + 1 = -1, -5, -10$	$1 + 1 = 3, 10, 100,$ or more
Defensiveness	$1 + 1 = \frac{1}{2}$	
Compromise	$1 + 1 = 1\frac{1}{2}$	

If you and I are hostile to each other, we'll come up with nothing—or worse, be like the guy who wrecked his car to keep his brother from driving it.

Or we could compromise. People think that's a good thing, but it's actually a form of lose-lose. In a compromise, we both "give a little"—in other words, we both lose something. The whole is less than the sum of the parts.

Take two people and measure the weight each person can carry with one arm. Add up those numbers. Then ask the two people to interlock their arms and measure the weight they can carry together. You'll be stunned; the second number will be far higher than the first.

That's positive synergy.

And you can make it happen in teams, study groups, friendships, classrooms, families—anywhere people are trying to succeed together. But you can achieve it only if you truly believe that "together is better." If you believe other people are weird because they're different, or you think you don't have anything to learn from others, or you just hate group work, synergy does not happen. Synergy starts with the paradigms in your head.

WHAT STUDENTS WHO SYNERGIZE *DO*

Former Supreme Court Justice Oliver Wendell Holmes said, "Many ideas grow better when transplanted into another mind than in the one where they sprang up." One big purpose of college is to bounce ideas around with other students and tap the minds of professors, fellow students, and friends. If you practice Habit 6, you:

- Value differences.
- Build complementary teams.
- Go for the 3rd Alternative.
- Remove barriers to synergy.

Value Differences

Most of us don't like it when people disagree with us. If somebody says, "I disagree with you," what's your reaction?

You get defensive. You fire back or withdraw. You avoid that person. After all, disagreeing with you is hateful and wrong.

But if you practice Habit 6, you *love* it when someone disagrees with you. Let me explain.

Diversity is a beautiful thing. While I was in college, I moved to Washington, D.C., one summer to work for a U.S. Senator as part of a political science program. My roommate was a guy named Rob. Although we had a lot in common (we both liked school and we were both immature), we were very different. I was on the football team and he was in student government. I liked lifting weights and he liked to read. He was the smartest guy in his school and I wasn't.

I worried how things would turn out, but it was an incredible experience. Rob was the most intelligent guy I had ever known, and I learned a ton just listening to him. He talked about *The Brothers Karamazov* by Dostoyevsky, the idiosyncrasies of the U.S. Supreme Court members, and why you can't think beyond your vocabulary. Meanwhile, he didn't know a thing about getting into shape, so I taught him everything I knew about lifting weights, agility training, and eating well. By valuing and tapping into each other's strengths, we both grew and became lifelong friends.

When people hear the word "diversity," they typically think about race and gender. But there is so much more to it: language, upbringing, class, religious beliefs, experiences, age, food, music, dress styles, learning styles, lifestyles, and on and on. When you think about all the different ways we can be different, we are each a "minority of one." So we have three ways to deal with diversity: We can shun it, tolerate it, or celebrate it.

The Shunner. If you're a shunner, you think people with different politics, religion, or tastes in music are just wrong. They're strange and inferior. You avoid them, make fun of them, or even bully them. To you, diversity is a threat or a weakness.

The Tolerator. Tolerators believe everyone has the right to be different. "You do your thing and I'll do mine. You leave me alone and I'll leave you alone." You respect the fact that people are different, but you don't see any value in those differences.

> "He who cannot put his thoughts on ice should not enter into the heat of dispute."
>
> —Friedrich Nietzsche, German philosopher

229

The Celebrator. If you're a celebrator, you're excited about differences. You know you can learn a lot from different opinions and ways of life. You're mature enough to know you don't have to go along with those differences; you can be curious and even delighted by what others bring to the party.

People with the Habit 6 paradigm realize that if two people have the same opinion, one of them is unnecessary. They celebrate diversity.

So where do you fall? Do you respect people with different beliefs, or do you think they're brainwashed? Can you listen to a teacher you don't agree with and still learn from that person? Can you get excited about having a roommate who isn't very much like you at all?

What about economics? Do you think most rich kids are spoiled and arrogant, or do you look down on the poor, believing they bring it on themselves? These are tough questions. Most of us are biased in one way or another whether we know it or not.

Do you really believe there is strength in differences?

What if Sergey Brin and Larry Page were the same kind of person? Would Google be what it is? Would there even *be* a Google?

Let me tell you about A.B. Combs Elementary School in Raleigh, North Carolina. It used to be a failing school: low scores, lack of discipline, falling enrollment. It was in a multiethnic neighborhood with children from dozens of countries, many of them struggling with English. (The 800 students at A.B. Combs come from 50 cultures from around the world and speak more than 20 languages.) Some people blamed the school's weaknesses on its "diversity"—a recipe for racial strife, fights, and discrimination.

But just a few years later, A.B. Combs was named the number-one magnet school in America. Now scores are high, discipline referrals are way down, and enrollment has hit the ceiling; a waiting list is in place. What happened?

A.B. Combs started to teach the 7 Habits to students.

Habit 6: Synergize quickly became a favorite. (Kindergartners love to say, "Synergize.") The students and teachers began to see diversity as a huge advantage, not a weakness. Now they actively celebrate their diversity with songs, national flags in the halls, art on the walls, an annual international festival—but most of all in the way they treat each other.

A.B. Combs' success is not just about cultural diversity. Starting with kindergartners, teachers identify the unique talents and personality strengths of each child. From Day 1, students are told they are leaders—leaders of music, dance, sports, photography, math, science, or even friendliness, courtesy, and safety.

They find ways to showcase their talents every day, and two or three times a year educators and business people from around the world come to witness this school in action. All students—not just a gifted few—are treated as important. Their differences are valued, not suppressed.

Make it a habit to value the differences in people. For a start, look at your circle of friends. What strengths do you see in them? When was the last time you told them you admire their unique talents? If you want to make big deposits in their Emotional Bank Accounts, compliment them in front of others: "Hey, does everyone know what a great guitar player Rick is?" or "I'm glad Melissa's in our group because she's so good at graphic design."

Another way to value diversity is to become familiar with the theory of multiple intelligences, as described in the following activity.

> "Allowances can always be made for your friends to disagree with you. Disagreement, vehement disagreement is healthy. Debate is impossible without it. Evil does not question itself."
>
> —Craig Ferguson, talk-show host

Mural at A. B. Combs Elementary School

Just How Intelligent Are You?

One form of diversity we often overlook is the different ways people learn. Howard Gardner proposes at least eight different types of intelligence:

1. **Spatial:** Ability to judge spacing. This category includes artists, designers, architects, and puzzle solvers.
2. **Linguistic:** Ability with words, written and spoken. Authors, storytellers, public speakers, teachers, and linguists exhibit this type of intelligence.
3. **Logical-Mathematical:** Ability to deal with logic, numbers, and reasoning (a lot like IQ). Scientists, physicists, engineers, doctors, and economists are found here.
4. **Kinesthetic:** Coordination, sense of timing, good reflexes, hand dexterity. Athletes, dancers, surgeons, musicians, builders, soldiers, and actors demonstrate this intelligence.
5. **Musical:** Sensitivity to sounds, tones, rhythms, and pitch. This category includes instrumentalists, singers, composers, and conductors.
6. **Interpersonal:** Sensitivity to others' moods and motives; the ability to cooperate, get along, and be "team players." These people like discussion and debate. Salespeople, politicians, and social workers excel in these areas.
7. **Intrapersonal:** Ability to self-reflect and decipher one's own feelings. These people are internally calm and can work alone. Psychologists, lawyers, writers, and theologians fit well here.
8. **Naturalist:** Ability to relate information to one's surroundings. This category includes naturalists, farmers, and gardeners.

Carefully consider the intelligences above. Identify your top one to three intelligences, starting with your strongest.

1.

2.

3.

Consider your strongest intelligence. At what age did you first notice it? Write down a specific situation that showed your intelligence in this area.

_____

_____

_____

Now think about a close friend. Which types of intelligence does he or she possess that you value? Write down a specific way he or she has displayed one of these intelligences.

_____

_____

_____

Of course it's hard to appreciate—much less celebrate—people's differences without learning what they are, so get to know the people around you. You'll like college better, and a diverse group of friends might even help you succeed in college. Listen to Ken, a student at Penn State:

> *I did not go to school on a scholarship, so working during the school year was essential to pay the bills. I started working in food service. At a big school, the fear is that you are just an isolated "number." Working in the different food-serving areas on campus put me in touch with not only a diverse student population, but also a lot of the local people who held the permanent jobs. So I had a lot of acquaintances from all over the place, and I got to know the local-area people's cultures and happenings. I attended a few of their festivals. They became my friends. I never felt alone or isolated. I felt like I was an integral part of a larger community and valued. It helped me to appreciate the school more, and kept me sane in the process.*

Like Ken, you'll find that college is about studying and learning "people" as well as "subjects." If you want to practice Habit 6:

- Get to know people from different cultures.
- Sit by a different person in class each week.
- Join study groups with people different from you.
- Go to plays, concerts, art exhibits, and games you don't normally attend.
- Go to the library and skim publications on many different subjects.
- Go to campus lectures that have nothing to do with your major.
- Find out who the best teachers are and attend their classes.
- Before criticizing or rejecting other people's ideas, seek to understand them. Listen empathically. Put aside your biases.

> "Be genuinely interested in everyone you meet, and everyone you meet will be genuinely interested in you."
>
> —Rasheed Ogunlaru, British author and life coach

DID YOU KNOW?
The Six "Gains" of Diversity

Aaron Thompson, professor of sociology at Eastern Kentucky University and coauthor of *Diversity and the College Experience,* says that diversity benefits you in six ways. It:

1. **Expands global awareness.** College is a great opportunity to get to know people from diverse groups and cultures.
2. **Enhances social development.** Hanging out only with people just like you is boring.
3. **Prepares students for future career success.** You'll need to be comfortable with all kinds of people if you're going to succeed on the job.
4. **Increases your knowledge base.** Research shows that we learn more from people who are different from us than from people who are the same.
5. **Promotes creative thinking.** You're more creative when you hear things from many different points of view.
6. **Enhances self-awareness.** You see the panorama of the world around you and get a better feeling for your place in it.

For sure, valuing differences doesn't mean agreeing with them. I think it's interesting that Sergey Brin and Larry Page constantly disagreed but were amazingly synergistic together. Maybe it was because they disagreed.

Still, you have to use good judgment. It's one thing to value differences and another to adopt different values, especially unprincipled values. Leslie learned this lesson firsthand. She was lonely her first year, so she joined a sorority as a way to make friends. Once pledged, however, she found everybody was into fashion, popularity, gossiping, and drinking, none of which was her thing.

At first, Leslie felt like an outcast in the sorority, even though she tried her best to fit in. She started dressing the way the others dressed, talking the way they talked, and partying the way they partied. This went on for about a month, but then one night Leslie went out with her sorority sisters and thought, "They look like sleazebags. Is that how I look?"

So she left the sorority house and made different friends in her classes—people who had values like hers but were diverse in other ways. Her new friends introduced her to all kinds of new foods, music, and films, which helped Leslie grow tremendously.

Tap into the strengths of others. Have the humility of Ralph Waldo Emerson, who said, "Every individual is in some way my superior." As American advertising director, William Bernbach said, "An idea can turn to dust or magic, depending on the talent that rubs against it." Let your mind rub up against other bright minds. Diversity is beautiful—so go find some.

> "Be a Columbus to whole new continents and worlds within you. Opening new channels, not of trade, but of thought."
>
> —Henry David Thoreau

AND THEN BLITZEN HERE SAID, "YOU KNOW, GUYS. IF WE *REALLY* WORK AS A TEAM, IT'S EIGHT AGAINST ONE."

LESSON ON LEADERSHIP: Master Teachers

One of the great things about college is the incredible variety of talents, opinions, and expertise among faculty members. A student named Mary Ann has a great suggestion:

I was a music major. Music consumed my focus. I spent hours upon hours in practice rooms going through my music over and over. I studied the lives of great musicians. I lived music. The music building was a huge part of my world.

Then I got some advice from my brother-in-law. He was very successful in business, and said he had one suggestion for me while attending college. He said, "Find out who the great minds are, then take a class from them. Don't worry about what topic they teach. It may have nothing to do with your major. Soak in what they say. Observe how they teach and interact with people. You are bound to learn something."

I have done as he said, and his advice proved to be mind-stretching and invaluable. I took a history class from a professor who I heard was great. She was a master storyteller. I learned so much that I took another from her. Her ideas opened new ways of thinking to me.

How can you learn from the great minds on your campus? How could it help you to take a class from a master teacher who isn't in your major field of study?

233

Build Complementary Teams

Have you ever been part of a great team—drama, sports, music, or something else? Was it a service club, a church group, student government, a study group, a school committee, or even just your family? What did it feel like to be on a great team? What made it great?

It was the people, wasn't it? Together, you did things no one could have done alone. A great team is complementary—that is, each person's talents complement everyone else's talents and make up for any weaknesses. ("Complement" means to complete. Don't confuse it with "compliment," which means to say nice things about someone.)

When I started my M.B.A. program, people told me I'd never succeed without a good study group. "What do you suggest?" I asked. The answer: "A group with different strengths." So I joined a really diverse group. One member was a genius about operational issues, another was great with numbers, and another had sales and marketing experience. I was good at bringing food. All these minds working together made one very smart study group, and we all did well in school. We enjoyed each other so much that we met nearly every weeknight for two years.

Typically, you'll have five types of people on a team, and all of them are important:

- **Plodders** are sure and steady; they stick to a job until it's done.
- **Followers** support the leaders. If they hear a great idea, they run with it.
- **Innovators** are the creative "idea" people. They offer the sparks.
- **Harmonizers** cooperate well, providing unity and synergy.
- **Show-offs** are fun to work with, but they can be difficult sometimes. They often bring the diverse thinking you need to succeed together.

DID YOU KNOW?
Why Geese of a Feather Flock Together

You can find complementary teams everywhere in nature.

Did you ever wonder why geese fly in a V formation? Scientists have discovered why, and it's fascinating. By flying in formation, the whole flock can go 71 percent farther than if each bird flies alone.

When a goose flaps its wings, it creates an updraft for the goose that follows. When the lead goose tires, it rotates to the back and allows another goose to take the lead. The honking of the geese conveys information to the leader: "Let's stop to eat" or "Let's all aim for that golfer!"

When a goose falls out of formation, it immediately feels the resistance of flying alone and gets back in place. When a sick or wounded goose falls out of formation, two geese follow to help and protect it.

Good teamwork, I'd say.

Some people like to try to go at it alone. But think about it: Presidents of nations surround themselves with a cabinet. CEOs create boards of diverse people with assorted strengths. If the smartest people aim for diversity, why not do it as a college student?

Elena went back to finish nursing school after several years of work as a certified nursing assistant. At first, the program intimidated her somewhat.

The first day, I met Lisa, about my age and in a similar situation. But she was totally different mentally. She's very open and free, where I'm more of a detail person. She talked about what she was learning about nursing from reading Leonardo da Vinci's diaries, and I'd be telling her about the right way to put a patient in a bathtub. Most of the students thought Lisa was up in the clouds, but I was fascinated. And she liked my practical way of thinking. We really hit it off and studied together most of the time.

One semester we took the same class from different professors, and they were so different we'd laugh about it. Were we really studying the same subject? We would catch different things from the lectures. Lisa gave me her professor's big ideas and I would add my little insights, and when we put them together, we were the top students in both classes.

You can build a complementary team whenever you're pulling together a study group, selecting roommates, deciding on project partners, picking an intramural team—or choosing someone to marry.

Let me make one more suggestion about complementary teams: Pull together a personal "board of directors" for yourself. What do I mean by your own board of directors?

Recruit for yourself a team of advisors who have a lot of different strengths and your best interests at heart. You might choose a professor who can help you with your college plan, a financial advisor, a faith leader, a confidant who can counsel you on your love life, someone who cares about you unconditionally (Mom), and so forth.

> "The people on your personal board of directors are not only useful for helping you move up, they are also helpful in correcting you when you need a sanity check. EVERYONE should have a PBOD… If you don't have a network like this, get one. You will go nuts without it."
>
> —Holly Goodwin, MIT

Your Personal Board of Directors

Identify 10 people who can advise you on how to get the most out of college. They don't have to be personal friends—they can be a student advisor, professor, librarian, or doctor. Here are some ideas:

CATEGORY	PERSON
Financial	
Health/nutrition/diet	
Academics/graduation	
Career	
Social/emotional	
Work	
Friend supporter	
Family supporter	
Faith leader	
Other	

> "I am indebted to my father for living, and to my teacher for living well."
>
> —Alexander the Great

These people might never meet each other, but you could get two or three people together to advise you from time to time. It could be casual, like over lunch. If you're trying to decide on a major, you could get your mom and dad on the phone with your girlfriend by your side to talk it through. If you're feeling depressed, you might get your two best friends together to help you work through it. There is wisdom in councils.

A wise old friend once told me that if I got my parents to advise me on every major decision in life, I would never make a serious mistake. It's the best advice I ever got. People who care about and love you can give you perspective on the tough choices.

Of course, before you can build a team of people whose strengths complement yours, you need to know what your strengths are.

Many surveys measure your competencies—your skills. Just as important are your character strengths, such as wisdom, courage, and social intelligence.

What is unique about your personal character? What "signature strengths" of character can you build your life on?

Find out by taking the Values in Action Inventory (VIA).

The VIA asks you questions that assess your character strengths. It then gives you your top five "signature strengths" in order, from strongest to weakest. You'll be fascinated by the results.

To take a free survey of your own personal strengths, go to viacharacter.org.

Go for the 3ʳᵈ Alternative

Unfortunately, instead of using the strengths of others to build on our own strengths, we're used to thinking in terms of two sides: my strengths against yours. We are 2ⁿᵈ Alternative thinkers. It's "my team" against "your team." It's my party, my country, my clique, my opinion, or my side against yours.

This two-sided way of looking at things infects all of our thinking. We see our lives as "pass or fail," "win or lose," "go big or go home." Surveys ask, "Are you for the Republican or the Democratic solution? Do you favor or oppose legalizing drugs? Is it right or wrong to use animals for research? Are you for us or against us?"

But life is not just a choice between A and B. We always have a better way—a 3ʳᵈ Alternative.

Osman came from Pakistan to study electrical engineering, but he didn't understand how expensive it was to live in the U.S.A. He had no money. Soon he had to clean toilets and give blood just to get by.

Looking for ways to save money, Osman noticed that students were selling used textbooks online for a lot less than the college bookstore was charging. But still they cost too much.

He and his friend Phumbhra were always kicking around ideas. One day when they were watching a show on Netflix, a 3ʳᵈ Alternative hit them: "Netflix rents movies. Why don't we rent textbooks?"

Many students don't need their textbooks after the course is over, but bookstores buy them back at only a fraction of the original price. And strapped college students have a tough time paying more than $100 for some books.

Osman and Phumbhra realized they could rent books for only a fraction of their cost and make money off them indefinitely. That was the beginning of a healthy online business, featuring more than a million textbooks for rent. Many of the books come back highlighted, but Osman thinks that makes them more valuable. The renters "want somebody else to do the work," he says.

Osman got his degree and now runs his own businesses, expanding them every day. It all started with classic 3ʳᵈ Alternative thinking. (Schmit, "Chegg CEO Rashid")

"The really good idea is always traceable back quite a long way, often to a not very good idea which sparked off another idea that was only slightly better, which somebody else misunderstood in such a way that they then said something which was really rather interesting."

—John Cleese, actor

Instead of throwing their hands up over a hopeless dilemma, Osman and Phumbhra found a solution that was better than anything they had thought of before. Why? *Because they were looking for it.* As this story shows, there's always a 3rd Alternative.

Going for a 3rd Alternative requires a lot of humility. People who insist that their way is the best way won't get there. Their sights are too limited, and they can't see the future because their pride gets in the way.

If you practice Habit 6, you're always looking for 3rd Alternatives, even when you're making decisions like where to go on vacation or how to decorate your apartment.

MAJOR BREAKTHROUGH IN THE INVENTION OF THE CHAIR

WAIT A MINUTE, GUYS. WHAT IF WE PUT THE LEGS ON THE BOTTOM?

But going for the 3rd Alternative is most useful when dealing with real problems—like a study group where no one agrees on anything, or when you and your significant other have a big disagreement.

Here are the steps to a 3rd Alternative:

Step 1: Define the problem. Scientist and inventor Charles F. Kettering observed: "A problem well stated is a problem half-solved." Make sure you understand the real problem. Suppose a professor won't let you sign up for her class because she says there's no room.

"When you say there's no room in the class for another student, do you mean there aren't enough chairs? If so, could I bring my own chair?"

Step 2: Listen to their views. Listen empathically to others' views first. Let everybody talk until they feel "heard." You have two goals: (1) Make sure you understand everyone's best thinking, and (2) make sure everyone feels understood. Include everyone, because some people have trouble speaking up. Give them a chance to share their ideas.

Step 3: Share your views. Feel free to share your best thinking with others. Because you have listened to them, they might influence your views. Expand on their ideas. Make sure you feel understood.

Step 4: Brainstorm. Now that you've heard everyone's best thinking, ask this question: "Is everybody willing to look for an even better idea—one nobody has thought of yet?" Then let everybody brainstorm, which means generating ideas without stopping to judge or reject them. You don't want to kill creative thinking by shutting people down. Let the creative juices flow.

> "I never miss a good chance to shut up."
>
> —Will Rogers, humorist

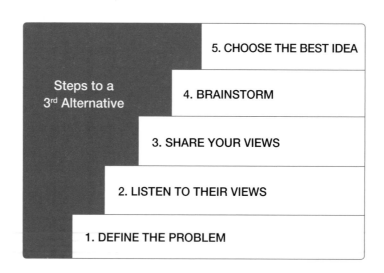

Steps to a 3rd Alternative

5. CHOOSE THE BEST IDEA
4. BRAINSTORM
3. SHARE YOUR VIEWS
2. LISTEN TO THEIR VIEWS
1. DEFINE THE PROBLEM

Step 5: Choose the best idea. You'll be surprised by the great ideas that come from synergy. Once people feel heard, they come up with amazing insights. Now you need to synthesize and form a solution. Consider all of the ideas that everyone has shared. Build on them. Take bits and pieces from different ideas and put them together in new ways. Eventually, a superior idea or solution will emerge, and you'll know when you find it because it will be exciting.

Talking Stick

LESSON ON LEADERSHIP: The Talking Stick

When visiting South Africa years ago, Stephen R. Covey was first introduced to the "Talking Stick." No, the stick did not talk. What it did was allow others to talk.

After Stephen had given a presentation on empathy and synergy, some tribal leaders said to him, "Stephen, we already practice a lot of your principles."

To show him, they presented him with one of their Talking Sticks. They told him that whenever a serious or controversial problem came up, the tribal council would gather to try and solve it.

They would pass the Talking Stick around. Whoever held the stick could talk until he felt satisfied that everyone understood his point of view. Then he would pass the stick to the next person.

Once everyone was heard, they would brainstorm ideas for solving the problem.

Stephen was impressed. From that day, he carried the Talking Stick wherever he went and used it to teach the principles of empathy and synergy. Kings, presidents of nations, and CEOs of great corporations have held the Talking Stick in their hands during important meetings.

So let's try going for a 3rd Alternative on a simple problem. Suppose you have a roommate, and the small refrigerator in your apartment isn't big enough for the two of you. You feel like you need a crowbar to get anything in or out. Your roommate feels the same way, but neither of you wants to give up space.

Step 1: Define the problem.

You: "Our refrigerator is not working for me. I can't fit anything in it. I can't find anything in it. I just found my jar of salsa, and it has all kinds of things growing in it. I had totally forgotten I even had it because it was buried behind so many other things. Can we please do something about it?"

Step 2: Listen to their views.

Roommate: "I don't like it either. But I think you're creating the problem with all your bulky bottles of mayonnaise, mustard, and ketchup. They take up tons of space, and it takes two months for you to go through one of them. Two of them have been

239

almost empty for weeks, so it's mostly air taking up all the space. How about buying the small bottles like I do? That would save a bunch of space."

You: "That would save some space, but…"
(Wait—don't get defensive!)

Roommate: "Yeah, half the time your stuff spoils before you get to the bottom of a jar and you end up throwing it out."

You: "Okay, so you think my bottles are taking up too much space, and they're mostly empty or rotten anyway. So I shouldn't buy them—I should get small bottles like you." (You're not being sarcastic. You're just showing you understand the other viewpoint.)

Roommate: "Exactly."

Step 3: Share your views.

(Now that you've shown you understand, calmly share your opinion.)

You: "I think there's a big problem with your milk. I don't drink milk, and it seems you usually have two half-gallon jugs in there at a time. They take up more than half the space, and I think I should have equal space. Also, my food budget is really tight. I've priced the large bottles of things like mayonnaise, and they cost a lot less than the small bottles you buy."

Step 4: Brainstorm.

You: "Maybe there's a better way to do this—a way we haven't thought of."

Roommate: "Well, what about this: We could buy bigger bottles and split the cost."

You: "Hmm. That way we'd have half the number of bottles in the fridge, and we wouldn't have to keep checking to see whose label is on which bottle."

Step 5: Choose the best idea.

Roommate: "Well, yeah. That's a lot better. Half the bottles, less chance of stuff going bad."

You: "Works for me. Half the cost and no more gross stuff in the fridge."

That was a simple example, I know, but do you see how it works? Instead of starting a big fight over fridge space, you and your roommate save money and your food stays fresh longer.

Tougher problems involving more people might be harder. But you can take the same steps to get to the 3rd Alternative with any problem—and the synergistic solution will excite you. It's almost always better than anything you could come up with alone.

"It was impossible to get a conversation going. Everybody was talking too much."

—Yogi Berra, baseball player

LESSON ON LEADERSHIP:
Students Synergize for a Cause

Going for the 3rd Alternative is not only more productive but also more enjoyable. Here's an example from a small university in California.

Students in the College of Law were required to work for free with low-income clients in a community law center. One day, a Latino baker named Rafael came in for help. He had been unjustly fired from his job. The students took the issue to court, but they lost the case. Rafael's job was gone.

When the word about Rafael got around the campus, students from many departments came together to look for a 3rd Alternative. Business students volunteered to help him open his own bakery. Finance students helped him prepare a business plan and obtain a small loan. Language students volunteered to interpret for him. Even law-school alumni got involved in supervising the legal and business contracts.

Soon Rafael didn't need his old job back; he was ready to stand on his own. Genuine synergy across every department of the university helped Rafael make a new life for himself.

Have you ever experienced positive outcomes from working in a group? Describe that situation to a classmate, including how it made you feel, and how listening and brainstorming helped the group function more smoothly.

Here's one caution in going for the 3rd Alternative: Don't turn the discussion into an all-day gripe session. You'll know you've arrived at the 3rd Alternative when everybody:

- Has a firm change of heart.
- Feels new energy and excitement.
- Sees things a new way.
- Feels the relationship has been transformed.
- Loves the solution—a better solution than anyone could come up with alone.

Remove Barriers to Synergy

I can hear you say, "Sean, this stuff about synergy makes sense, but people don't really do it. My study group doesn't work. Some of the members of the group are lazy, some have big egos and want to take all the credit, and some don't have any idea how to get along. And those are the good ones."

Of course, you can't control other people, but you can work within your Circle of Influence to take down some of the barriers to synergy.

The great French scholar Max Ringelmann once did an experiment with his students. He asked each one to pull on a rope attached to a scale so he could measure the weight one person could pull. After he added the individual scores, he asked the students to line up and pull on the rope together.

To his surprise, the team total was far less than the combined total of the individual scores.

What had happened?

Ringelmann concluded that the students in the second experiment just weren't trying very hard. When you're in a group, nobody can tell how much effort you're putting out, so you tend to put out less effort than you would if you were working alone. Today this is called the Ringelmann Effect, or *social loafing*.

As a college football player, I saw a lot of social loafing in practice. For example, while running 100-yard wind sprints, I'd notice that everyone would start to slack off at the same time (me too). We sort of knew if we all loafed together, the coaches wouldn't notice. It was a bad habit, but it was fun to see what we could get away with.

But from time to time, one guy would ignore the unspoken cues to take it easy and would sprint as hard and fast as possible. He'd beat everyone else by 10 yards and, suddenly, the rest of us were exposed as social loafers. We'd feel guilty and pick up the pace on the next sprint.

This strategy also works with your study group or group projects. If someone else is loafing, give it all you've got and watch what happens. Most people are decent; they sense the unfairness of what is happening, and they pick up the pace if you do it first.

Besides social loafing, you might run into these roadblocks to synergy:
- Ego
- No Private Victory
- Win-lose thinking
- Cliques

Ego. Synergy requires humility. A team of "me, me, me" players produces negative synergy. People who think their ideas are always the best hold back progress. Prejudice stops up people's creative juices. You need to focus on people's strengths, not their weaknesses.

Look into yourself. It takes humility to say, "I may not have the best answers," "Our team isn't up to this job—we need someone to help us out," or "I apologize. I was wrong." Model this humility for others.

No Private Victory. Another roadblock to synergy is insecurity. If you're insecure, it's difficult to be open to the opinions of others. You feel threatened by differences or other people's strengths and successes. Getting to synergy requires you to be vulnerable. When you're brainstorming with others, for example, you can't predict where the conversation may end up. You have to be open to anything.

That is why people who don't win a Private Victory have difficulty with synergizing. Private Victories always precede Public Victories. If you struggle with getting along with other people or being a team player, win a Private Victory first. Take charge of your life and stop being a victim (Habit 1). Figure out

YOU KNOW GUYS, IF YOU REALLY THINK ABOUT IT, WE HAVE MORE IN COMMON THAN WE DO DIFFERENCES!

what you want to do with your life and what you stand for (Habit 2), and get organized (Habit 3). This will increase your personal security and prepare you to Synergize and win Public Victories.

Win-Lose Thinking. When people think win-lose, they get trouble instead of synergy. That's why win-win thinking has to come before synergy.

I love LEGOs, and the LEGO Corporation fascinates me. It's one of the most trusted companies in the world. I believe their strength comes from synergy. At LEGO, people have a Habit 4 mindset; they Think Win-Win.

For 100 years, LEGO sold bricks only in packaged sets, like the popular *Star Wars* collection. But many customers (mostly adults who were children at heart) pleaded with the company to let them design their own sets and order the pieces they needed online. In response, LEGO created a software product to make it possible. The problem was that customers could buy only prepackaged sets, not individual pieces.

Then curious things happened. Somebody began hacking LEGO's computer systems, stealthily rewriting the program code so they could order parts individually.

LEGO caught on quickly, and the company lawyers were ready to go to war against the hackers. But LEGO is a highly effective company.

Instead of going after the hackers, the LEGO people thought, "If these guys want to purchase individual pieces so much that they're willing to risk being caught and punished, they must really, really like LEGOs. Maybe we should approach them and make them our friends instead of our enemies. Perhaps they have ideas we can use."

So in a spirit of win-win, they met with the hackers, seeking first to understand and valuing the different opinions. The hackers were invited to join LEGO's advisory board for product development. Now these volunteers design many of LEGO's products. The sour situation turned into a sweet display of synergistic thinking.

That's what successful people do: They thrive on other people's good ideas. They're abundant—they don't get jealous when someone else's better idea wins. So help everybody to think abundantly—starting with yourself.

Cliques. Too often people become part of a clique of some kind that ostracizes other people who don't fit in. Cliques attract people who think, act, and talk alike about money, popularity, race, dress, residence, interests, and so on.

In college, I experienced all kinds of cliques. I remember one group of popular girls who all had money and were fashionable. I don't think they realized how they were behaving, but they made it clear that girls with less money or fashion sense were lesser beings and didn't belong to their little club.

You'd hope that cliques would not last after high school, but they do. Having a tight group of friends isn't wrong, but excluding others for superficial reasons is absolutely wrong. Synergy cannot exist where cliques prevail. I encourage you to get to know all kinds of people and choose friends from all walks of life.

LEGO Headquarters

Photo reprinted with permission from LEGO Group.

"There never were in the world two opinions alike, no more than two hairs or two grains; the most universal quality is diversity."

—Michel de Montaigne, French philosopher

Barriers to Synergy

Identify specifically what your barriers to synergy might be. Write them in the barrier wall below.

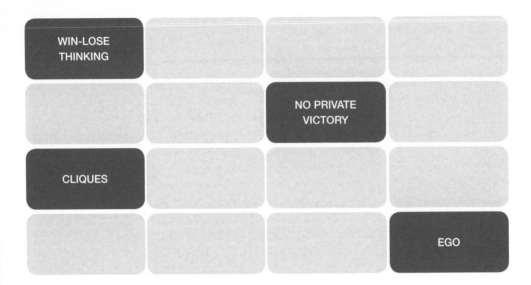

WIN-LOSE THINKING

NO PRIVATE VICTORY

CLIQUES

EGO

Now come up with some ideas for taking down those barriers:

GET

WHAT SYNERGIZING GETS YOU

If you think about it, nobody ever accomplishes anything worthwhile all alone. Even the Albert Einsteins and "lone geniuses" of the world freely admit they couldn't do what they do without standing on the shoulders of the giants who came before them. Teams run businesses. Teams win elections. Teams even write books. (Just ask some authors. If they don't admit it, they're lying.) And the list goes on. Accomplishing something worthwhile depends on synergy.

Synergy is the ultimate habit—the point of all the other habits. It's the reward, the delicious fruit of effective living. (If you doubt that, think about the synergy that happens in a happy marriage or family.)

Here's what synergy gets you:

- Effective solutions to your problems.
- Less work for you because everybody's contributing.
- Better relationships.
- Greater learning, and more appreciation for the wealth of diversity in the people around you.

What I Want to Get

Reflect on the principles and concepts of Habit 6: Synergize. Think of ways you can apply each See and Do of Habit 6 (listed in the summary that follows) to any groups you belong to or any relationships you want to work on. What results do you hope to Get as you better live this habit?

	WHICH SEES OR DOS CAN I APPLY?	WHAT RESULTS DO I HOPE TO GET?
GROUP 1		
GROUP 2		
RELATIONSHIP 1		
RELATIONSHIP 2		

IN SUMMARY

Synergy happens when two or more people produce something greater than either could alone. Synergy is an essential paradigm and process for thriving in today's interdependent, high-touch, global economy.

In this chapter, we learned what synergy is and isn't. To summarize:

SYNERGIZING IS NOT...	SYNERGIZING IS...
Tolerating differences.	Valuing differences.
Working independently.	Working interdependently.
Thinking you're always right.	Staying open-minded.
Compromising (1 + 1 = 1½).	Finding new and better ways (1 + 1 = 3, 10, 100, or more).
Aimless brainstorming.	Getting results.

Habit 6: Synergize

Principles: Diversity and Collaboration

The key concepts of synergizing are described in the See-Do-Get table below.

	INEFFECTIVE STUDENTS	EFFECTIVE STUDENTS
What They *See*	• It's my way, or no way; alone is better. • Different points of view are wrong. • My way is the only way.	• Together is better. • Differences create opportunities. • We can create a higher way that is better than your way or my way.
What They *Do*	• Do it their way; go it alone. • Disregard people's opinions that are different from theirs. • Shut their office doors. • Go for compromise.	• Value differences. • Build complementary teams. • Go for the 3rd Alternative. • Remove barriers to synergy.
What They *Get*	• Compromise at best. • Negative synergy. • Increasing problems. • Frustrated team members.	• *Effective* solutions to your problems. • Less work for you because everybody's contributing. • Better relationships. • Greater learning, and appreciation for the wealth of diversity in the people around you.

Now that you know more about the paradigms and habits of synergy, you will discover many opportunities to apply the principles.

Try some of the Baby Steps on the next page to experiment with synergy. I also recommend following the advice in the Academic Protip at the end of this chapter: "How to Read College Textbooks."

COMING ATTRACTIONS

A car has four tires. If one tire is out of balance, all four tires wear unevenly. It's the same with people. Our lives are made up of four parts, and if one part is out of balance, everything goes bad. That's why the habit of renewal and balance is so important. It's up next!

Baby Steps

1. Teach to Learn. Using the chart on page 246, teach the key concepts of Habit 6 to a friend, classmate, or family member within the next 48 hours.

2. The next time you disagree with someone, try taking the steps to a 3rd Alternative.

3. When you meet someone with a disability or impairment, go out of your way to get acquainted.

4. Discuss a challenge you're having with a friend or a person you trust. Ask for his or her insights. Bounce ideas around. See if you can come up with new and better ideas for dealing with your challenge.

5. Do you know someone whose background is totally different from yours? What can you learn from that person? Find out.

6. Brainstorm with friends and come up with something fun, new, and different to do this weekend, instead of doing the same thing again and again.

7. What's your biggest barrier to synergy—social loafing, ego, win-lose thinking, prejudice, or ignorance? For one whole day, try letting down that barrier and see what happens.

8. Choose one professor you admire and would like to get to know. Go outside your comfort zone and visit that professor sometime this week.

9. Go online and read about the same topic in at least three or four different publications. What's different about them? What do they emphasize? What do they have in common?

10. Go online and read about a major political or social conflict in the world today. Brainstorm and write down 3rd-Alternative solutions to the conflict.

Academic Protip

College is a Habit 6 experience. Your college textbooks introduce you to new and diverse minds, presenting new ideas that might or might not appeal to you but always shake up your paradigms.

Although you might be afraid of that big, heavy textbook, look at it as a chance to go for a walk with someone who has thought deeply about the subject and has a whole new landscape of ideas to show you. Professor Janet N. Zadina is the best person we know to guide you through the steps of reading college textbooks effectively.

Dr. Janet N. Zadina,
Tulane University

» How to Read College Textbooks

By Dr. Janet N. Zadina,
Tulane University

College is all about reading—a lot of reading. You'll read more than you ever have before and probably more than you ever will again. Even people who love to read sometimes feel overloaded in college. If reading isn't your favorite thing, you might feel like your brain is being squashed.

So how do you deal with it?

Think of it this way. Reading a textbook is like taking a road trip. When you're going for a long drive, you plan it before you start. You get clear on your destination. You look at a map to find the best route. As you travel, you pay attention to road signs so you don't get off track. When the traffic gets bad or the road gets bumpy, you slow down and concentrate harder so you don't crash and burn. Plus, you take a break occasionally to refuel or nap for a while so you don't run out of energy.

Follow the same strategy when you read a textbook as you would when you take a long drive. Here are three keys to effective reading:

1. Make a plan.
2. Focus as you read.
3. Pace yourself.

Make a Plan

Just as you would look at a map before taking a trip to a place you've never been before, look at the map of the book. Where's the map? The table of contents. It tells you where you're going. It's like looking at a Google map from the highest point—you can see all the major landmarks.

Then skim through the book, paying close attention to the headings, the visuals, and anything in bold or italics. These are like road signs on a journey; they help you find your way through the author's argument.

Divide the number of pages in the book by the number of days in the term to arrive at the number of pages you must read daily. You can't drive 5,000 miles in a single day, so plan to read a certain amount each day and stick to your plan.

Some maps are too complicated or confusing to be much help. Often you need a simpler map to get oriented to the territory. Likewise, when you're facing an advanced textbook, look for something easier to help you get started. Go on the Internet and find simpler material that gives you the background you need to understand the more difficult textbook. (Do this in addition to reading the textbook, not instead of.) Check out videos on YouTube that provide background on the subject.

This preview work will help you understand the main points of the book and get a handle on the issues the book is talking about before you plunge in.

Focus as You Read

Driving a car is different from riding in a car. Passengers can afford to be passive, ignoring the road ahead, talking, texting, or sleeping. But drivers are active. They watch the road, take note of signs and landmarks, keep an eye on speed, slow down, or even backtrack if they miss an important turnoff.

The same is true for reading college material. You can't afford to be a passive reader, letting the words fly by like the scenery on the road. You're an active reader, paying close attention to the road the author is taking you down. You watch for important ideas, which are usually marked by headings, or for obvious signs marked by words that show the direction the author is going.

Some of these obvious signs show that the author is taking a new path: "by contrast" or "instead" or "however" or "in my opinion." Other signs show that the author is adding new information: "furthermore" or "moreover" or "in addition." Other signs show that the author is about to arrive at an important destination: "in conclusion" or "in summary" or "to sum up." You could almost draw a map of the author's argument by following these road signs.

Active readers slow down or speed up just as drivers do. As an active reader, you skim quickly through material you already know or understand easily, but you slow down for difficult material you have to learn. If you don't get it, you backtrack until you do get it. You look up unfamiliar words, search for help on the Internet, and ask other people to help you understand it.

If you're an active reader, you don't stop to underline or highlight things. Research tells us this method doesn't help your memory. And don't try to reread the whole book to prepare for exams.

Instead, take notes as you read. Keep notepaper beside your book and divide the paper into two columns. In the right column, note key words and important ideas. When you finish reading, write questions in the left column—questions you might be asked on a test. Then cover up the right column and mentally answer the questions based on the reading you've done. This little trick will help you remember what you've read, and you'll also have a review sheet to help you get ready for exams later on.

Finally, active readers keep the distractions to a minimum. When you're driving, you can't eat a burger, drink a Coke, text your friends, listen to music, check social media, carry on a conversation with your passengers, and drive the car safely. The same is true for reading. Eliminate all distractions. Yes, all distractions. That means your phone, texts, and especially those headphones on your head.

Pace Yourself

Reading is hard brain work. It uses a great deal of fuel and a big part of the brain's resources. It's a gym workout for your brain.

- Break up your studying throughout the day. Read in short spurts using a timer. Start with 20 minutes at a time; then take a 5-minute break. Get up and move around. Work up to cycles of 45 minutes with 15-minute breaks. You'll increase your reading time through practice.
- Study every day so you don't have to do a lot of reading all at once.

249

- Take breaks, including a nap if you are studying three hours or more. A brief nap helps you learn.
- Don't sacrifice nightly sleep to study. Nighttime sleep helps you learn because the brain consolidates new information while you sleep.

Most of all, don't worry if you find yourself unable to read everything. College reading is not the same thing as reading a romance novel from cover to cover. Nobody's going to hold you accountable for reading every word. Your goal is to get the important ideas down.

Your brain has two basic capabilities. Your working memory is short and very limited—that's why you have trouble remembering phone numbers. If you try to commit everything you read to memory, you'll immediately overload that tiny space. That's why taking notes as you read is so important.

But the other part of your brain is an unimaginably huge network of neurons connected by nerve pathways. This part of the brain is "plastic"—that is, it changes as a result of experience. The more you do something, the more territory it gets in the brain.

Picture a field of tall grass. Now walk through it. You'll leave a very small path. Now walk through it again. That path will get bigger. The more times you walk through the field, the bigger and more well-defined the path becomes. If the pathway gets a lot of traffic, it becomes a road and eventually a superhighway.

The same is true for your brain. The more you read, the easier it gets as your brain creates new superhighways of information. So don't give up because the reading is hard at first. To become a better reader, just keep on reading.

Dr. Janet N. Zadina used to teach at a community college. Fascinated and concerned about the reading problems of her students, she decided to go back to school and study cognitive neuroscience—the study of how the brain learns. Today Dr. Zadina is assistant professor in the department of neurology at Tulane University. She has produced groundbreaking books including *Six Weeks to a Brain-Compatible Classroom and College Reading: The Science* and *Strategies of Expert Readers*. She writes about new developments in her blog, brainresearch.us, and provides workshops internationally on learning and the brain.

References

Schmit, Julie, "Chegg CEO Rashid Applies Netflix Concept to Textbooks," *USA Today*, January 12, 2009. http://usatoday30.usatoday.com/money/companies/management/entre/2009-01-11-chegg-rashid_N.htm

Thompson, Aaron and Joseph B. Cuneo, *Diversity and the College Experience*, Kendall Hunt Publishing, 2009.

Sharpen the Saw
The Habit of Daily Self-Renewal

"A long, healthy, and happy life is the result of making contributions, of having meaningful projects that are personally exciting and contribute to and bless the lives of others."

–HANS SELYE

IN THIS CHAPTER, YOU WILL DISCOVER WAYS TO:

- Stay fit and healthy.
- Build rewarding relationships.
- Keep your mind sharp.
- Make your life meaningful.

Also, look for the Academic Protip...

- How to Manage Your Money

Habit 7:
Sharpen the Saw

is the habit of staying sharp physically, emotionally, mentally, and spiritually.

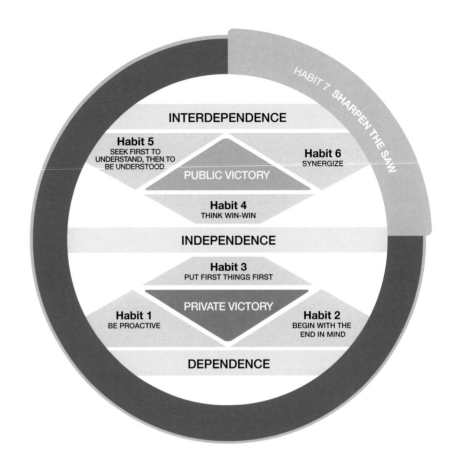

What I Wish
I'd Known in College

"I wish I'd known the meaning of the 'Dry Clean Only' clothing tag."
—Sarah, Indiana Wesleyan University

"Take advantage of the opportunities, travel, study abroad, sign up for the classes that you are interested in even if they don't 'count.' The price you pay, the extra money, the extra time will not be that big of a deal to you in five years. I promise."
—Courtney, Utah State University

"The friendships you will make in college will last a lifetime. Your relationships with classmates, dorm mates, and roommates will grow and evolve until you eventually feel like you've created a new family."
—Pam, Northeastern University

"I'm glad for all the times that I didn't make my life all about studying. All of those camping trips and other things I did with friends are wonderful memories to have now and I honestly don't remember which classes I got A's in and which I got B's in."
—Amy, Kirtland Community College

"I graduated a semester early. I wish I would have slowed down and had more fun."
—Sherri, University of Miami

REAL CHOICES:
Burning Out

You may have seen a thread like this on a college chat board:

I'm in my junior year of college. I also have a part time job. I've gained a ton of weight in the last year and I'm really trying to change my lifestyle so I've been working out at the gym nearly every night.

Now, I really do love both my major and my job. However, I'm so burned out by my schedule. It's only the second week of classes but I feel completely overwhelmed by everything. I have so much reading and papers due already. I normally have great time management skills (and an alright 3.7 GPA), but this semester is already kicking my butt. Most nights when I get home I just want to sit down and cry.

I have no clue what I want to do after I graduate. I'll probably keep working at my current job, or I'll have to find another if I can't get a real full-time position. I already come home most nights so exhausted the thought of school does nothing but make me want to cry.

I just feel so lost in my life. I'm burned out with everything and constantly stressed.

All I want to do right now is sit at home in my PJ's, stare at the TV, and eat my body weight in ice cream. Blah. Can anyone else relate to this?

REPLY 1:

I can relate. I'm in nursing at community college and am feeling extremely burned out and unhappy as of late.

I'm only working about 10 hours/week in addition to school, but sometimes I feel like that is even too much. And the LAST thing I want to do after spending 8 hours at a clinical is to come home and work on the mountains upon mountains of homework I have.

I've been struggling lately with school because I can't decide if I like what I am doing or not. And if not, what else can I do? I'm very unsure if I am just so stressed out and overwhelmed and that is causing me to not like nursing or if I actually just don't like it.

REPLY 2:

I feel the exact same way! I don't have a job, but I'm taking 20 credit hours this semester (17 at my university, 3 at community college), so I feel like I have SO much going on. I've been burned out on school for a while now, but I'm so incredibly burned out this semester.

After I graduate I'm planning on going to nursing school, but I'm applying for the Walt Disney World College Program for the fall so that I can have some

253

sort of a break! I think I'd literally go crazy if I couldn't take a break. But, since I don't know if I'll get into the program or not, I'm constantly stressed about life after college. I'm also stressed about other stuff, so life for me really isn't very fun right now either.

So many college students feel exactly like this.

Life is a big balancing act for them. It's hard to get everything under control. Some focus so much on school, partying, or work that everything else suffers. Some are so obsessed with grades that they give up on sleep, food, friends, and everything else.

It's okay to be out of balance for a period of time, but if it goes on too long, you risk burning out and breaking down.

Habit 7: Sharpen the Saw is the habit of renewal, continuous improvement, and balance. It's about staying sharp in the four major areas of your life—your body, your heart, your mind, and your spirit. If you neglect any one of these, it's like speeding down the street with one flat tire. All four parts need constant renewal.

In this chapter, you'll learn how you can keep the stress under control and enjoy your life in college instead of burning out.

> "My point is, life is about balance. The good and the bad. The highs and the lows. The piña and the colada."
>
> —Ellen DeGeneres

PEOPLE WHO PRACTICE HABIT 7:

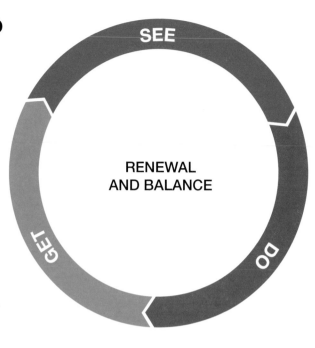

RENEWAL AND BALANCE

GET

- Physical endurance.
- Richer relationships.
- Lifelong learning.
- A life filled with meaning.

SEE

- I must continuously renew my body, mind, heart, and spirit to be healthy and happy.
- I'm doing all right, but I can do better.
- Balance is best.

DO

- Stay fit and healthy.
- Build rewarding relationships.
- Keep your mind sharp.
- Make your life meaningful.

THE PARADIGMS OF SHARPENING THE SAW

Picture a lumberjack dripping with sweat as he tries to cut down a big dead tree with a bow saw. He's been at it for hours but has cut through only a third of the trunk. He is weary.

His neighbor comes up to watch (as neighbors sometimes do). The neighbor notices the saw is dull. "Why don't you stop and sharpen your saw?" he asks.

The lumberjack says, "I can't. I don't have time to sharpen the saw. I need to cut this tree down immediately."

"It'd probably go faster if you sharpened the saw."

"Why don't you mind your own business?"

And the neighbor shrugs and goes home.

So it is with life. We get so busy we don't stop to "sharpen" our bodies, minds, emotions, or spirits. We become dull, and it actually takes longer to do everything. Have you ever been too busy driving to take time to get gas?

But if you have the paradigms of Habit 7: Sharpen the Saw, you think this way:

- I must continuously renew my body, mind, heart, and spirit to be healthy and happy.
- I'm doing all right, but I can do better.
- Balance is best.

I Must Continuously Renew My Body, Mind, Heart, and Spirit to Be Healthy and Happy

If you don't use a muscle for a long time, it atrophies—it weakens and shrinks. If you've ever worn a cast on a leg or an arm for a while, you know all about atrophy. To keep your muscles from atrophy, you need to use them all the time.

255

There's a principle at work here: the principle of renewal. It applies to everything in your life. Listen to Greg:

> *My first exam was supposed to be an hour, but it took me 25 minutes to ace. Everybody else was sweating, and I was done and with an A+. This was the usual story for me. I had always gotten good grades in school and I didn't feel like college was any harder, so I started slacking off.*
>
> *After a couple of months I was the video-game champion of my dorm floor. Long nights of hard, concentrated work, I'll tell you that. I was too tired for classes so I only showed up on test days. I flunked a test or two, but I wasn't worried.*
>
> *By the end of my first year, I was on academic probation and about to lose my scholarship. My brain was deep-fried mush from pizza and no sleep and nothing but games. But when they told me the money was going to go away, that snapped me awake. I saw myself as a slacker, and it wasn't me.*
>
> *Deep down I knew my life wasn't working. My second year was totally different. I still play games, but only after I take care of the stuff that really matters—decent study time, decent hours, and decent food. (The sight of pizza makes me a little ill right now.)*

If you start out healthy but go on a cheap cheese-and-pepperoni binge for a month, you will feel awful. It's unavoidable. If you have a bunch of good friends, but then go for months without any contact, your pool of friends will dwindle over time. If you're smart in history but stop reading or keeping up with the news, you will lose the very thing you're good at.

Renewal is a principle. You can't avoid it; you can't change it. If your phone goes dead, it stays dead until you recharge it. If you don't renew yourself, you run the same risk.

You have four basic human needs that require attention every day: physical, social-emotional, mental, and spiritual. They're interconnected. If you don't meet the needs of your body (food, exercise, and sleep), your emotional, mental, and spiritual life also suffers.

"Everyone is a house with four rooms, a physical, a mental, an emotional, and a spiritual. Unless we go into every room every day, even if only to keep it aired, we are not a complete person."

—Native American Proverb

PHYSICAL
Food
Exercise
Sleep
Hydration
Regular checkups
Hygiene

SOCIAL-EMOTIONAL
Friends
Family
Study groups
Social media

MENTAL
Schoolwork
Class discussions
Lectures
Journals
Literature
Skill development

SPIRITUAL
Service
Meditation
Art
Music
Nature
Inspirational reading
Religious worship

If you purposefully care for each of these areas every day, you have the Whole-Person Paradigm. You're caring for the "whole you," not just part of you. You don't neglect yourself.

Let's do a checkup on how well you Sharpen the Saw in these four areas:

Sharpen the Saw Checkup

How well are you sharpening the saw? Circle the scores that apply to you.

	Hardly Ever				Most of the Time
PHYSICAL (BODY)	**TIME**				
I eat nutritiously.	1	2	3	4	5
I get enough sleep.	1	2	3	4	5
I pace myself so I'm not constantly under stress.	1	2	3	4	5
I get enough physical exercise.	1	2	3	4	5
I manage my finances well.	1	2	3	4	5
SOCIAL-EMOTIONAL (HEART)	**TIME**				
I make an effort to make new friends.	1	2	3	4	5
I am a good friend.	1	2	3	4	5
I have a good time with my family.	1	2	3	4	5
I handle my emotions well, including controlling my anger.	1	2	3	4	5
I take steps to reduce or avoid undue stress.	1	2	3	4	5
MENTAL (MIND)	**TIME**				
I work hard in school.	1	2	3	4	5
I am learning new lessons all the time.	1	2	3	4	5
I keep up on current issues and trends in the world.	1	2	3	4	5
I am well-rounded; I know about more than one subject.	1	2	3	4	5
I take initiative to learn new skills on my own.	1	2	3	4	5
SPIRITUAL (SPIRIT)	**TIME**				
I find time to serve others.	1	2	3	4	5
I have a creative outlet—writing, drawing, designing, building, etc.	1	2	3	4	5
I regularly read motivating, inspiring literature.	1	2	3	4	5
I regularly do things that rejuvenate my spirit: meditating, singing, praying, playing or listening to music, spending time in nature, etc. I take initiative to learn new skills on my own.	1	2	3	4	5
I treat others kindly.	1	2	3	4	5

KEY

Add up your score for each of the four dimensions.

IF YOUR SCORE IS...	THEN...
20	Your saw is sharp. Either that, or you did the scoring backward.
16–19	You're doing okay, but there's room for improvement.
12–15	No wonder you're feeling blah.
8–11	You're running out of fuel.
4–7	Your doctor, your psychiatrist, and your mom are on the phone…

Look at the total for each dimension. Are some areas high or low? Which dimension do you need to work on the most?

So how did you do? Are you giving all of the four areas the attention they need? Is anything screaming for attention?

Of course, we know better than to neglect these things. We're not stupid. But life intrudes: "I'll start eating right and exercising when summer break comes around, but for now, I need to plow through this semester." Or "I don't have time for any social life right now. I'll worry about that later." Or "I have so much on my plate right now that I never have time for myself."

With ineffective paradigms like these, you'll spiral downward in life or at best stay stuck where you are. You simply can't do well if you don't eat right, take breaks, keep up with your studies, spend time with people, do something to calm your spirit, and get some sleep. It sounds like a lot to handle, but not if you're good at Habit 3: Put First Things First.

Obviously, sharpening the saw is a Quadrant 2 thing. That means it isn't urgent, which is why people don't do it. You have to act on it because it won't act on you. Smart students make Sharpen the Saw a top priority.

I'm Doing All Right, But I Can Do Better

Chances are you're doing fine caring for your "whole person"—better than you give yourself credit for. So don't beat yourself up. Still, you can always do better.

The paradigm of a highly effective student is "continuous improvement." You're not satisfied with the status quo. You want to get better.

Most of us are pretty good at keeping up with the outside world. You know that yesterday's smartphone won't work for you tomorrow. You

> "Months are different in college, especially freshman year. Too much happens. Every freshman month equals six regular months—they're like dog months."
>
> —Rainbow Rowell, author

259

understand the latest memes. The music you listened to last month is no good this month.

But your inside world needs upkeep too. Are your friendships getting better or going stale? Is your mind getting brighter or dimmer—or burned out entirely? Could you be more fit and healthy tomorrow than you are today? Are your savings growing or shrinking?

If you have the Habit 7 mindset, you're always looking for ways to improve your capacity. Life gets better instead of stagnating—or worse.

Balance Is Best

It's maybe the most common whine you hear from college students: "My life is totally out of balance. It's too much, it's too hard, I'm burning out, I just want to sit here and eat my weight in ice cream."

Effective college students believe that a balanced life is a better life. If you live the 7 Habits, there's no reason for your life to be out of balance. Sure, you might lock yourself in your room for a couple of days and live off pizza if you've got a big class project to do, but that sort of thing will be the exception, not the rule.

You don't want to party away and forget your studies, but you don't want to look back after four years and think, "I never had any fun." You don't want to spend so much time studying that you neglect ever having meaningful conversations, but you also don't want to spend so much time with friends that you get lousy grades. You have to find a balance.

A young friend of mine recently shared that she didn't want to live with her roommate anymore because all her roommate ever did was study. Her roommate seemed to care way more about grades than relationships. In reality, with a little more effort and planning, this roommate could have done well with both her studies and her relationships.

Don't believe the lie that you can't maintain some sense of balance in college. You can. People do it all the time. This doesn't mean you won't have days and weeks now and then where you're working around the clock. You will. But overall, you strive for balance. And when you're balanced, you feel better, so you just do better.

WHAT STUDENTS *DO* WHO SHARPEN THE SAW

At this point you may be thinking, "This is all common sense." And you're right. But common sense is not always common practice. Just because you know something does not mean you Do it effectively.

In fact, our surveys show again and again that people have a lot of trouble with Habit 7. Most often they say, "I don't have time!" But as the lumberjack should have known, sharpening the saw is a great time-saver.

I'm going to point out a few simple things you can do to stay sharp every day in each of the four areas. I won't go into depth (there are whole books on this subject), but I hope some of these tips will help you care for the "whole you."

Stay Fit and Healthy

Too many college students are worn out, dragged out, burned out. If you don't Sharpen the Saw in this area, you won't have the energy to do well in school. And as your immune system collapses, you'll get sick with frequent colds or mono or something worse.

Whether or not you like its shape, height, color, or condition, your body is yours. So you might as well take good of care of it. Of course, you can't avoid all physical problems, but you can work within your Circle of Influence to prevent problems.

Sleep. Get plenty of it. Research shows that sleep deprivation leads to depression, lower grades, accidents, and emotional problems. When you're tired, you're more likely to blow things out of proportion. That rude little comment someone made about your haircut suddenly seems unforgivable, or that looming history exam becomes more than you can bear. That's what happens when you're a walking zombie.

Here are a few basic tips on sleep:

- Get what you need. Many students get only about six hours of sleep a night—some much less. Experts say you need at least eight hours or more a night, and no less than seven for sure. They also say that your memory is being rewired and rebuilt during deep "Stage 3 and 4 sleep." That's why you can be confused by a lecture, wake up the next day, and suddenly it's all clear to you. Not enough sleep? You can wake up depressed, anxious, and unable to pay attention. What's worse, you might actually lose some of what you learned the day before. (Paller and Voss)

- Go to bed early. Get up early. There's wisdom in the old saying, "Early to bed and early to rise, keeps a man healthy, wealthy, and wise." College students who perform the best also have the earliest bedtime and waking times. (Eliasson, et al.)

- Be consistent. For example, if you typically get to bed around 10 or 11 p.m. most weekdays, don't go to bed at 3 a.m. every Friday and Saturday and sleep till noon. Weekend binge sleeping messes with your sleep patterns and makes you drowsy, tense, and nervous. (Oginska and Pokorski)

- Relax before bed. Take a bath, write in your diary, read the comics. A few minutes of chill time before bed can make all the difference. Stay away from your tablet or smartphone screen just before bed; research shows that light from the screen interferes with the brain chemical melatonin, which makes you go to sleep. (Wood, et al.)

- Reduce caffeine and sugar intake, especially late at night. Caffeine in soda, coffee, tea, or energy drinks can keep you awake, especially if you consume too much in the evenings. The same is true of big doses of sugar. (Lorist, et al.)

Sometimes you'll want to stay up late to relax or finish homework, or maybe you work the graveyard shift and can't get as much sleep as you'd like. Do what you can to get some sleep. If you're feeling depressed, confused, or stressed out, a steady series of a good night's rest should help.

> "There's that moment every morning when you look in the mirror: Am I committed or am I not?"
>
> —LeBron James

SORRY, I DON'T MEAN TO BE SHORT WITH YOU. I ONLY GOT 15 HOURS OF SLEEP LAST NIGHT.

READY TO BLAST YOUR DELTS?

Nutrition. College means no time and no money. People with no time and no money don't eat, or they eat only noodles and frozen pizza. We all know this stuff will make you sick after a while. What to do?

What do the 7 Habits teach you?

Be Proactive. Find a source of good food—fruit, vegetables, and protein. Maybe there's a local produce market or a co-op where you could buy a lot for not much, saving both time and money.

Begin With the End in Mind. If you're putting on pounds, maybe you should think about your own "end." Keep in mind the trim, fit, healthy person you could be.

Put First Things First. Eat the good stuff before you pig out on junk.

As a kid, I loved soda pop, doughnuts, and chips—all chips. The pounds added up. I felt sluggish. Then I came across my mom's eating guide, which she based on solid principles of nutrition. Next to the "food groups" were little check boxes for the "recommended daily servings." I remember it exactly.

Food Group	Daily Servings
Grains (bread, rice, cereal, pasta, etc.)	☐ ☐ ☐ ☐ ☐
Fruits (any sort)	☐ ☐ ☐
Vegetables (any sort)	☐ ☐ ☐ ☐
Dairy (milk, cheese, yogurt, etc.)	☐ ☐ ☐
Proteins (chicken, fish, beef, beans, etc.)	☐ ☐
Fats (butter, oil, etc.)	☐ ☐ ☐
Water	☐ ☐ ☐ ☐ ☐ ☐ ☐ ☐

After watching what I ate for a few days, I realized I was eating the Great American College-Guy Diet of bread, meat, and fat—no fruit, vegetables, or dairy, and not enough water. So I started following Mom's program religiously. Every night before bed, I'd check off what I had eaten that day. I still ate a lot, but different kinds of food like fruits and veggies. I also started lifting weights and running. My body changed quickly, and the extra weight I was carrying melted away in a few months. I felt so much better.

Some rules for keeping yourself physically sharp:

1. Eat a healthy breakfast.
2. Eat at least five servings of fruits and vegetables daily. Eat a variety.
3. Eat whole grains like oatmeal, brown rice, and whole wheat instead of processed grains like enriched flour (white bread) and white rice.
4. Don't take in so much sugar, processed foods, and fried foods—like soda pop, french fries, and rainbow-colored cereal.
5. Get at least two servings of protein each day from meat, chicken, fish, eggs, beans, or soy products.
6. Eat some healthy fats each day (fish, nuts, olive oil, sunflower oil, canola oil).
7. Spread out your calories. You're better off eating several smaller meals throughout the day than eating one big meal at lunch or dinner.
8. Drink plenty of water.
9. Don't get into fad diets. They're unsustainable. You'll temporarily lose weight, but in the long run, you'll gain it all back, if not more.

"Life expectancy would grow by leaps and bounds if green vegetables smelled as good as bacon."

—Doug Larson, Olympic medalist

On that last note, please avoid the extremes. College seems to breed eating disorders like anorexia (starving yourself), bulimia (stuffing yourself and then purging), and binge eating. You could die. Anorexia has one of the highest death rates of any psychological disorder (Arcelus, et al.). If you're suffering, do not waste another minute—your college health center can help you.

Exercise. You might think you don't have time to exercise, but in reality you don't have time not to. Without it, your brain slows down and you get sleepy during the day and can't sleep at night—you just feel awful. And you lose time.

Even if it's just a few minutes a day, *do something*. Try at least one or two of these simple things:

- Clear your mind. Yoga or meditation relaxes the body, improves circulation, and reduces stress.
- Work your heart. Swim, power walk, cycle, jog, or do aerobics to burn calories and build up your heart and lungs.
- Lift weights. You'll build muscles, of course, but you'll also burn calories, increase bone mass, and build your endurance.
- Take a break. Exercise tears muscle fiber; then at rest, the muscles repair themselves. Avoid training the same muscle group two days in a row.

Omar, a student at Claremont Colleges, has a unique way of sharpening the saw without putting much time into it.

Every morning he cycles to school with Jaimin, a classmate who lives nearby. En route, they talk about their classes and what they've been reading. They stop at the mosque in Pomona for prayer. After that, they get back on the bikes and pick up the pace, racing each other to the campus.

Omar says, "This way I Sharpen the Saw all four ways at once. The bike is exercise, the prayers are spiritual, and we socialize while we learn from each other. Body, spirit, social, and mental. We call it 'multi-sharpening.'"

Avoiding Harmful Substances. During high school, I was recruited by a prominent West Coast college to play football. One weekend they invited me to visit their campus. My host was a big, 240-pound athlete whose job was to show me a good time and get me to go to his school. Although he knew I didn't drink, he took me to a frat party where everyone was getting wasted. I had a good time and drank a lot of soda.

Afterward, he took me to a movie with his friends. During the movie, he passed out, having downed too many bottles. He then began to vomit uncontrollably. Three of us had to carry him to the parking lot. I thought he was going to die. An ambulance was called, and he spent the night in the hospital.

He was supposed to show me a good time? But he turned me off completely, and I decided to play ball at a different school.

The choices you make about chemical substances, legal or illegal, will impact everything about you—your body, mind, heart, and spirit. When making decisions about alcohol, tobacco, and drugs, think hard about the short- and long-term risks you're taking:

"The word 'aerobic' came about when the gym instructors got together and said, 'If we're going to charge $10 an hour, we can't call it jumping up and down.'"

—Rita Rudner, comedian

On average, each cigarette shortens a smoker's life around 11 minutes.

WELL, I GUESS IT'S TIME TO RENEW MYSELF.

SUBSTANCE	POSSIBLE SHORT-TERM RISKS	POSSIBLE LONG-TERM RISKS
Alcohol	Loss of coordination Poor judgment Memory lapses Blackouts Vomiting and choking Coma Drunken-driving arrests Motor-vehicle crashes Accidental injury Sexual assault Alcohol poisoning Sudden death	Broken relationships Family problems Inability to hold a job High blood pressure or stroke Brain damage Liver damage Sexual problems Chronic depression Cancer of mouth or throat Premature death
Tobacco	Immediate increase of blood pressure and heart rate Narrowing of arteries Carbon monoxide in blood Oxygen starvation in cells Bad breath Inability to smell or taste Disgusting public smoker's areas	Cancer of lungs, larynx, esophagus, mouth, bladder, cervix, pancreas, kidneys; chronic lung disease; heart disease; discoloring of teeth and gums; tooth loss; low birth weight in children; problems getting or holding a job; wasting thousands of dollars a year; higher insurance costs; disfiguring surgeries; premature death
Marijuana	Impaired coordination Difficulty thinking Disrupted learning and memory Lung irritation similar to the effects of tobacco smoke More phlegm production Chest illness Lung infections Fourfold increase in heart-attack risk Risk of death or injury while driving	Loss of connection among brain areas responsible for learning and memory Higher likelihood of dropping out of school Difficulty getting or holding a job
Prescription Drugs	Respiratory shutdown Fatal seizures Irregular heart rate Circulatory-system failure Feelings of paranoia or hostility Dangerous driving Sudden death	Addiction Increased tolerance; need for higher and higher doses Extreme weight change Long, painful withdrawal Premature death

This table sums it up. Of course, the same or more serious risks apply to other common substances that are often abused: date-rape drugs, cocaine, methamphetamines, LSD, heroin, and PCP. Athletes use steroids to bulk up their bodies, but also encounter wide-ranging health risks including heart and liver problems, skin damage, strokes, hair loss, and aggressive mood swings. Using e-cigarettes ("vaping") is less dangerous than smoking regular cigarettes, but the nicotine in them is just as addictive and still harmful to the brain. (Condon)

When these substances are mixed—alcohol and prescription drugs, for example—the effects can be extremely harmful.

> "College is a fountain of knowledge, and the students are there to drink."
>
> —Old Proverb

Drinking, Smoking, Drugs—And You

When it comes to drinking, smoking, and taking drugs, try using the 7 Habits along with your self-awareness, imagination, and conscience to help you answer some important questions. Write your answers in the spaces below.

1. Be Proactive. Know the risks. Get educated. If someone pressures you to participate, remember that you have the freedom to choose. Nobody can make you do anything—it's entirely your choice. What will you choose to do about drinking, smoking, and taking drugs?

2. Imagine going to a big party tonight. Begin the party with the end in mind. How do you want the evening to end? What risks are you willing to live with?

3. Put First Things First. What's more important to you: your health and safety, or a momentary good time that might not turn out so well? If you start abusing alcohol, tobacco, and drugs, which quadrant are you moving into? Are you sure you want to go there?

4. What about people who try to pressure you into substance abuse? Are they win–win thinkers? Will you win or lose if you abuse alcohol, tobacco, or drugs?

5. What do you need to understand about people who rely on or abuse substances to have fun?

6. What are the 3rd Alternatives to getting caught up in alcohol and drugs?

7. How might using drugs affect you spiritually, emotionally, mentally, and physically?

ACTIVITY 46

Living conditions. What about your physical surroundings? Ask yourself:

- Do I feel safe?
- Do I have enough light?
- Do I have enough space?
- Do I have enough quiet?
- Do I have enough privacy?
- Are things clean and orderly?
- Do I have inspiring pictures or posters on the walls?

Granted, you might not be able to say yes to all of these questions. Maybe you can't afford a better living space, but what can you do within your Circle of Influence? Clean up regularly? Bargain with your landlord to paint the place in exchange for one month's free rent? You can do a lot about your place besides complain about it.

Appearance. I'm not one to recommend spending a lot of money on clothes while in college, but I'm not one for wearing the same clothes for four years either. Your appearance is up to you, but you might want to consider the 7 Habits.

Are you proactive? Are you in charge of your appearance? If not, who is? Who's choosing your clothes? Are you dressing the way *you* want to or the way other people do?

What's your end in mind when you put on a certain outfit? What's your priority—to impress, to fit in, to keep warm? The more you think like a professional, the more you will want to look professional. First impressions are often lasting ones, and your appearance is your "letter of recommendation" for whoever looks at you.

Is it a win for the people around you if you're a slob? If laundry for you is an annual chore, or if your socks are generating their own life forms, you might try to show a little empathy for others and clean yourself up.

Sex. I know this is a very personal, potentially life-changing topic. Making decisions about sex is hard for everyone, no matter how much they joke about it or act like it's a casual thing. How can the 7 Habits help you with sexual issues?

Be Proactive. Are you educated about sex? Do you really understand the consequences of having sex? What do you know about pregnancy? Are you ready for that possibility—for all of the deep and even wrenching feelings that come with having or not having a baby? Are you ready for all the changes to your body, and all the changes to your future?

What do you know about disease? Are you aware that there are several million new cases of sexually transmitted diseases on American campuses every year? Are you ready to be a new case yourself? Do you know what these diseases are—what they can do to your body, and how some of them stick with you for life? Are you okay with telling future boyfriends or girlfriends that you have an STD?

What's your real end in mind when it comes to sex—a long-term, committed, loving, and growing relationship, or just a quick exchange of bodies?

If you're pressuring somebody to have sex (if you think that's a win for you), how is it a win for the other person? Is the idea just to use him or her to have some fun, or is "no deal" the best decision for now?

"Nearly half of the 20 million new sexually transmitted diseases (STDs) are diagnosed each year among young people aged 15–24 years. Long-term effects of these diseases include infertility, tubal scarring, ectopic pregnancy, and chronic pelvic pain."
–U.S. Centers for Disease Control and Prevention, 2012

What about empathy? Do you really understand the feelings of your partner? Do you care?

Obviously, sex has a big impact on your body, mind, heart, and spirit. With the proactive mindset, you know you're free to decide whether to have sex or not. But you're not free to choose the consequences of having sex. They're out of your control.

Just be smart. What more can I say?

Money. I know you don't have any, but let's Be Proactive about it.

The basic principle for managing your money—whether you're a student or not—is to spend less than you take in. It sounds so obvious and simple, yet the average student carries not only student loans, but also thousands of dollars in credit-card debt, the most expensive kind of debt. These debts will eat away at your future. If you're proactive, how do you handle a credit card?

What's your end in mind for money? Do you blow it as soon as you get it? Or do you save some of it? Do you have a picture of yourself as financially strong and independent some day? (You don't have to be rich to be independent.)

How are you going to get there? What Quadrant 2 activities should you be doing now to make sure you're financially independent someday?

Because so much of your success in college and in life depends on your finances, I recommend you take advantage of the Academic Protip at the end of this chapter: "How to Manage Your Money."

There's a lot more involved in keeping yourself physically sharp, but let's pause and consider what you could do about it now.

The Physical Dimension

Assume you're an exhausted college student (no imagination necessary), and the doctor just told you you're on the edge of total collapse. How would you change your habits about exercise, diet, or sleep?

Assume you have a big test coming up in three days. What will you do to keep yourself physically ready for it?

Assume you want to graduate from college with the brightest future possible. How will you deal with drugs and alcohol? What about managing your money?

THINGS TO
DO IN COLLEGE

- Sneak on top of the highest building on campus.

- Stay up all night working on a paper. When you're done, Instagram a view of the library at sunrise.

- Befriend someone who makes you question everything.

- Attend a student protest. Be loud.

- Cram 50 people into your dorm room for a birthday party.

- Get a selfie with your school mascot.

- Sit through an entire lecture wearing a disguise.

–Buzzfeed.com

Build Rewarding Relationships

You always hear people say they had more fun in college than any other time in their lives. It's true. College can be a blast.

It's ironic because college students usually have a job and a huge load of coursework. You may be gasping for relief and thinking, "Where's the fun in this?" I have some ideas for you.

Take a Break. If you're not stressed at least a little bit, you're not pushing hard enough. Still, every brain needs a break, so build it into your Quadrant 2 planning time.

Get together with somebody and dance, hike, cook, see a chick flick, go to the opera, or watch stupid videos on YouTube. Of course, if you're having too much fun, learn to say no a little more often and stay out of Quadrant 4.

Think of yourself as a rubber band: If it's not stretched, it serves no purpose; if stretched too far, it snaps.

Build Friendships. College is a great place to meet friends and develop lifelong relationships. It's also an easy place to blend into the walls and talk with no one. It's your choice. So make some friends, join a club, or run for office. If you do college alone, you're missing half the reason for going in the first place.

Of course, no one you try to make friends with is perfect; neither are you. To build a strong relationship, start with yourself and work in your Circle of Influence. In other words, making good friends requires being a good friend. You can't make people like you, but you can make yourself more likeable.

If you're struggling to connect with others and make friends, it may be helpful to ask yourself a few questions:

- Have you been told that you're obnoxious, too loud, inappropriate, or that you just won't shut up?
- Do you ask people about their lives, or does every conversation revolve around you? Can the people with you barely get a word in?
- Do you talk only about one subject?
- Are your grooming standards questionable?
- Do you swear or complain a lot?
- Do you feel you're better than everyone else?
- Are you always putting yourself down?
- Are you way too serious, or do you try to turn everything into a joke?

If you answered yes to any of these questions, consider making some adjustments. Focus on things you can control, not on things you can't. You can't control your height, features, or general body type. But you can control your personal hygiene, manners, dress, appetites, and the way you carry yourself.

As a minimum, challenge yourself to make a deposit in someone's Emotional Bank Account every day. I'm not talking about grandiose acts of service; I'm talking about a phone call, a compliment, or a thank-you note. Two things will happen: You'll make more friends, and you'll feel good about yourself.

Date Intelligently. College is a time when a lot of people start pairing off, sometimes for life. If you get serious with somebody, great—just bring the 7 Habits along with you as you start on the momentous journey of love.

My friend Durelle Price teaches seminars on "intelligent dating." (Yes, there is such a thing.) She compares love to buying a car. Do you walk onto the lot and let the salesperson pick your car out for you? No. Usually, you have your end in mind, a mental wish list of things you've got to have—color, make, model, reliability, economy—and another list of things you can do without.

Durelle thinks people ought to begin romantic relationships "with the end in mind"; that is, they should put at least as much brainpower into choosing a lifetime partner as into buying a car. What's on your "must-have" list: Smart? Athletic? Music-loving? Religious? Funny? Parent-approved?

It can't hurt to have the 7 Habits on your list: "I want to be with someone who is proactive, purposeful, and good at planning; who wants both of us to be winners, has empathy for me, and hugs me." You could do worse.

College romances are emotional roller coasters. Your heart is smashed on the ground one minute, and you're 9 miles high the next, but you can sharpen the emotional saw without getting too badly injured.

Most dating relationships are a complicated web of feelings. You can expect to feel hurt, puzzled, frustrated, abandoned, inspired, stupid, deliriously happy, or embarrassed all in the same conversation. One college counselor used to shed buckets of tears with his students who were agonizing over love. He'd go home and tell his wife, and then she would cry all night. But after a few years, he now says, "Toughen up. Love is war. Pick yourself up and move on." Don't be so reactive. Remember, you can choose how you feel. Use your Empathic Listening skills, and be prepared to go your separate ways (no deal) if you have to.

In close, intimate relationships, remember: you're proactive. You are in charge of yourself—no one else. You don't have to do anything. You might get a stunning wound or two, but remember—no one can really hurt you at your core because you are an independent human being.

> "True romance is not Romeo and Juliet who died together but Grandma and Grandpa who grew old together."
>
> —Old Proverb

My Dating Wish List

What things would you like in a dating relationship?

	MUST HAVE	CAN DO WITHOUT
1		
2		
3		
4		
5		
6		

ACTIVITY 48

YOU KNOW, NOT *EVERYTHING* IS A LAUGHING MATTER, PAUL.

As you know, there are four types of relationships: win-win, win-lose, lose-win, lose-lose. If a dating relationship is based on anything other than win-win, you need to fix it or break it off.

Sometimes no deal is the best deal, difficult as it may be. One way to know when it's time to break off a romantic relationship is to watch for red flags—warnings that something isn't right. Take such warnings seriously.

Here are a few red flags to watch out for:

Ultimatums. I had a girlfriend in college who would call me the night before I'd be playing in a big game on national TV and say, "Are you committed to me or not? You need to decide by tomorrow morning or I'm leaving." Well, tomorrow would come and she'd back off. But then, two weeks later, she'd give me another ultimatum. Finally, I could see the red flag, and we broke up. I only wish I'd done it sooner.

"You can go out with me or study for that test" or "Either you have sex with me or I'm leaving you"—such ultimatums are a sign of a dependent personality, and you should exit quickly.

The Rescuer Complex. One form of lose-win relationship is called a "rescuer complex." A student named Jennifer got sucked into this and still can't see her way out.

I was with a guy for two years. Most of the two years was horrible. He had lots of problems and I tried to change him. I would drive around late at night looking for him to make sure he was all right. For some reason, I couldn't leave him alone.

Life finally caught up with him, and now he is in jail. I still love him with all my heart and would do anything for him. I hope after he gets help, he will be a better person and we can work out our problems.

I'm a sympathetic person. I believe in giving people second chances, but if you can't stop playing mom or dad to somebody, you're losing out. In strong relationships, people build each other up.

Lies. If someone's constantly lying to you, that's one whopping red flag. My colleague Annie interviewed a student named Angie about her boyfriend. Here are a few lines from that interview:

Annie: *Does your boyfriend go to school here?*
Angie: *No, he went to school somewhere else. He says he graduated early, but I don't know if he graduated or dropped out.*
Annie: *What does he do?*
Angie: *Um, he says he works, but I know he doesn't. Like, he's not very honest.*
Annie: *I'm gonna ask you a funny question. Is this the kind of person you want to end up with?*
Angie: *Yeah. No. But he's not... you know. It's just that he's not honest with me. He always lies about things to make himself look better or to get out of problems he has created.*

Unfortunately, it's hard to see red flags when your paradigms are fuzzy. As comedian Jim Carrey put it, "You know what the trouble about real life is? There's no danger music." He's right.

"You don't have to wait for someone to treat you bad repeatedly. All it takes is once, and if they get away with it that once, they know they can treat you like that, then it sets the pattern for the future."

—Jane Green, author

A person with a win-lose approach to a relationship:
- Makes you cry.
- Says things that make you feel stupid, embarrassed, or worthless.
- Prevents you from spending time with your family and friends.
- Keeps you from doing things you want to do.
- Acts super jealous or possessive.
- Shoves, shakes, slaps, or hits you.
- Always insists on being alone.
- Threatens to harm you or himself/herself.
- Lies or hides things from you.
- Tries to belittle you into doing things you don't want to do.

Spend Time with Family. For some, being away from family for the first time and dealing with homesickness is one of the hardest challenges of college. For others, it's nonstop family problems. And still for others, there's no time for the family. Some students face all these challenges at once.

Whether your family situation is "good" or "bad," college can be a good time to strengthen family relationships. For some, going away to college improves relationships. You miss a meal or two and start missing your parents too. Meanwhile, your parents might relax a bit, mellow out, realize they can't control everything their child does, and miss having you around. So sometimes all it takes is time and distance to heal the wounds.

If you've got rough family relationships, be proactive about it. Stop blaming your family; focus on yourself and what you can do. Make deposits: send a letter of thanks for all they've done for you, apologize for your own mistakes, text them when you pass a test. Let them know that you care about your family. Some won't respond, but you can feel good about yourself and your proactive efforts.

Maybe you feel like you don't have any time for your family. I don't believe it. You might be short on time, but everyone has time for a thank-you, a note, or an "I love you." You can make family time a Big Rock in your planning. You can write a class paper about your family. You can involve your family in your schoolwork. You can talk about what you're learning. You can teach them the 7 Habits.

Deal With Low Times. A growing challenge for college students, male and female, is depression. There are at least two types of depression: (1) occasional low spirits or feelings of dejection, and (2) ongoing forms of psychological depression that stem from physiological causes.

Everyone experiences the first form of depression, what we call the "blues." Lots of things can make you feel this way: cold weather, the flu, being overworked, or more serious things like a failed class, a breakup, or a fight with parents. Usually, these feelings don't last, and if you're proactive and mature, you get in the habit of deciding how you will feel.

But the chronic form of depression doesn't just wear off, and you can't tough it out. Nor is it a sign of weakness. It's sometimes the result of cycles of stress, sexual abuse, chemical anomalies in the brain, substance abuse, or severe family problems. Often depression has genetic roots. According to the

> "The home is the ultimate career. All other careers exist for one purpose, and that is to support the ultimate career."
>
> —C.S. Lewis

National Alliance on Mental Illness (NAMI), the symptoms of this kind of depression include:

- Big changes in sleep, appetite, and energy.
- Lack of interest in activities that were once a lot of fun.
- Feelings of sadness, guilt, worthlessness, hopelessness, and emptiness.
- Regular thoughts of death or suicide.

Depression and some types of mental illness often do not manifest themselves until adulthood. Having these symptoms for a steady period of time may or may not signal chronic depression. If you are depressed, you can be treated through counseling, nutrition, exercise, medicine, or a combination of these things.

Surprisingly, fewer than half of depressed people actually seek help. When people get sick from an infection or virus, most are willing to go to a doctor and take medication. They talk openly about it. But when they become emotionally ill or depressed, they refuse to talk about it, mistakenly thinking they can cope on their own. But listen to mental-health expert Sherri Wittwer: "There is no shame in having a mental illness. Mental illness is no different than any other illness such as asthma or diabetes. What we do know is that treatment works, recovery is possible, and there is hope." I couldn't agree more. Don't be afraid to open up and share that you're struggling, because you're not alone. Depression is everywhere, and any stigma associated with it is long gone.

If you have emotional issues you can't cope with, go to the student health center or a family doctor. See a mental-health specialist.

Take Time for Yourself. Here's one last insight about keeping yourself sharp emotionally.

Often we feel guilty when we take time for ourselves because we're frequently told to think of others first. But when you need to sharpen your saw, it's not selfish to take time to think, revisit your goals, and meditate. That's one of the great advantages of Habit 3: weekly planning time is *your* time.

When you live with roommates or have family members around all the time, you owe yourself a little solitude. Again, you may have to be creative. I have a friend who was a radio addict until he realized that turning the radio off would give him some quiet time when driving to and from school. It was the only time he had to think. Everyone deserves an hour or so a week just to think, reevaluate how things are going, self-reflect, and plan. Your creative self needs solitude and quiet to grow.

The Social-Emotional Dimension

Imagine a world where people can hear every word you say about them. How might you choose your words differently?

What one thing could you do to sharpen your social-emotional saw that would bring you the most relief?

Keep Your Mind Sharp

If college doesn't sharpen your mental saw, I don't know what will. (I do know some people who came out duller than they went in, but that's a different story.) One great thing about college is that you really learn how to learn—a skill that will help you grow the rest of your life.

Ben grew up with no idea of going to college. It just wasn't in his sights.

There were two groups of people at my high school. The ones we called "gunners" came from upper-class families, and they were all "gunning" for college and fancy jobs. Guys like me came from the other half. We were going to work right after high school like our moms and dads had done, mostly in the refinery.

So I went to work in the refinery too, and it was great. I liked the work and the guys around me. But one of my friends started taking night classes so he could qualify for a new job at the refinery, and he wanted me to come with him. So I did, and I really enjoyed the classes. Then it became obvious that I wasn't going anywhere in the refinery without a degree of my own, so I applied and got in.

What surprised me was how much I liked it. There were some classes I could do without, but the engineering courses fired me up. There was something exciting about the experiments and the designing and making things work or work better.

Now I'm a hydraulics engineer at the plant and making a lot more money than I ever thought I would. But that's not the point. I read everything I can find on the science of hydraulics, and in just two years, I've actually made some real improvements in our plant. My friends now call me "Gunner." I kind of like it.

People who don't go to college sometimes joke about it. "I got my diploma in the real world," they say. Of course you can learn anywhere; with the Internet, you can learn just about anything you want to know right now.

But there's something about walking on a campus, interacting with great minds, talking things through with other students, hearing well-known lecturers in person, browsing through libraries, and soaking up new ideas. These things are hard to describe to people who have never experienced them. And they're hard to beat.

> "I'm hungry for knowledge. The whole thing is to learn every day, to get brighter and brighter. That's what this world is about. You look at someone like Gandhi, and he glowed. Martin Luther King glowed…. I think that's from being bright all the time, and trying to be brighter."
>
> —JayZ

273

In fact, college is so good at keeping your mental saw working that you probably feel like giving it a rest. So here are some ideas for staying mentally sharp.

Stay Well-Rounded. It's no coincidence that Bill Gates, founder of Microsoft, is one of the world's greatest innovators and one of the world's greatest thinkers. "I try to make time for reading each night. In addition to the usual newspapers and magazines, I make it a priority to read at least one newsweekly from cover to cover. If I were to read only what intrigues me—say, the science and business sections—then I would finish the magazine the same person I was when I started. So I read it all." ("Personal Glimses," *Reader's Digest*, April 17, 1996.)

What does he mean by "I read it all"? He means that he keeps his mind sharp and exercised by reading different stuff all the time.

One downside of college is that you might end up hyperfocused on one subject. You do this so you can become an expert, but you also become very narrow and uncreative if all you think about is accounting or chemistry.

While you're in college, try to open your mind to new things each week. Skim magazines not in your field for 15 minutes, walk down a different aisle in the library and read the titles on the book spines, or attend a lecture outside your major. Study a world map regularly or a different country each month.

In the new science of "neurobics," people exercise their brains by doing a few new things every day, like brushing their teeth with a different hand or folding their arms the opposite way. Try it. Learn how to juggle or play the guitar to stimulate new brain growth. If you have the time and money, study abroad for a semester, pick up an internship in another state, visit museums, or take fencing lessons. You can learn a lot online, but the brain needs input from all five senses to stay sharp.

LESSON ON LEADERSHIP: The Well-Rounded Benjamin Franklin

Benjamin Franklin

Benjamin Franklin was an author, scientist, diplomat, postmaster, and inventor. His inventions ranged from bifocals to musical instruments, lightning rods, a stove, and an odometer. He was curious why ships took longer to sail from Europe to America than they did in return, so he investigated and mapped the Gulf Stream. He also helped found the University of Pennsylvania and the first fire station in America. And that's just a start.

A few years ago, 500 scholars gathered from around the world to hold a celebration in honor of Benjamin Franklin. They broke the sessions into 10 categories: (1) statesmanship; (2) education and the study of nature; (3) science, invention, and engineering; (4) mass communication; (5) finance, commerce, and industry; (6) printing, advertising, and arts; (7) religion and humanities; (8) medicine and public health; (9) agriculture; (10) music and recreation.

They found he had made major contributions in all 10 areas.

Franklin's life was interesting because he was interested in just about everything.

Be a Lifelong Learner. When you get your diploma, you'll be so glad to be done with papers and tests and homework and lectures that you'll just want to stare at the back of your eyelids for a week or so. It's only natural.

But don't stay there too long. Too many graduates shut their last book and never open another one. What happens to them?

I don't have the statistics, but my experience in 25 years of business is that about 20 percent of people allow their minds to decline to the point they're not even competent anymore. They flat out don't do what they need to do to keep up. Another 60 percent do just enough to keep their heads above water. But that last 20 percent? They proactively take steps on their own initiative to expand their minds, develop new skills, read the latest information, and get ahead of the game. Some of them even create new knowledge. They are the innovators. We're always looking to them for guidance, for the next new direction.

Be one of them. Be a self-starting, lifelong learner—a pioneer, an explorer, and an innovator. It's so much more fun than being reactive and constantly saying, "Why didn't I think of that?"

So, what's your end in mind for your mind? Do you see yourself getting smarter, wiser, and more interesting? Or dumber and dumber?

Developing your mind is a Big Rock, so get it into your schedule every week.

"Once you stop learning, you start dying."

—Attributed to Albert Einstein

The Mental Dimension

Assume your current knowledge and skills will be obsolete in two years. What new learning avenues will you explore?

Make Your Life Meaningful

What deeply inspires you—a great song? a good book? being in nature? What makes your life meaningful—family? friends? making a difference in someone's life? When I talk about spirit, I mean that inner self that lurks far beneath the surface of your everyday self. Your spiritual dimension is your core, where your deepest convictions and values lie. It is the source of purpose, meaning, and inner peace. Sharpening the saw in the spiritual area of life means taking time to renew and awaken that inner self. As Pearl Buck, winner of the Nobel Prize for Literature, wrote, "Inside myself is a place where I live all alone and that's where you renew your springs that never dry up."

College is a time when people start thinking about important questions, such as "Who am I? What do I stand for? What do I believe in? What is truth?" We read or hear ideas about things we never heard before—ideas that provoke us, light up our minds, or make us angry or confused. In some cases, for the first time, we really think about what we believe and why we believe it, and our beliefs get abruptly pushed and shoved around.

What a great time to sharpen your spiritual saw—to get clear on what you believe and what makes your life meaningful.

That's why some college students let go of religion and others get more into it than ever. "What do I believe? Will religion be part of my life? If so, why? If not, why?"

Your decisions about your values, standards, philosophies, religion—those things that give meaning to your life—are yours to make, and they are intensely personal. But those decisions can have a significant impact on who you are, what you do with your life, and what values your children (if you choose to have them) will be raised with.

Too many people go through life not knowing what they believe in or what values or principles they stand for. They waffle and change with the tides and trends of the day. As Alexander Hamilton said, "Those who stand for nothing fall for anything."

DID YOU KNOW?
Healthy Religion

Did you know that belonging to a formal religion can help you to be healthier? Dr. Peter Gott cites a range of research that supports a positive relationship between religion and better health. According to Gott, most formal religions:

- Encourage healthful behavior and positive lifestyle choices.
- Provide active social support for people.
- Promote feelings of self-worth and the inner confidence that one can control one's life and actions.
- Encourage practices such as prayer and meditation that can help people deal with unpleasant situations and relieve stress and depression.
- Cause positive emotions that favorably influence the immune system.
- Give hope by promoting a positive outlook that enables believers to better cope with the vicissitudes of life.

Dr. Gott concludes that organized spirituality "is associated with health benefits, not because of divine intervention but because the various aspects of a religious life promote behavior and attitudes that are healthful." (Gott)

Keeping your spirit alive—whether at school, at work, or elsewhere—depends on how well and often you sharpen your spiritual saw. There are so many ways to do it. Here are a few ideas shared by students:
- Meditating
- Spending time in nature
- Listening to inspiring music
- Writing poetry
- Doing service
- Praying
- Thinking deeply about what matters most
- Writing in a journal
- Religious worship
- Reflecting on your goals or Personal Mission Statement

Often the thing that can rejuvenate your spirit the most is studying in a major or working in a job that ignites the fire within you.

I'm thinking of Lori, a nontraditional student if ever there was one. Growing up, Lori disliked school and didn't do well. Her life centered on kids. Even though caring for them was a minimum-wage job, she liked working in a day-care center and couldn't wait to get back to the children each day.

"Time spent in nature is the most cost-effective and powerful way to counteract the burnout and depression we feel when we sit in front of a computer all day."

—Richard Louv, journalist

Children flourished around Lori, especially the littlest ones who were the most insecure when their parents dropped them off. She had a way of communicating with them. When she suspected one of them was being abused at home, it broke her heart. But people didn't listen to her—after all, who was she? Just a part-time worker with no educational background and no professional status.

That's when she knew she would have to step up and become something more. She applied for admission to college with a plan to be a school psychologist. Once in college, she found a new job working in a school with underprivileged students where she felt deeply needed and valued. In fact, she could hardly get her studies done because she spent so much energy on those kids she loved.

Meanwhile, many of her psychology classes were in theory, statistics, and research methodology—all required, but a big turnoff for Lori. "I don't want to be a researcher." She also didn't like to write, and all those papers were total torture.

Before long, Lori was fed up with school. All she wanted to do was work with the kids; she could do without all the homework and research. On the other hand, she knew she needed to get a degree, preferably a master's degree, to become certified and make enough money to support herself.

Fortunately for Lori and the children she now counsels, she paid the price to finish her degree. She is now certified and making a huge difference in the lives of many children. This daily work with children was her method of sharpening her spiritual saw, and it gave her the stamina to make it through college. Although she now earns a lot more than she did as a day-care worker, the money was never her inspiration. The children were.

Lori could have dropped out. But she was a 7 Habits person, an effective person with a spiritually compelling mission. Sure, she had trouble—lots of it, but quitting was not one of her habits.

To sharpen your spiritual saw, you must find ways to keep your mission always in sight. You review it. You set goals to fulfill it. You plan your weeks around it. That's why I say weekly planning is essential to keeping your spirit alive.

Here is another way a college student, Lance, sharpened his spiritual saw:

Early in the winter semester, I started to think maybe I should drop out. Things weren't going well in my head. It was freezing on campus and I felt like I was running from one mess to another, from my mom's house to my classes, and not being able to get interested in anything. One day my class got canceled, so I wandered into the arts building to get out of the cold for an hour, and there was this empty classroom. I just sat down... collapsed really.

Then I heard music coming from up above. The classroom was under the concert hall, and I guess an orchestra was rehearsing. I'd never heard classical music before, but it kind of filled me up where I was empty.

I came back most days to that empty classroom just to listen for a while. It was my safe place, where I could be alone and hear that music. I don't know why, but it got me through one of the hardest times in my life. Now I listen to recordings of the great classics, and it has this effect on me where it lifts me up. That lift is all I need sometimes.

> "The best way out is always through."
>
> —Robert Frost, poet

The Spiritual Dimension

Assume that you have a year to live. What legacy would you want to leave? What would you do to make sure of that legacy?

WHAT YOU GET BY SHARPENING THE SAW

It's hard to argue against Habit 7: Sharpen the Saw. It doesn't take a genius to know that you should take care of yourself—body, heart, mind, and spirit. The hard part is doing it.

For many college students, the barrier to sharpening the saw is lack of time. They're too busy driving the car to stop for gas.

That's the wrong paradigm, though. Sharpening the saw will actually save you time by preserving your health and overall well-being. How?

In his book *Spark*, Harvard Professor John J. Ratey shows, after many years of hard research, that proper exercise all by itself helps you learn better, cut stress and anxiety, and banish depression and attention deficits. Notice that exercise is just one thing you can do to sharpen the saw, but it affects your emotional, mental, and spiritual life as well. If you sharpen the saw in one area, you're sharpening the whole person.

And you can save even more time by "multi-sharpening." Take your younger brother on a 10K run for charity. While you're running, talk about a book you're reading. Now you've sharpened all four saws at once!

So don't let lack of time be your excuse. You might spend only three or four hours sharpening the saw in a week made up of 168 hours. But those few hours will dramatically increase the effectiveness of every other hour of the week.

"A sound mind in a sound body is a short but full description of a happy state in this world."

—John Locke, philosopher

279

What I Want to Get

Think back on the principles of Habit 7 and the activities you have completed in this chapter. Identify one or two actions that would help you most as a student. What results do you hope to get as a result of doing these things?

	CHANGES I WANT TO MAKE	WHAT I HOPE TO GET
PHYSICAL		
SOCIAL-EMOTIONAL		
MENTAL		
SPIRITUAL		

IN SUMMARY

Sharpening the saw represents your commitment to preserving and enhancing the greatest asset you have—you. Habit 7 is based on the principle of renewal. In physics, the second law of thermodynamics (entropy) says that everything breaks down—including you.

So if you let your mind go dull, your body become malnourished, your friends go cold, and your spirit wither away, you'll get sick—a sickness of body, mind, heart, and spirit; a sickness of the whole person. Habit 7 is the cure.

Habit 7: Sharpen the Saw
Principles: Renewal, Continuous Improvement, Balance

	INEFFECTIVE STUDENTS	EFFECTIVE STUDENTS
What They *See*	• I'm so busy, I can't stop to Sharpen the Saw. • I will Sharpen the Saw later.	• I must continuously renew my body, mind, heart, and spirit to stay current. • I'm doing all right, but I can get better. • Balance is best.
What They *Do*	• Neglect their health. • Fail to maintain friendships. • Fail to update their knowledge and skills. • Live a meaningless life.	• Stay fit and healthy. • Build rewarding relationships. • Keep a sharp mind. • Make life meaningful.
What They *Get*	• Illness, lack of energy. • A list of former friends. • Outdated skills and knowledge. • Lack of meaning.	• Better health. • Lasting relationships. • Lifelong learning. • A life of contribution.

Try some of the Baby Steps to experiment with sharpening the saw. I also recommend following the advice in the Academic Protip: "How to Manage Your Money."

COMING ATTRACTIONS

If you don't have enough time to get everything done, if you have a relationship challenge of some kind, or if you can't find the right job, then read on. The final chapter pulls all the habits together to solve these problems and many more. (You'll also like it because it's short.)

Baby Steps

1. Teach to Learn. Using the summary chart on the prior page, teach the key concepts of Habit 7 to a friend, classmate, or family member within the next 48 hours.

2. Identify a new talent or skill you want to develop: _____
    Do something about it this week.

3. For three consecutive days, count how many servings of fruits and vegetables you eat. If you're not getting five or more, adjust your diet.

    Day 1:

    Day 2:

    Day 3:

4. One night this week, get a solid eight or nine hours of sleep and see how good you feel the next day.

5. Think of an old friend or family member you've lost contact with. Call or text to say you're thinking of him or her.

6. Go to a museum, a recital, or an ethnic restaurant you've never been to before. Expand your horizons.

7. Go to a religious service you've never experienced before. What did you discover? How did the people, the place, and the practices affect your spirit?

8. Which person inspires you most? What is it about that person?

9. Watch the sunset tonight or get up early to watch the sunrise.

10. Go on a one-on-one outing with a family member. Catch a ball game, go shopping, or see a movie for old times' sake.

Academic Protip

If you're a college student who doesn't worry about money, you're pretty rare. One of the main reasons for dropping out is a lack of finances.

Here's someone to help you get the most out of the money you have and maybe make more. At the Crotonville Academy in New York, Joe Knight teaches General Electric's business leaders how to understand money. (You'd be surprised how many leaders don't understand it.) Joe is also an old friend of mine, and his advice on money management is the best I've heard. When it comes to money, I couldn't find a better teacher of college students than the man who teaches the world's top businesspeople.

How to Manage Your Money

By Joe Knight, Business Literacy Institute

Money is a big cause of stress for most college students. You're paying high tuition, you're borrowing to do it, and you have less time to earn income while you're in college.

The good news is this: By going to college in the first place, you're making a long-term investment in yourself. Never doubt that. People ask if college is worth it. In financial terms, I can tell you that it's worth a million dollars to the typical college graduate. That's not just a guess; it's based on actual research findings.

At this writing, it costs about $30,000 to get a four-year college degree at a public university. If you were to invest that money at current bank rates, it would take you 90 years to make a million dollars. So unless you can afford to wait 90 years, your investment in college is worth every penny, believe me.

The bad news is… well, there isn't any if you'll follow one simple principle and never forget it: Make a profit.

Make a profit. If you don't make a profit, you cease to exist, at least financially. It's no different for you than it is for a major corporation. For an individual, profit is simply what we call savings. If you want to

be successful financially, you have to earn more than you spend. If you save something out of every dollar you get, you build what we call "net worth"—the money you have minus the money you spend.

For a while, most students have a negative net worth—they owe more money than they have—but that's okay because they're going into debt (usually on student loans) and expecting to make a profit in the future. But if you go into debt just to create more debt, say, by buying an expensive car or binge shopping for clothes, you dig yourself into a hole you might never get out of.

Your goal is to create a positive net worth someday—to have more money than you owe. That might not happen for a while, even years. But by saving something out of every dollar you get, you develop the habit of making a profit and you gradually move toward a positive net worth.

So figure out a way to live on less than your income and build your net worth over time. You can't spend more than your income for very long—that's an unbreakable principle. I hear your question: "But how can I save if it takes all the money I have just to live?" Even if all you can save is a dollar a month, put it aside. Get into the habit.

Avoid unnecessary debt. Don't go into debt unless it's absolutely necessary. Any debt you take on will damage that goal of positive net worth.

Joe Knight, Business Literacy Institute

If you have a credit card, don't charge more than you can pay off within a month. If you have debt left on the card after a month, the bank will start charging you some of the highest interest rates around. If you make only the minimum payment each month instead of paying off the entire balance, you'll end up paying for things again and again.

If you don't pay off your credit card, you hurt your credit rating. That rating is a number that tells people if you can be trusted to pay your debts. If you miss payments now, you can destroy your credit rating at a young age, and it will take you years to recover. You might not even be able to borrow money for school or a car or a home in the future.

Here are a few dos and don'ts for using credit cards:

DOS	DON'TS
Get a debit card instead of a credit card. With a debit card, you draw out money already in your bank account. With a credit card, you're going into debt.	Don't have more than one credit card.
Before charging anything, make sure it's a "need," not a "want."	Never use your credit card for cash advances.
If you think you really need to buy something, wait 10 days. By that time, you probably won't need it.	Don't use your card carelessly. Limit your credit-card purchases.
Shop for a card that has zero or low annual fees. (Check the fine print.)	Don't fall for "too good to be true" offers for a second or third credit card. "Too good to be true" offers are always untrue!
Shop for a card with low interest rates. (It's in the fine print.)	Don't increase your credit limit. Charge within your means.
Ask questions before signing on the dotted line: Are there any hidden fees? Does the interest rate increase after a certain time or for any other reason?	Don't share your credit card with friends or relatives, or take it places where you won't be using it.
Find out when the interest starts adding up.	Do not miss a payment; credit-card companies will charge you a penalty. Missing even once affects your credit. If you can't pay it all, pay something.
Read the fine print. If you don't understand it, ask.	Above all, don't charge more than you can pay off in one month.

Make a budget. A budget is just a simple plan for staying in control of your money. Go through your expenses for a week or a month—rent, utilities, tuition and fees, books, food, activities—and figure out how much it will take you to live. Follow these steps:

1. Record your spending for one week in this table.

ITEM	AMOUNT	REASON	WHERE/WHEN
TOTAL EXPENSES			

2. Analyze your spending:
   - Put a check mark next to each item you needed (as opposed to something you wanted). Did you spend more on needs or wants?
   - What spending patterns do you see? For instance, do you buy things on impulse or by plan? Do you spend too much when you first get paid?

3. Subtract your expenses from your income. Put the difference in the "Profit or Loss" box.

INCOME	
EXPENSES	
PROFIT OR LOSS	

If you have money left over, you've made a profit. That's for your savings account. If the answer is zero, you have no profit and no savings. If your expenses exceed your income, you've lost money and you're in trouble.

Now you can make a budget. Here's a budget that can work for a whole college term. Just fill it in.

My Budget

Savings: *How much can I put aside?*	$
Education: *What does school cost?*	$
Tuition and fees	$
Books	$
Lab fees	$
Health insurance	$
School supplies	$
Computer (laptop)	$
Miscellaneous	$
Living Expenses: *How much money do I need to live?*	$
Housing (mortgage/rent)	$
Utilities: water, gas, electricity	$
Phone	$
Wi-Fi or cable	$
Food: *How much can one pizza cost?*	$
Groceries	$
Eating out/fast food	$
Campus meal plan	$
Other Living Expenses: *Can't live without them!*	$
Personal care	$
Laundry and dry cleaning	$
Clothing/shoes	$
Gifts	$
Membership/subscriptions	$
Credit-card payment (Pay it in full every month if at all possible.)	$
Transportation: *Getting from here to there!*	$
Car payment	$

Gas and oil changes	$
Car maintenance	$
License and registration fees	$
Campus parking fee	$
Bus, taxi, subway, carpool	$
Car insurance	$
Entertainment: *Are we having fun yet?*	$
Movies	$
Concerts	$
Sports events	$
Parties	$
Cable TV	$
Music/videos	$
Sports/recreation equipment	$
Unexpected Expenses: *Crap happens...*	$
Traffic tickets	$
Car repairs	$
Medication	$
Dental care	$
Library or other fines	$
Anything else?	$
Total Expenses	$
Total Income	$
Total Balance: Expenses Subtracted From Income	$

If your expenses exceed your income, you can (1) cut your expenses, (2) increase your income, or (3) both.

If you can't make a profit, go back through your budget and start cutting expenses. Remember the basic principle—never spend more money than you bring in.

Make some money. Get a part-time job and increase your income. Work so you learn this important process of earning money and saving some. If you get a $200 paycheck, put $5 or $10 in a savings account. It's good training for life.

If your budget isn't working and you can't cut anymore, go to your employer. Work out your schedule so you have more blocks of time for your job. Go to the job-service center at your college to find out about jobs you can do at school, allowing you the flexibility for work and study.

Find the best terms for a loan. If you do borrow for college, find the best student-loan terms you can get. Go shopping for a loan. Ask about the terms of the loan: What's the interest rate? How long do you have to pay it back? How often do you have to make a payment? Then compare the terms of each lender. You might find you get better terms if you shop around.

Pay off student loans. Your loan payments will be a big part of your budget. If the payments are too big for you to handle, go to the lending agency and find out if you can adjust the payments. On the other hand, if you have enough to pay off the loan, do it as soon as you can and save yourself a fortune in interest payments.

Don't drop out. If you really get into money trouble and have nowhere to turn, go to the student-services office at your college. They'll help you work it out. Lots of students drop out because of money; don't be one of them. Remember, if you drop out, you just threw away a million dollars over a lifetime.

Have some fun. I think college is fun even if you don't have money—that's just part of being a college kid. There are so many things you can do for fun without spending money. Take a hike. Ride a bike. Lie down, look at the stars, and talk. Get together with friends and hang out or watch TV if nothing else. It doesn't take a lot of money to enjoy life as a college student.

Joe Knight is president of the Business Literacy Institute in Los Angeles. He has an M.B.A. in finance from the University of California, Berkeley, and is author of the Harvard Press best-seller *Financial Intelligence: A Manager's Guide to Knowing What the Numbers Really Mean*. A respected teacher of financial principles, Joe regularly instructs some of the world's top executives.

References

Arcelus, Jon and Alex J. Mitchell, et al., "Mortality Rates in Patients with Anorexia Nervosa and Other Eating Disorders," *JAMA Psychiatry*, vol. 68, no. 7, July 2011.

Condon, Timothy P., "The Neurobiology of Nicotine Addiction," Centers for Disease Control and Prevention, http://www.cdc.gov/tobacco/icsh/meetings/summary120808/neurobiology/

Eliasson, Arne H., Christopher J. Lettieri, "Early to Bed, Early to Rise! Sleep Habits and Academic Performance in College Students," *Sleep and Breathing*, Feb. 2010, 71–75.

Gott, Peter H., "The Link Between Faith and Health," *USA Today*, July 22, 1999.

Lorist, Monique M. and Jan Snel, "Caffeine, Sleep, and Quality of Life," in J.C. Verster, et al., eds., *Sleep and Quality of Life in Clinical Medicine*, Totowa NJ: Humana Press, 2008, 325.

Oginska, Halszka and Janusz Pokorski, "Fatigue and Mood Correlates of Sleep Length in Three Age-Social Groups," *Chronobiology International,* vol. 23, no. 6, 2006, 1317–1328.

Paller, Ken A. and Joel L. Voss, "Memory Reactivation and Consolidation During Sleep," *Learning & Memory,* Nov. 2004, 664–670.

Ratey, John J., Spark. *The Revolutionary New Science of Exercise and the Brain*, New York: Little, Brown and Company, 2013

Wood, B., and M.S. Rea, et al., "Light Level and Duration of Exposure Determine the Impact of Self-Luminous Tablets on Melatonin Suppression," *Applied Ergonomics*, vol. 44, no. 2, March 2013, 237–240.

Putting It All Together

"If you want a place in the sun, you've got to put up with a few blisters."

–ABIGAIL VAN BUREN

IN THIS CHAPTER, YOU WILL DISCOVER HOW TO:

- Apply the 7 Habits to your life challenges.
- Climb the 7 Habits "spiral staircase" and make your life a continuous success.

Putting It
All Together

is about applying all 7 Habits to the challenges and opportunities of your college life.

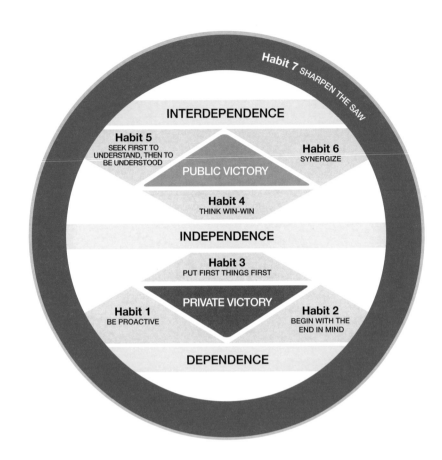

What I Wish
I'd Known in College

"You don't know what you don't know until you go to college—wow, did it impact my awareness in life."
–Sam, Georgia Tech

"University helped me grow up a lot. I conquered mathematics and got my first 4.0 GPA in college. Also loved the football games."
–Merrill, University of Utah

"Don't dwell so much on what's 'going to happen.' You don't know what's going to happen. I know tons of people who are succeeding in jobs they never majored in. Just focus on what you're doing now and enjoy it."
–Laila, Arizona State

"It's really, really easy to ditch class. Seriously. Nobody cares. But if you fall behind, it's a bugger to catch up. So get your butt to class."–Jon, Claremont Graduate University

"The university is where I got excited about life."
–Dean, University of Chicago

"College set the foundation and pattern for an adult life of learning, examination, thought, open-mindedness, soul searching, progress, repentance, service, compassion, love, accountability, spiritual roots, etc., and gave me the tools to magnify all of those as well as marketable skills to support me and my family. And set in concrete a love (and sometimes guilty pleasure) for all things written."
–Paul, American River Community College

REAL CHOICES:
Going Back to School

With a wife, children, and no college degree, Zac was approached by a small business to be their director of marketing. He was grateful. "Wow, this is exactly the career opportunity I need. If I work here for a few years, I might be able to get a good marketing role inside a large company, and do it without a college degree." But deep inside, Zac knew he was fooling himself—that without a degree he would be at a serious disadvantage when competing for any top marketing position in a larger corporation, which was his goal. So he decided to go back to school.

Zac's father said, "Do you have any idea how difficult it's going to be with a family to provide for?" He was quick to point out the negatives. But Zac had already made up his mind.

Indeed, it was tough. Finances were a big struggle. In Zac's words, "I had a mortgage to pay and a new baby in the house. We had to cut back. I sold my new truck and got a cheaper car. We used up our savings and had to borrow additional money from my father-in-law."

Academically, Zac struggled too. He made it a point to concentrate hard in class, take good notes, and do the reading, but he hadn't realized how much writing he would have to do. His first class required several papers. At first, the load discouraged him, but he got a lot of help from teachers and tutors. As the semester progressed, his writing did too.

One thing that set Zac apart from the other students was his graphic-design experience. When grading papers, his teachers paid a lot of attention to graphics, and Zac excelled at that. He brought that strength to team projects and was a big help to other students. He rose to the top of his class.

All through this ordeal, he made sure to spend a few minutes every day with his two children. He and his wife tried to help them understand why their dad was so involved elsewhere, but those deliberate few minutes a day made a big difference to feelings in the family. Early mornings he jogged and lifted weights with his wife, a valuable time for talking and connecting.

At graduation, Zac had a tremendous feeling of accomplishment. Due to his strong grades

Zac Cheney and his family. Photo courtesy of Zac Cheney.

and his work experience, he got a job at a multinational company where he has found his niche and blossomed.

We've come to the final chapter. I want to explore with you the story of Zac and how the 7 Habits helped him beat incredible odds and come out a success.

First let's see how far we have come.

You now know the College Success Formula. You have a compelling "why" for being in school. You're on your way to developing strong academic skills and life skills.

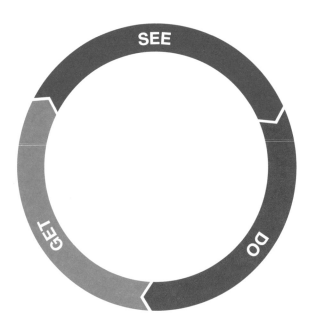

You know about See-Do-Get—that the way you See things impacts what you Do, and what you Do impacts the results you Get. In fancier academic-style terms, "your paradigms determine your behavior, and your behavior determines your situation in life."

You also know that your life is governed by principles you cannot change. If your paradigms are in line with those principles, you'll succeed in school and in life, no matter what happens to you.

And because the 7 Habits are based on timeless and proven principles, the more you develop those habits, the more effective you will become.

Now let's see how all 7 Habits work together. While each habit is powerful by itself, taken together they can help you meet successfully any challenge you face.

Zac knew the 7 Habits well. Although he faced a demanding few years in college, and although others, like his dad, worried that he wasn't up to it, he made the proactive choice to go for a better, more meaningful life (Habit 1). And that required a college degree.

His end in mind was clear—to become a valued, respected marketing professional who could make a great contribution (Habit 2). He made a plan with clear priorities and tradeoffs: His expensive new truck was not a priority. He had always made saving money a Big Rock, which was now a big help (Habit 3). He complemented the strengths of others with his graphic-design skills (Habit 4). He was a good listener and learner (Habit 5) and didn't hesitate to go for synergy with teachers, tutors, and project groups (Habit 6). And he carefully planned time for exercise and connecting with family (Habit 7).

Without the 7 Habits, Zac could have made it anyway. But I think his chances of giving up on his dream or dropping out were high. With the 7 Habits, life and school became much easier.

THEN I REALIZED THAT NO ONE, ON THEIR DEATH BED, EVER WISHES THEY SPENT MORE TIME GATHERING POLLEN.

WHEN WORKER BEES GET PHILOSOPHICAL

Apply the 7 Habits to Your Life Challenges

Zac's story reminds of one of my favorite old movies, *The Three Amigos*. It's a classic! I first watched it when I was in college.

The movie is about a battle between the good guys—the Amigos—and a crazy villain named El Guapo. Toward the end, one of the Amigos desperately tries to rally the villagers to stand up to El Guapo: "In a way, all of us have an El Guapo to face someday. For some, shyness might be their El Guapo. For others, a lack of education might be their El Guapo. For us, El Guapo is a big dangerous man who wants to kill us."

He's right. We all have our El Guapos to conquer. Your El Guapos right now might be:

- Balancing your life—school, work, friends, family.
- Getting everything done on time.
- Dealing with tough family issues.
- Coping with brain-stretching academic demands.
- Overcoming self-doubt.
- Facing discouragement, homesickness, or depression.
- Managing on very small amounts of money.

Zac had to face a lot of these El Guapos. They're common challenges, whether you are fresh out of high school, have been in the workforce for years, just got out of the military, or sent your last child off to school and went back to college yourself. Everyone has to deal with them. The question is how.

I am absolutely convinced that the 7 Habits can help you beat just about any El Guapo. No, the habits don't cure cancer, pay your bills, or take your final exam for you. But they can help you face any challenge successfully.

I did think my dad was crazy a time or two when he was teaching them to me. But through years of tough college work, a competitive career, and parenthood, I now see more than ever the value of each habit by itself and in combination with the others.

Let's say you're carrying a full load of classes, but you don't have the money to pay tuition for next term. So you ask your boss if you can work more hours. Then you score low on a test and feel you need to study more. But your time already seems maxed out. How are you going to deal with it all?

Let's see how the 7 Habits can help.

> "The further you get away from yourself, the more challenging it is. Not to be in your comfort zone is great fun."
>
> —Benedict Cumberbatch, actor

295

HABIT	HOW TO APPLY EACH HABIT TO MANAGING LIMITED TIME
Habit 1: Be Proactive	Focus on your Circle of Influence; don't waste time in your Circle of Concern. Blaming a teacher or a boss won't help. Take charge of your time.
Habit 2: Begin With the End in Mind	Make a plan for acing your tests. You have only so much time—what's the best you can do with it?
Habit 3: Put First Things First	Avoid unimportant activities. Get into Quadrant 2 so you spend most of your time where it counts right now—on effective study and work. Also, remember that studying more does not mean studying better.
Habit 4: Think Win-Win	Bargain for a raise in return for taking on new responsibilities—not more hours—at work. Make deposits in your Emotional Bank Account with your boss.
Habit 5: Seek First to Understand, Then to Be Understood	Do more focused listening in class and take good notes. You'll save study time and improve your test scores.
Habit 6: Synergize	Get a network together of people who can study with you and help you understand the material you'll be tested on.
Habit 7: Sharpen the Saw	Take a little time each day for each of four things: (1) keeping fit and healthy, (2) connecting with friends and family, (3) reading something you're *not* studying, and (4) doing something to lift your spirit (meditation, nature, prayer, music—whatever inspires you).

> "There's no limit to how complicated things can get, on account of one thing always leading to another."
>
> —E.B. White, author

Do you see how the 7 Habits, taken together, can make a real difference to a personal challenge like managing your time? And you probably have even more insights to add.

Life was complicated in another way for Audrey, a student with a serious boyfriend. Her problem was juggling the demands of school with the usual issues that come up in a close and growing relationship. Parker was a great guy and she wanted to spend time with him, but she wasn't exactly sure how she felt about him. Sometimes he was sweet and other times seemed not to care at all. He got hurt when she was too busy for him, but their schedules were tough. The situation was confusing for Audrey.

Here's how Audrey might apply each habit to her relationship challenge:

HABIT	HOW TO APPLY EACH HABIT TO A RELATIONSHIP CHALLENGE
Habit 1: Be Proactive	Start with yourself. Carry your own weather in the relationship. Decide that you are going to act calm and pleasant, no matter how others behave. Don't be reactive. Make sure your actions are principle-centered.
Habit 2: Begin With the End in Mind	Put into perspective how important this relationship is to you. Think about what you would want him to say about you on your 80th birthday. Treat him the way you think is right, no matter how he treats you.
Habit 3: Put First Things First	If the relationship is a top priority for you, plan time together each week for building this relationship. Choose a time when you won't be rushed.
Habit 4: Think Win-Win	What's a win for him in this relationship? What's a win for you? Keep both in mind as you get to know each other better. Don't allow trivial quarrels or little annoyances to ruin big relationships. Make deposits; apologize for withdrawals.
Habit 5: Seek First to Understand, Then to Be Understood	Listen to him sincerely. Use your ears, eyes, and heart. Reflect what he says and feels. Check by asking, "Do you feel understood?" When he feels understood, ask him to listen to you sincerely. Hold your tongue until you are calm.
Habit 6: Synergize	Learn to brainstorm solutions together. If you're both trying and you work hard enough, you can almost always find a better and higher way to resolve any problem.
Habit 7: Sharpen the Saw	Keep yourself in good condition. Renewing yourself physically, emotionally, mentally, and spiritually results in better judgment and more confidence. It gives you the inner peace and courage you need for managing your emotions.

Consider one more example. Sara yearned for a better job but realized the economy was difficult—even crazy. After working as a low-paid tech-support person for three years, she had had enough. It was time to try for something new—not an easy goal for a single mom.

HABIT	HOW TO APPLY EACH HABIT TO THE CHALLENGE OF FINDING A JOB
Habit 1: Be Proactive	Take the initiative to get the job you want. Find a company you want to work for. Find out what their problems are (every company has problems) and figure out how you can be the answer to a problem they care about.
Habit 2: Begin With the End in Mind	Get an appointment and describe your "end in mind"—how you can help them achieve an important goal or solve a big problem.
Habit 3: Put First Things First	Make preparing for your interview a Big Rock. Do the online research and investigation to learn as much as you can about the needs of the company you're interviewing with.
Habit 4: Think Win-Win	During the interview, describe clearly how you can help the company win. Then don't be shy about describing what a win is for you—in terms of compensation, benefits, child care, whatever you really need.
Habit 5: Seek First to Understand, Then to Be Understood	Before going to an interview, study the organization with empathy. Put yourself in their place. What do they do? What are their challenges? How can you contribute?
Habit 6: Synergize	During your interview, share why you believe you could be a solution to some of their problems. Point out the unique strengths you offer.
Habit 7: Sharpen the Saw	Look sharp for your interview. Show what an emotionally mature person looks like. Be smart, well-prepared, and well-read. Be inspiring. Talk about your vision and why the job would be meaningful for you.

These three quick examples show you how the 7 Habits apply to challenges of all kinds—in school, at work, and in your personal life. If you have any doubts, give it a try. Think of a challenge you are currently dealing with. It could be anything—studying for a big upcoming test, working out a problem with a friend, choosing a major, or coping with a setback. Now think through the questions on the next page.

© Randy Glasbergen / glasbergen.com

"If I start applying now, I figure I might land a job by the time I finish grad school."

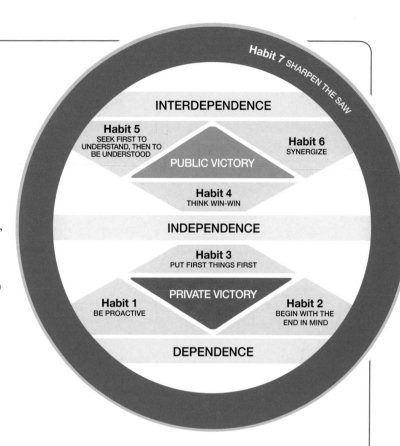

HABIT 1: BE PROACTIVE

- What is within my Circle of Influence? What is not?
- If I use my initiative, what could happen? What will happen if I don't?
- What resources do I have for dealing with this problem?
- Am I carrying my own weather, or am I letting others' moods dictate mine?

HABIT 2: BEGIN WITH THE END IN MIND

- What outcome do I want here?
- What is my mission here? How does this relate to my Personal Mission Statement?
- Do I have a written plan for dealing with this issue?

HABIT 3: PUT FIRST THINGS FIRST

- Which quadrant am I in when dealing with this issue?
- What one thing would make the biggest difference in dealing with the issue?
- What Big Rocks should I put in my calendar to deal with this issue?

HABIT 4: THINK WIN-WIN

- How will my actions affect other people?
- How will I show courage and consideration in dealing with this problem?
- What's the balance in my Emotional Bank Account with these people?

HABIT 5: SEEK FIRST TO UNDERSTAND, THEN TO BE UNDERSTOOD

- Do I really understand the situation at hand?
- Have I gathered all the facts and feelings of those involved?
- What do I need to communicate to others so they understand my needs and feelings?

HABIT 6: SYNERGIZE

- Who can help me with this issue?
- Who has strengths I don't have?
- Are there 3rd Alternatives to pursue?

HABIT 7: SHARPEN THE SAW

- **Physical:** Do I have the strength and physical resources necessary to deal with the challenge?
- **Social-Emotional:** Am I emotionally ready to handle the issue? Which friends will support me?
- **Mental:** What facts or research will help me deal with this issue?
- **Spiritual:** How does this challenge affect me spiritually? What can help inspire me to make a good decision?

Applying All 7 Habits

Identify a personal challenge. Describe how each of the 7 Habits might help you with that challenge.

CHALLENGE

HABIT	HOW CAN THIS HABIT HELP ME ADDRESS THE ISSUE?
Habit 1: Be Proactive	
Habit 2: Begin With the End in Mind	
Habit 3: Put First Things First	
Habit 4: Think Win-Win	
Habit 5: Seek First to Understand, Then to Be Understood	
Habit 6: Synergize	
Habit 7: Sharpen the Saw	

How did that go?

"A circle goes around, but never goes anywhere, while a spiral goes around, but constantly rises."

—Jarod Kintz, humorist

Climb the 7 Habits Spiral Staircase

Sometimes I hear people say, "Oh, yeah, I did the 7 Habits years ago. I know all about them." It's like they went to a theme park: "Been there, done that." As for me, I've been learning about the 7 Habits since childhood. Trying to live the 7 Habits has made a great deal of difference in what I get out of life. I avoid dumb mistakes, I grab great opportunities, I have wonderful friends who advise me, I hold "synergy sessions" for coming up with cool ideas at work, and I have family meetings. But I'm still far from "graduating" from the school of the 7 Habits.

For example, I think I'm a pretty proactive dad—but then I start thinking about all the things I could do proactively at home. I know this because my kids tell me. Furthermore, I'm constantly meeting other parents whose examples inspire me and show me how far I have to go.

Think of your life as an upward spiral, like a staircase going up forever. Imagine that each step is labeled with one of the 7 Habits—Habit 1: Be Proactive, Habit 2: Begin With the End in Mind, and so forth. Of course, you'll soon run into Habit 1 again, but this time is different because you've progressed.

Many students come from difficult backgrounds. If you've had a tough life, your first step toward becoming proactive might be nothing more than showing up to class every day. One day you might remember to Be Proactive, but the next day you slip back to being reactive. If you persist and stay hopeful, you can keep going up the spiral staircase as it rises to the sky.

Don't compare yourself with others. Taking a Baby Step might require a lot more effort from you than from someone else. Applaud your steps, even your Baby Steps. One day you will look down the steep spiral staircase and be amazed at how far you have come.

So when you finish this book and the course, don't walk away feeling like you've "been there, done that." Make mastering the 7 Habits an ongoing upward spiral in your life.

So Now What?

Before you close the back cover, I want you to take one final look at what you are you going to do with the 7 Habits.

Near the end of each chapter, you're asked to review the concepts found in that chapter and identify (1) what you already do well in relation to the habit, (2) what one or two things you can do better, and (3) what you hope to get from making the improvements.

Now quickly review the entire textbook. Skim the pages. Look at the headings. Review some of your responses in those end-of-chapter activities. What did you put in your draft Personal Mission Statement? How did your weekly planning go? How effective have you become at listening empathically? What are you doing well? Where are you falling short? Be honest with yourself, but don't be too critical either.

Retake the 7 Habits Self-Assessment at FranklinCovey.com/tc/resources or in the "Foundations" chapter to see how you have grown. Compare your scores to the scores you got at the beginning of the course.

> "Everyone thinks of changing the world, but no one thinks of changing himself."
>
> —Leo Tolstoy, novelist

Now, think back on the principles you've learned and the activities you've completed in this book. Identify the one or two actions that would help you most as a college student. Go for leverage. Of all the things you could do, which one or two will make the most difference? What results do you hope to get from doing these things?

ACTIVITY 54

What I Want to Get

Two Things I Am Doing Well	1.
	2.
Two Things I Hope to Do Better	1.
	2.
What I Hope to Get by Doing Better	1.
	2.

> "It was about this time I conceived the bold and arduous project of arriving at moral perfection…. But I soon found I had undertaken a task of more difficulty than I had imagined."
>
> —Benjamin Franklin

As we discovered in the "Foundations" chapter, if you want to make minor improvements, work on changing your behaviors (your Do). If you want to make major improvements, work on your paradigms (your See). If you struggle with working on your paradigms, start with the Dos. Try the habits for a week. Test any of the principles. Sometimes it takes a few months to form a habit, but you should start seeing results in about a week. Then keep going. Eventually, doing the Dos will start to change your Sees.

As you move up the spiral staircase, be patient with yourself. Sometimes life really is "two steps forward, one step back." You may be feeling proactive and patting yourself on the back one minute, then wondering why you were so reactive the next.

The "Franklin" in our company's name, FranklinCovey, honors Benjamin Franklin. That great leader identified 13 virtues that would improve his life, and he worked on one each week until he got to Number 13. Then he would start over again on Number 1.

You might want to do what he did and focus on one habit a week, then start over. Or you could work on the habits you feel are most important to you, like saying no to Quadrants 3 and 4 or using proactive language. Keep at it and you will become more effective.

For now, you're just beginning. So are many others. The 7 Habits are spreading rapidly around the world, so you will probably hear the language of the habits for the rest of your life. Lots of people are trying to do the same thing you're trying to do. As you awaken to the value of these principles, the day will come when the habits are just as natural to you as breathing.

A Final Word

To end, let's go back to where we began and see where we have been.

Think back on John Stephen Akhwari, the Olympic marathon man from Tanzania who kept going until he hit the finish line, injured and hurting, long after the medal ceremony was over. What about you? Can you persevere to the end?

Think back on Franklin McCain and his college friends who had the proactive courage to change their lives and the lives of countless others—just by sitting down in a diner and ordering a meal. Are you courageous enough to create your own future?

Think back on Norman Borlaug, who went to college, unleashed his talents, and fed a billion people. What end in mind do you have for your life?

Think back on John Wooden, who put first things first by turning down the most prestigious job in the NBA to fulfill his mission of transforming the lives of young college students. What "yes" of yours is so strong that you would say no to millions of dollars?

Think back on Wendy Kopp, who helped college students and children win by finding each other in the classroom. Where could you benefit from thinking win-win with other people?

Think back on Kelsey, who didn't understand her mother's concerns until she had a baby of her own.

"I thought yesterday was the first day of the rest of my life but it turns out today is."

—Steve Martin

Remember how Google started with the teamwork of two guys who loved to argue—Sergey Brin, a Russian party animal, and Larry Page, a quiet guy from Michigan? Life is an interdependent reality, and those who make the most of others' talents go farthest in life.

All these people are like you and me: They wake up each day and choose what they will do with the next 24 hours. Sometimes when we think in terms of leadership, we think in BIG terms—big numbers, big influence, big impact. But leadership doesn't have to be big at all to be important. Being a leader can simply be about leading your own life or about making a difference in the life of one other person.

Dr. Stephen and Sandra Covey on their wedding day.

My father was world-acclaimed. He used to disguise himself on airplanes just to get some privacy. *Time* Magazine called him one of America's 25 Most Influential People. He met with major world leaders around the globe. He was also humble.

And he would tell you without any hesitation that the real hero in my family is my lovely mother, Sandra Covey. I watched her raise nine children, including me. I watched her raise funds to build an arts center to further her love of art and music and bring opportunities to others. And I've watched her deal with a back problem that has left her in a wheelchair.

Still, she chooses her own weather each day. And she shines! She is in every way my father's equal. But she does it quietly.

So it doesn't matter whether you touch millions or one person. It doesn't matter whether you are famous or unknown. It doesn't matter whether you are a high-profile business leader, a single mother attending school, or a returning vet. What does matter is what you choose to do with the hand of cards that life has dealt you. What matters is what you do with the opportunities, gifts, and talents you've been blessed with.

The longer I live, the more I see genius in everyone. Everyone has unique, one-in-a-million talents. They are often buried or undeveloped, but they are there, and college can be the catalyst to unleashing them. In my experience, for every person who exaggerates his or her importance, there are 10 who sell themselves short.

We've all heard of financial identity theft, where someone steals your identity and uses your name and records. That is a frightening experience for anyone. What's worse is the identity theft that happens when people forget who they really are. Too often people believe that their self-worth depends on how well they stack up compared to others.

The reality is, every person has infinite worth and potential—including you. So stop thinking other people are better than you. They aren't. After all, most problems in the world begin when people begin to think they are better than someone else—*or not as good!* The truth is, we are all equals. We all share the same infinite worth.

As we end this book, I'm reminded of an unforgettable scene from the movie *Signs* where Graham, a disillusioned religious leader, asks his brother Merrill whether or not he believes in miracles.

> **Graham:** *People break down into two groups.... Are you the kind who sees signs, sees miracles? Or do you believe that people just get lucky?*
>
> **Merrill:** *I was at this party once. I'm on the couch with Randa McKinney. She was just sitting there looking beautiful, staring at me. I go to lean in and kiss her… and I realize I have gum in my mouth. So I turn, take out the gum, stuff it in a paper cup next to the sofa, and turn around. Randa McKinney throws up all over herself. I knew the second it happened it was a miracle. I could have been kissing her when she threw up. That would have scarred me for life. I may never have recovered.*
>
> *I'm a miracle man.*

So how about you? Do you believe in miracles, or do you believe people just get lucky? Or as Albert Einstein put it, "There are two ways to live your life. One is as though nothing is a miracle. The other is as though everything is a miracle."

As for me, I'm a miracle man. I believe that you are a miracle in one way or another. I also believe you can make a great contribution to this world in some way, large or small.

Someday, when it comes time to graduate from your two-year, four-year, or umpteen-year program, you will likely be invited to attend a commencement ceremony. A commencement is a beginning. In other words, you begin your future. It is my hope that your future will be so bright you'll have to wear shades. And I wish you all my best on your quest to become great teachers, paramedics, sign-language interpreters, scientists, entrepreneurs, graphic designers, chefs, horse whisperers, or whatever—as well as devoted mothers, fathers, husbands, wives, partners, brothers, sisters, and friends.

Live long and prosper.

> "I am not what has happened to me. I am what I choose to become."
>
> —Carl Jung, psychiatrist

THE 7 HABITS OF HIGHLY EFFECTIVE COLLEGE STUDENTS INDEX